# FATHERLAND

Kritik: German Literary Theory and Cultural Studies / Liliane Weissberg, *Editor*

## BOOKS IN THIS SERIES

*Walter Benjamin: An Intellectual Biography,*
by Bernd Witte, trans. by James Rolleston, 1991

*The Violent Eye: Ernst Junger's Visions and Revisions on the European Right,*
by Marcus Paul Bullock, 1991

*Fatherland: Novalis, Freud, and the Discipline of Romance,*
by Kenneth S. Calhoon, 1992

Kenneth S. Calhoon

# FATHERLAND

## novalis, freud, and the discipline of romance

WAYNE STATE UNIVERSITY PRESS  DETROIT

LIBRARY OF CONGRESS CATALOGING-IN-PUBLICATION DATA

Calhoon, Kenneth Scott, 1956–
  Fatherland : Novalis, Freud, and the discipline of romance /
Kenneth S. Calhoon.
      p.    cm. — (Kritik)
  Includes bibliographical references and index.
  ISBN 0–8143–2367–7 (alk. paper)
    1. Literature—Psychological aspects.   2. Psychoanalysis and
literature.   3. German literature—History and criticism.
4. Romanticism (Literature).   5. Fathers in literature.   6. Autonomy
(Psychology) in literature.   I. Title.   II. Series.
PN56.P92C35   1992
809'.9145—dc20                                                         91–39468
                                                                              CIP

DESIGNER: S. R. TENENBAUM

*Cover Art: Phillip Otto Runge, FALL DES VATERLANDS (1809).*
*Courtesy of Hamburger Kunsthalle.*

# Contents

ACKNOWLEDGMENTS 3

TEXT NOTES | Translation • Abbreviations 4

INTRODUCTION 5

## 1
### The Politics of Infanticide: Goethe's "Erlkönig" 25

## 2
### The Political Novalis 49

## 3
### The Philosophical Unconscious 71

## 4
### The Stones Speak! The Romantic Archaeology of the Psyche 97

## 5
### Allegories of Plot 117

## 6
### "Kubla Khan" and the Oriental Hallucination 142

EPILOGUE

**The Romantic Mother and the Fatherless Society** 161

Notes 166

Index 185

# Acknowledgments

So many friends and colleagues have read and commented on parts of this manuscript that to attempt to thank all of them by name would mean risking any number of embarrassing omissions. I must, however, acknowledge an inordinate debt to Helmut Schneider and Ashish Roy, two long-distance companions whose enduring friendship is paralleled by an abiding intellectual presence that often borders on inspiration. Special thanks also to Liliane Weissberg for her persistent encouragement, and to Wolf Sohlich for hours upon hours of meaningful conversation. Finally, to Cristina and Martha, who share their lives with me and have watched this labor with unwavering patience, I reaffirm my love.

# Text Notes

## TRANSLATION

All translations from German are my own, unless otherwise indicated. Where *Heinrich von Ofterdingen* is concerned, I have had the benefit of consulting Palmer Hilty's English rendering of Novalis's novel, and though my translations generally deviate from Hilty's, I have cited him whenever I have modified my version in light of his, however minor that modification.

## ABBREVIATIONS

*HA*    Goethe, Johann Wolfgang. *Werke: Hamburger Ausgabe*, ed. Erich Trunz. Munich: C. H. Beck, 1976.

*PH*    Novalis [Hardenberg, Friedrich von]. *Henry von Ofterdingen*, trans. Palmer Hilty. New York: Ungar, 1964.

*SA*    Freud, Sigmund. *Studienausgabe*, ed. Alexander Mitscherlich, Angela Richards, James Strachey. Frankfurt: Fischer, 1973.

*Schriften*    Novalis [Hardenberg, Friedrich von]. *Schriften*, ed. Paul Kluckhohn, Richard Samuel, Gerhard Schulz, Hans-Joachim Mähl. 3d ed. Stuttgart: Kohlhammer, 1977–84.

*SW*    Schelling, Friedrich Wilhelm Joseph. *Schellings Werke*, ed. Manfred Schröter. Munich: C. H. Beck, 1965.

# Introduction

## FAMILY ROMANCE AND THE FATHERLAND

What began for me as an attempt to clarify a Romantic quest in light of psychoanalytic theory has become that of situating Freud's thought within a discourse that Romanticism helped constitute. This study examines Romanticism and psychoanalysis in terms of a shared economy of longing and disappointment of which mourning is a profound index. In the decade following the French Revolution, the aesthetic liberalism espoused by many German writers was a labor of mourning for the fallen king, much in the way that self-control, the dominion of the Freudian superego, follows the internalization of the father, whose death, even when only symbolic, recalls an actual, prehistoric patricide. Freud's "discovery" of psychoanalysis was itself a mourning labor undertaken in the wake of his own father's passing, yet his theorizing was framed by political events that impressed themselves on especially those writings where his own dreams came under scrutiny. Freud's theoretical resurrection of his father's ghost seems meant to resist the specter of populist, anti-Semitic uprisings against the class, culture, and ideology that Jakob Freud represented. Moreover, the eclipse of contemporary politics by Freud's own "family romance" enabled him to describe this momentous personal loss with a word suggestive of the condition of quest and, at that time anyway, was the apparent fate of the Jews—the "lack of a fatherland" (*Vaterlandslosigkeit*).[1]

5

The epic borrowing to which Romanticism owes its name marks the appropriation of a narrative space across which theory is projected in the form of quest.[2] To the extent that psychoanalysis is born of the desire to *ground* the father—to locate as well as justify him—it too is implicated in the romance it elucidates.[3] "Family romance" is a term Freud used to explain how children, faced with doubts about their parents' legitimacy, develop fantasies in which their mothers and fathers are replaced by persons of nobler, more heroic stature (*Der Familienroman der Neurotiker*, 1908). The need to supplant an actual parent with a fairy-tale counterpart coincides with the emergence of a critical faculty that causes children to see their parents realistically, to recognize the inevitable flaws and limitations of those they previously idealized. Forced to abandon the exalted image they once held of their parents, children imagine themselves the offspring of knights, princesses, wealthy strangers, and other figures worthy of the most unquestioning adoration. Freud understands these imaginings as compensatory by-products of a painful but necessary process of enlightenment—"the working loose of the developing individual from parental authority" ("[d]ie Ablösung des heranwachsenden Individuums von der Autorität der Eltern," *SA* IV:223). Later, when children acquire a rudimentary understanding of sexual reproduction, their fantasies of illegitimacy concentrate on the father, as only his identity remains in doubt once the mother's body is recognized as a site of incontestable origin. Implicit in Freud's account are two successive definitions of legitimacy—the one rational, the other sexual—and what initially resembles an allegory of Enlightenment is interrupted by an obstetric reorientation that makes the maternal womb the focal point in a continued quest for the legitimate father.

That Romanticism conceived of itself in terms of this reorientation can be seen in *Heinrich von Ofterdingen*, the novel written by Novalis (Friedrich von Hardenberg, 1772–1801) and published in its incomplete form one year after the author's death. Set in Germany during the Christian crusades, *Ofterdingen* is a quest-romance that begins with a dream and continues as a journey through topographies that emulate the original dream-scape. What evolves into a pilgrimage to Jerusalem is at once a return to that most originary locus of which the dream is evocative—the womb. Finding himself in a deep cavern before a luminescent fountain, the excited Heinrich immerses himself in a shimmering fluid, which transports him out of the cave and leaves him, entranced, beside a spring amidst a multitude of flowers. One of these is the blue flower, the most persistent symbol of German Romantic longing, which responds to Heinrich's approach by metamorphosing into a graphic image of autoeroticism.[4] Here the youth stirs to his mother's voice and returns her embrace, and this momentary union of child and mother is compatible with the narcissism of the dream imagery. The dream simulates both the experience of being born and sexual ecstasy, representing an act of self-creation that had its corresponding moment in contemporary German philosophy.

Freud's small treatise on family romances first appeared in a collection of essays published by Otto Rank in 1909 entitled *Die Geburt des Helden* (The Birth of the Hero), a title that well describes *Heinrich von Ofterdingen,* in which the hero is repeatedly presented with scenes of heroic birth (his own and that of others), through dreams and various tales embedded in the larger narrative.[5] Like Freud, who sought an explanation of myth in the neurotic romances of individuals, Novalis derives the familiar forms of epic adventure from the secrets of conception of birth. The dream in which those secrets are revealed begins as a romance that leads the hero to the first in a series of apertures or recesses in the landscape that suggest the reproductive cavity:

> Bald kam er vor eine Felsenschlucht, die bergan stieg. Er musste über bemooste Steine klettern, die ein ehemaliger Strom herunter gerissen hatte. Je höher er kam, desto lichter wurde der Wald. Endlich gelangte er zu einer kleinen Wiese, die am Hange des Berges lag. Hinter der Wiese erhob sich eine hohe Klippe, an deren Fuss er eine Öffnung erblickte. (196)

> Presently he came upon a rocky gorge that slanted uphill. He had to scramble over moss-covered stones, which an ancient stream had swept down from above. The higher he climbed, the lighter the forest became. He finally reached a small meadow, which lay at the slope of the mountain. Behind the meadow a cliff loomed, at the foot of which he spied an opening. (*PH* 16)

The opening marks a meandering passageway that takes Heinrich to a subterranean fountain, which eventually emerges as a spring above ground. The ensuing adventures constitute a series of displacements that make explicit the full meaning of the word "source" (*Quelle*), implicating herein the disciplines concerned with uncovering sources—for example, philology, geology, archaeology, and ultimately psychoanalysis. The "romance" of *Heinrich von Ofterdingen* is the translation of theory into narrative, the metonymic development of the metaphorical implications these disciplines provide.[6]

Romance is a topographical overlay that transforms inquiry into travel, but one that superimposes a regressive geography on the Romantic concern for origins—historical, linguistic, archaeological, sexual. Even philosophy, for Novalis the "drive to be at home everywhere" (Trieb überall zu Hause zu seyn, III:434), is enveloped by the nostalgic compulsion of the novel in question, described as an eternal quest for home: "Wo gehn wir denn hin? Immer nach Hause" ("Where are we going? Ever homeward, 325). Heinrich's own Oriental journey, as a voyage to an original site of conception, is an expression of the "will to knowledge regarding sex which," following Foucault, "characterizes the modern Occident."[7] This "family romance" proceeds from the discovery of an irrefutable maternity. This discovery is the lesson of the dream, and the passion with which Heinrich recounts the experience to his parents leads the father to invoke the moment of his son's conception, thereby insinuating himself into the scene of sexual origin: "Mutter, Heinrich kann die Stunde nicht verläugnen, durch die er in der Welt ist" (Mother, Heinrich cannot deny the hour thanks to which he is in the world, 199). The elder Ofterdingen recollects the romantic circumstances of Heinrich's conception, as well as an elaborate dream of his own—a dream of fatherhood that, significantly, predates his courtship of Heinrich's mother. This dream, which replaces the fountain at the heart of Heinrich's dream-cave with a beautiful maiden hewn in marble, juxtaposes images of petrification and order to the fluid intermingling of forms that suffuses Heinrich's dream and even suggests a certain *ecriture féminine*.[8] One dream claims the child for the mother's body, the other for the father's mind. The instruction of the latter is that certain knowledge about maternal identity is an obstacle that demands heroic detour.

Beginning as an excursion from the birthplace of his father to that of his mother (Augsburg) and continuing by way of Loreto, the "displaced" birthplace of the Virgin Mary,[9] Heinrich's journey develops into a pilgrimage to the land made holy by the miracle of fatherless birth, a destination that in turn promises a vantage point from which the fatherland would appear as a distant romantic vision. The German crusaders who seek to enlist Heinrich in their next campaign tempt him with the image of a repatriated Jerusalem where they would soon celebrate victory "with wine from the fatherland" (bey vaterländischem Wein, 231). The enemy they describe is all but indistinguishable from the stormy seas they must cross before crossing swords, and *Vaterland* appears synonymous with a militaristic male fantasy rooted in a fear of inundation.[10] The voluptuous flood of Heinrich's dream is momentarily transformed into a source of abject horror. And although the youth does not join the crusaders (he returns to his mother instead), his poetic voyage to the Orient is concurrent with an erotically motivated subjugation of the feminine. The warriors' song makes

violent death the prerequisite for rejoining the mother; it lends the desire
for the mother a double edge that, within an oedipal framework, favors the
patriarchal:

> Die heil'ge Jungfrau schwebt, getragen
> Von Engeln, ob der wilden Schlacht,
> Wo jeder, den das Schwerdt geschlagen,
> In ihrem Mutterarm erwacht (233).

> Born on wings of angels flying,
> The Holy Virgin hovers mild,
> To whose embrace each soldier dying
> Awakens like a tender child.

Like the dreaming Heinrich, the soldier slain in battle awakens to a mother's embrace, a common denominator that leads one to regard the dream
and the wishes it represents rather more problematically. The crusaders,
for whom desire is but a prelude to conquest, manifest the fear of conflict
that accompanies the attraction constantly drawing Heinrich into a landscape that recreates the contours and openings of the maternal body. For
them, the threat of being engulfed and consumed transforms that body into
something more bestial: "glühende Felder, wirrer Wald, wehende Heide;
eine Landschaft, die sich 'spannt', die auf dem Sprung selber ist, ihn [der
über ihn dahinrast] zu verschlingen" (ardent fields, tangled forest, wailing
heath; a landscape that 'tenses' itself, one that is poised to devour whom-
ever races over it).[11] The setting of Snow White, but also of Goethe's
"Erlkönig," this animated landscape harbors the kind of domestic nightmare that Heinrich's journey assiduously circumvents, and his becomes a
quest for the conditions under which the continued presence of the maternal and feminine would be possible. What emerges, in other words, is a
search for a gentle, tolerant, and as such impassive, father.

This kind of father is familiar from "Hänsel und Gretel," a tale that
revokes the unique privilege of the natural mother by substituting a stepmother, thus vindicating fatherhood and creating a rational basis for the
family. The removal of childbirth as a central reference is the condition for
the paternal beneficence that appears at story's end with the death of the
witch, whose terrible oven manifests the ambivalence of a family structure
that traces its history back to the womb. Novalis's novel is replete with
widowed fathers, and the hero's eventual return to Thuringia would signal
a reversal of the initial movement from the city of his father (*Vaterstadt*) to
the site of virgin birth. The existing novel-fragment hints but vaguely at

that final destination, yet the ultimate substitution of the mother by the father is foretold in the exact middle of Part One when Heinrich ventures into the cave of a nobleman living in seclusion following his own return from the Orient. The cave recreates the topography of the womblike cavern of Heinrich's original dream, yet while the earlier experience mimics conception and birth, this second cave, which houses both a library and the tomb of the hermit's wife, replaces the natural origin with a rational one, suggesting too that the advance of reason entails the radical separation from the mother.

If *Heinrich von Ofterdingen* is any indication, Romanticism does not attempt to undo the Enlightenment by rewriting history from maternal origins, but rather acknowledges explicitly that the loss of the mother is the condition for writing history. The motif of the maternal crypt in Novalis's novel is a recurrent reminder that history is a commemoration of a departed mother. Heinrich's question to Sylvester toward the end of the existing fragment summarizes the condition that only death relieves: "Aber musste die Mutter sterben, dass die Kinder gedeihen können, und bleibt der Vater zu ewigen Thränen allein an ihrem Grabe sitzen?" (But did the mother have to die in order for the children to prosper, and shall the father remain sitting alone at her grave in eternal tears? 327).

The reference to the mourning husband and father evokes Lessing, whose famous expressions of grief at the loss of both wife and child due to complications during labor emblematize the Enlightenment's failure to absorb the irrationality of sexual procreation. His bitter concession that the contingency of birth stood in the way of even brief happiness led him to project the opposition of autonomy and natural necessity as the agon of his infant son, who died one day after a difficult delivery requiring the use of forceps. Lessing's insertion of choice into a situation that is irreducibly involuntary—all the while applauding the child's "good sense" (*Verstand*)—returns the Enlightenment to the conflict of which it was born:

> Und ich verlor ihn so ungern, diesen Sohn! denn er hatte so viel Verstand. . . . War es nicht Verstand, dass man ihn mit eisern Zangen auf die Welt ziehen musste? dass er sobald Unrat merkte?—War es nicht Verstand, dass er die erste Gelegenheit ergriff, sich wieder davon zu machen?[12]

> And I so hated to lose him, this son! he had so much good sense after all. . . . Was it not good sense that he had to be pulled into the world with steel forceps? that he immediately noticed mischief? Was it not good sense, that he seized the first opportunity to take his leave?

It is revealing that Lessing's *Nathan der Weise,* written shortly after the deaths of both wife and child, reestablishes the possibility of Enlightenment by means of the displacements that make up family romance—and this in a setting similar to that of *Heinrich von Ofterdingen.*[13] A Jerusalem beset by crusaders furnishes both authors with an appropriate context for framing the problematic relationship between *legitimacy* and *origins.* The Jewish Nathan, having lost his own wife and sons to a holocaust, has found new happiness in his adopted daughter Recha, a Christian child entrusted to him in infancy by the servant of her biological father. The latter, a Persian warrior who had married a German noblewoman and taken the name "Wolf" (the very nomenclature sounds a Freudian echo), turns out also to be the father of the Christian Templar and the brother of the Islamic Sultan.

The discovery of the truly original father appears as a fantasy that parallels and succeeds the establishment of Nathan's claim—supported by virtue and wisdom rather than the fortune of birth—to the title of "father."[14] The epic hero (Asaad, alias Wolf von Filnek) corresponds to and compensates for the bourgeois, essentially modern Nathan. The latter's absence from the final moment of reconciliation underscores the importance of the biological father's substitution of the adopted father. This "true" father, an almost mythical figure of vague provenance whom neither child ever knew, satisfies the requirements of the imaginary parent through whom, according to Freud, filial affection is ultimately preserved. As a creation of fantasy, the natural father is an archaic, simpler representation of the more complex and less tangible legitimacy embodied by Nathan. The representation is regressive: like a dream, it returns an idea to a sense perception, yet here the image (biological fatherhood) contradicts the idea it represents (rational fatherhood)—a paradox that vivifies the complications that finally forced the Enlightenment to be translated back into romance.

A virtual dress-rehearsal for *Heinrich von Ofterdingen,* the fairy-tale resolution of Lessing's *Nathan* suggests that the Enlightenment created problems only Romanticism could solve. Freud's discussion of "family romances" in effect traces the emergence of Romanticism out of the Enlightenment in terms of the imaginative compensation for the knowledge that, while the identity of one's mother is a matter of certainty, *"pater semper incertus est"* (*SA* IV:225). The editorial revisions by which the Brothers Grimm replaced actual mothers with stepmothers may represent the simplest attempt to nullify the threat to autonomy posed by natural childbirth.[15] The further substitution of the stepmother by the witch (as in "Hänsel und Gretel") unveils the genealogy of the "Romantic Mother."

In a variation on the theme of family romance, Freud theorizes that when a child finds his or her mother increasingly incapable of gratifying all needs, he or she protects the positive image of the mother by projecting whatever disfavor she has incurred onto an evil, threatening surrogate.[16] The stepmother and the witch of the aforementioned tale both deflect the anxiety of the hungry child away from the mother, though in different ways. While the stepmother places the refusal of nourishment at a safe remove from the natural mother, the witch with her gingerbread house not only restores an ambivalence appropriate to the natural mother, but she also associates this ambivalence with the erotic, indeed incestuous implications of the drive that is first satisfied at the maternal breast.[17]

The witch peering out from her cottage made of sweets represents, in the spirit of taboo, a prohibition from within, an internal fear that meets with equal force the desire it attends. Freud suggested the oxymoron "holy dread" (heilige Scheu) to characterize the emotional ambivalence that accompanies the contemplation of acts as tempting as they are forbidden, incest in particular (*SA* IX:311). The coinage, and especially Strachey's translation,[18] has a familiar ring to those versed in English Romanticism, given the prominence of "holy dread" in the closing lines of Coleridge's "Kubla Khan." This poem isolates its visionary transgressor through a ritual measure of encirclement and avoidance and depicts him as a Narcissus whose crime is an ecstasy of feeding:[19]

> And all shall cry, Beware! Beware!
> His flashing eyes, his floating hair!
> Weave a circle round him thrice,
> And close your eyes with holy dread
> For he on honey-dew hath fed
> And drunk the milk of paradise. (l. 49–54)

Rather more sublime than the gingerbread house, Coleridge's paradise is nonetheless the setting of some vaguely incestuous witchery—an erotic union between woman and devil consummated at the procreative opening of mother-earth:

> But oh! that deep romantic chasm which slanted
> Down the green hill athwart a cedarn cover!
> A savage place! as holy and enchanted
> As e'er beneath a waning moon was haunted
> By woman wailing for her demon-lover! (l. 12–16)

*Ofterdingen* repeatedly returns its heroes to those places in the land-scape—fissures, caves, and ravines—that resemble the female reproductive cavity, and in one instance the result is pregnancy, the conception of a new heir to the throne of Atlantis. (A longer discussion of Novalis's novel and Coleridge's poem comprises the final chapter of this study.) Both texts recall traditional fertility rites typically conducted at similar "romantic chasms," rites that by their mere choice of setting reveal the need for sustenance also to be a desire for the person who first satisfied that need—the mother. The fertility of the land and the fecundity of the womb collapse under the weight of a nostalgia for the epoch in which hunger and eros were as yet indistinct. The association in these texts of childbearing with elemental forces in the natural world, that is, with storms and subterranean convulsions, identifies the "womb of nature" (Kant) with the "Other of reason."[20] The ritual commemoration of birth (and of the maternal origins of agriculture) poses a general threat not only to a social structure based on patrilinearity but also to the Enlightenment dream of self-creation, which continues to inform such present-day expressions as "born again" and "self-made." The latter usage in particular demonstrates a resistance to the fact that we owe our lives to a realm governed by instinct and chance rather than reason and choice. The boast of being "self-made" connotes a hatred of debt that ultimately implicates the incommensurable indebtedness represented by the "accident of birth."[21]

## ELECTIVE PARENTHOOD
## AND THE BURDEN OF ENLIGHTENMENT

The emergence of the dream of autonomous self-creation accompanies the rise of the bourgeoisie and marks the historical juncture at which ascent within the social hierarchy ceased to be a matter of birthright alone. Yet class distinctions, which the "self-made man" had largely overcome, retained a powerful political and psychological significance for Jews, whose social mobility was still inhibited by the inexorable circumstances of birth. In the specific case of Freud, burgeoning anti-Semitism in Vienna had rendered certain professional titles as seemingly inaccessible as titles of nobility. The essay "Family Romances," which furnishes a model for reading Enlightenment ambitions into Romantic fantasies, also offers a kind of solace for the frustrations suffered by Freud and expressed by him in tones that resonate of the same ambitions. The model itself, in other words, reproduces the displacements characteristic of Romanticism.

Psychoanalysis renews, though under increasingly urgent political circumstances, the dialectic of enlightenment realized in Romanticism and forecast in Lessing's *Nathan der Weise*. Nathan looms large as a Freudian contemporary at the point where he defines the conditions of family romance, warning of the intolerable doubt that ensues when children compare their (fore)father(s) to the fathers of others—a comparison that brings an end to the age in which, following Freud, a child's parents are the "source of all faith" ("Quelle alles Glaubens," *SA* IV:223):[22]

> Wie kann ich meinen Vätern weniger,
> Als du den deinen glauben? Oder umgekehrt.—
> Kann ich von dir verlangen, dass du deine
> Vorfahren Lügen strafst, um meinen nicht
> Zu widersprechen?

> How can I believe my fathers less
> Than you do yours? Or conversely.—
> Can I ask of you that you accuse your
> Forefathers of lies, in order not
> To contradict mine?

Romanticism, with its more apparent maternal orientation, seems—in light of the complications threatened by Nathan—actually to have redefined the Enlightenment's search for the terms of paternal legitimacy. Finding himself failed by the promise of autonomy (and faced with doubts about his father), Freud repeated the Romantic move of diverting attention to the region of the mind where it was still possible to choose one's own parents.

Freud's dream of the yellow-bearded uncle, analyzed in *The Interpretation of Dreams* under the heading of "Dream-Distortion" (*Traumentstellung*), shows that the experience of anti-Semitism in Freud's professional life revitalized the contest between the Enlightenment desire for rational self-determination and the unalterable contingency of birth. This dream can be read as an attempt to invalidate birth by creating a rational structure in which the circumstances of birth are no longer relevant. The dream is further significant because it supplies a framework for the discussion of censorship, or rather the process of distortion in dreams, which he likens to the work of the political censor. A parallel emerges between the *fantasy*, which establishes a legitimate rationale behind the otherwise inscrutable machinations of the government bureaucracy, and the *theory*, which inserts a grammar and legality behind the seemingly nonsensical content of the dream. Just as the fantasy is a liberal one, so too is the theory, insofar as it makes censorship an internal mechanism less comparable to political repression than to manners, civility, that is, to strategy. To say that censorship foils interpretation is misleading because censorship is complicit in the initial formation of interpretable material. The hermeneutic principle according to which mystery and incomprehensibility foster understanding is one that psychoanalysis and Romanticism have in common, and this study as a whole is concerned with various disciplinary manifestations of an aesthetics that is also a psychohermeneutics.

The preliminary report (*Vorbericht*) to Freud's dream-analysis is a brief but suggestive tale of liberal frustration. Recounting his pleasure at being nominated to a professorship by two senior colleagues at the University of Vienna, Freud also reports guarding against undue optimism because many other men, equally if not more qualified than he, had been rejected by the official ministry. The bureaucracy is immediately shown to be an irrational and impregnable system in which there is no apparent correlation between merit and promotion. Yet Freud's own nomination appears immanently rational: "the expression of appreciation, not attributable to personal connections, on the part of two distinguished men" (Ausdruck einer durch persönliche Beziehung nicht aufzuklärenden Anerkennung von seiten zweier hervorragender Männer, *SA* II:153). Freud professes the middle-class faith in "careers open to talent,"[23] the belief that one's ultimate rank in society does not depend on the title one is born with and that in order to be recognized one need only be clever, industrious, creative, and honest. The ministry is shown to be a structure that resists upward mobility, and the opening sentences of Freud's *Vorbericht* contain a clear juxtaposition of liberal optimism and bureaucratic intractability.

The issue of anti-Semitism makes an unassuming entry when Freud introduces his friend "R.," a colleague in medicine who had visited him the evening prior to the dream. R. had been nominated to a professorship long before Freud, but once it became clear that a favorable decision was not forthcoming, he called upon the appropriate official to inquire whether the refusal to promote him was owing to "confessional considerations" (konfessionelle Rücksichten, 154). The official conceded that this was indeed a factor, and Freud, to whom the same considerations applied, saw his own resignation justified.

In the dream itself, Freud experiences great affection for R., whose visage is conflated with that of Freud's uncle, who appears with a yellow beard. Freud explains how his uncle Josef, his only uncle, had served time in prison on a criminal conviction, and Freud recalls that his father once referred to his wayward sibling as a "fool" (*Schwachkopf*, 155). Freud is puzzled by the dream's conflation of the uncle and his friend R. because under no circumstances could the latter be considered foolish. Nor was he a criminal. This observation prompts Freud to remember an earlier encounter with another colleague, "N.," also a Jew, who had been denied promotion presumably on the basis of a false charge of extortion. Freud now concludes that the dream employed the uncle to represent both colleagues—one as a fool, the other a scoundrel—thereby creating reasons other than being Jewish for their rejection. This clears the way for fulfilling Freud's professional aspirations: "unsere Gemeinsamkeit ist aufgehoben, ich darf mich auf meine Ernennung zum Professor freuen" (our common quality is suspended, and I may rejoice at my appointment to a professorship, 156).

An oblique family romance, Freud's dream brings the Enlightenment desire for a rational social structure into contact with the family romance inherent in Jewish law, according to which religious identity is passed on to children through the parent whose biological identity is certain.[24] (Lessing's Nathan, obviously incapable of giving birth, attributes his new found fatherhood to a virtue rewarded, not to "nature and fortune" [Natur und Glück].)[25] The dream effectively liberates Freud from the matrilinear inheritance of Judaism, a freedom that enables him to identify with his father and the bureaucracy simultaneously: the dream replicates R.'s rejection by subjecting him to the judgment pronounced by Freud's father over Uncle Josef. The father's verdict is the vehicle of patronymic transmission.

Students of Freud's own family romance have argued that his early identification with heroes, both historical (Hannibal) and literary (Karl Moor of Schiller's *Robbers*), compensated for what he perceived as an instance of shamelessly unheroic behavior on his father's part. Specifically, the young Freud had been greatly disillusioned by his father's account of having once yielded to an anti-Semitic bully who had blocked his path on the sidewalk, knocked his hat from his head, and ordered him to the side. Freud was ten or twelve when his father told him of this experience, and the disappointment he remembered feeling is typical of that which inspires family romance: "Das schien mir nicht heldenhaft von dem grossen starken Mann, der mich Kleinen an der Hand führte" (That seemed unheroic on the part of the big strong man who was leading me, his little son, by the hand, *SA* II:208).[26] But disappointment turned to admiration when Freud came to see in his father's obeisance an exemplary level of self-control and emotional autonomy (qualities that had profited Jews in times of adversity), and the rebellious figures he once esteemed were superseded by others who showed the same capacity for restraint his father had demonstrated. One of these was Winckelmann, the historian of art whose classical sensibility entailed a balance of character and willingness to compromise (he converted to Catholicism to gain employment at the Vatican), all of which produced a result that Hannibal's militancy had failed to achieve: it cleared a path to Rome—a desired destination that had eluded Freud for years despite numerous journeys to Italy.[27] As Freud's reward for the renunciation of a one-time rebelliousness, Rome (in its initial unattainability a cipher of Freud's *Vaterlandslosigkeit*) is a coordinate on a map that extends theory across space and shapes it as a journey.

Viewed biographically, Freud's project might be explained as a theoretical quest for the terms according to which his father's (in)action could be valorized; as a political undertaking, psychoanalysis appears as an attempt to insulate the values of liberalism against the gathering forces of populist reaction. Jakob Freud's encounter with the anti-Semite, while a matter of biography, demonstrates how inseparable for Freud the personal and political spheres had become, and to identify with his father under those circumstances was to renounce his earlier claim to radicalism.[28] Much of Freudian theory, in particular the theory of the superego, is concerned with describing the processes that provide for a similar renunciation and ensure the son's ultimate identification with paternal authority. Thus at the very moment liberalism was failing in the political arena, Freud was seeking to engrave onto the human psyche the inevitability of its triumph.

## ROMANTICISM AND PSYCHOHERMENEUTICS

The foregoing allows for a provisional thesis, namely that Freud's theories represent an attempt to work out the metaphorical implications of anti-Semitism; such implications were the legacy of the German Enlightenment, which had invested anti-Semitism with a powerful and enduring symbolic charge. A Romantic reading of psychoanalysis would accentuate the metaphoricity of the latter, much in the way that Romantics like Novalis and Friedrich Schlegel exposed the reliance of their philosophical contemporaries on metaphor, rhetoric, and on fictional models in general.[29] Psychoanalysis appears to renew the Romantic project of filling out metaphorical spaces. The prevalence of archaeological imagery in Freud's writing, for example, signals a dependence on the architectonics of surface and depth required by Romanticism for elaborating historical sedimentations of various kinds. Another example is narcissism, the discussion of which introduced strong sexual connotations into the chaste problematic of subject and object—an achievement common to Novalis and Freud.

Paul Ricoeur has argued that psychoanalysis became a hermeneutics—a theory concerned with decipherment and interpretation—at the point where Freud began to move away from a neuroanatomy that sought to localize psychical functions on a map of the brain and toward an "imaginary anatomy,"[30] that is, the topography of unconscious, preconsciousness, consciousness. Freud portrayed the interrelationship of these systems using schemata that suggest a spatial order, yet spatiality serves here as an "auxiliary representation" for designating sequence, a temporal direction.[31] This metaphorical space, according to Ricoeur, becomes the locus of hermeneutic labor: "I think the development of Freudian theory may be looked upon as the gradual reduction of the notion of a psychical apparatus . . . to a topography in which space is no longer a place within the world but a scene of action where roles and masks enter into debate; this space will become a place of ciphering and deciphering."[32] Ricoeur concentrates on a polarity in Freud's thinking: one side is a quantitative energetics of psychical forces; the other side is a hermeneutics whose object is not *force,* but meaning. In the *Interpretation of Dreams,* he notes, Freud must always resort to a "mixed language" that combines, without wholly reconciling, these energetic and hermeneutic components.[33] The metaphor of censorship exemplifies this dichotomy, for while it refers to the mechanism through which meanings are changed, disguised, weakened, or displaced, it also insinuates, by way of political connotations made explicit by Freud, the force with which the state counters dissent.[34] Censorship is at once an agency of repression and representation.

The result of Freud's efforts to nullify political crisis by integrating it into normal psychic development is that even his more technical discussions of dreams read like political allegories. Hence the repressive practice of censorship is removed from the realm of external politics and "liberalized," that is, reinscribed as an internal process that does not foil understanding but, under the right conditions, guarantees it. The censorship that helps constitute dreams, while disguising (and thus repressing) dream-thoughts, also creates the associations that become the object of, and incentive to, interpretation. The repression of desire (*eros*) produces the conditions of another desire—the desire to interpret or rather to make explicit the interpretations that disguise already implies. Psychoanalysis thus revives the basic hermeneutics of the parable, which enlists secrecy and difficulty in the interest not of obscurity, but of an understanding all the more profound.[35]

A similar dialectics of concealment and revelation is articulated by Novalis, whose description of incomprehensibility as stimulus (*Reiz*) has vast implications for an analytical project the aim of which is the recollection of desire. And much as Freud allowed the political turmoil surrounding him to be absorbed into an ancient mythological structure where wishes, now banished to the unconscious, were acted out, so does Romanticism seem to have resituated its political anxieties in a fairy-tale underground representing a distant, indeterminate age "where wishing still made a difference" (wo das Wünschen noch geholfen hat).[36] The history told by Novalis in his political writings is a narrative of the repeated deferral of wish fulfillment; the result is a pointed "erotization" of politics. For Novalis, however, the erotic is something mystical—always veiled—and his criticism of the Enlightenment opposes the destimulation that the removal of mystery entails. The whole of Novalis's writings is informed by a poetics that links strangeness with familiarity, mystery with understanding, and repression with pleasure, justifying ultimately the kind of authority that turns knowledge into enigma in the first place. Goethe's poem "Erlkönig" (1782), the first in a constellation of Romantic texts I shall discuss, demonstrates the peril that arises when the same authority tries to do the opposite—to turn mystery into rational knowledge.

The broad figurative structure of family romance identifies psychoanalysis as the heir to the Romantic narrativization of theory. The Romantic quest is the hermeneutic response to the nonidentity inherent in representation; the distance covered measures the difference within the metaphorical regimen of the "same-but-different."[37] Its goal is the spatial separation of double meanings: for example, the dual significance of "source" as natural spring and verbal relic (the nonidentity of which Romanticism asserts and mourns through the figure of Narcissus). Novalis's Jerusalem and Freud's Rome both fall within the topography that, according to Ricoeur, is not a real space within the world, "but a scene of action where roles and masks enter into debate . . . , a place of ciphering and deciphering." In Goethe's poem, this scene of action is a forest traversed at night by a father and son on horseback—an obscure place where conflicting modes of interpretation do battle over the life of the child. The outcome is a tragic rendering of the famous Wordsworthian inversion of Enlightenment patronymy ("The Child is Father of the Man"[38]): fear, emerging from the dark heart of the Enlightenment, is an inheritance passed on from child to father.

This pre-Romantic primal scene raises the specter of child abuse, but literally as specter: the Erl-king, whose erotic desire for the boy is unambiguous, and whom only the boy sees, is a tree-dwelling troll from Nordic folklore.[39] The seduction of the child is not hidden, only confined to the realm of childhood fantasy. The poem thus rehearses the pivotal moment in the development of psychoanalysis when Freud renounced his seduction theory, which attributed hysteria to actual scenes of abuse in childhood, or rather absorbed that theory into a more comprehensive oedipal structure that makes us suffer for not only deeds actually committed but also fantasies.[40] The poem sets two interpretive models in conflict: one treats the child's fantasy as the consequence of delirium (the child seems to be sick), and another regards the fantasy as the product of repression (as manifested in the repeated censorial gestures of the father). These explanations were commonly invoked to account for the French Revolution, either as a pathological aberration or as the normal "return of the repressed." The French Revolution both provides the context for reading the poem and underscores the political ramifications of the oedipal theory itself.

Among those who understood the French Revolution in terms of the return of the repressed was Novalis, who even adopted the terms "puberty" and "castration" to account for the forces of rebellion and reaction (II:465–66).[41] My second chapter focuses on his *Glauben und Liebe* (Faith and Love) and *Die Christenheit oder Europa* (Christianity or Europe), a set of fragments and a "speech" (Rede) respectively, which can be considered political writings at least to the extent that they address the French Revolution. These works have frequently been cited as examples of the reactionary politics of Romanticism—expressions of a regressive longing for the premodern unity of feudalism and medieval Catholicism. *Die Christenheit* begins with a paean to the beneficent embrace of the medieval church ("Es waren schöne glänzende Zeiten"/Those were beautiful shining times, III:507), a nostalgic accolade mimed by Georg Lukács in the opening sentence of *Die Theorie des Romans:* "Selig sind die Zeiten" (Blissful are the times).[42] Lukács, after World War II the fiercest critic of Romantic regression, represents a leftist lineage extending back to the early nineteenth century when Arnold Ruge and Theodor Echtermeyer excoriated the German Romantics for an introspectiveness borrowed from an indigenous mystical tradition whose historical moment had long since passed.[43]

The Freudian left, as represented by Herbert Marcuse's *Eros and Civilization,* views regression rather differently and indeed rehabilitates a critical usage of regression already practiced by the Romantics (and by Rousseau, for that matter). To dream is to regress; the hallucinatory recovery of perception in dreams causes wishes to appear already fulfilled, thereby reviving an era of childhood, however short-lived, in which gratification is never deferred. (This again corresponds to that fairy-tale world "where wishing still made a difference.") The "psychoanalytical liberation of memory," says Marcuse, enlists regression in the service of progress by tapping urges and desires denied by civilization—by confronting the inadequacies of the present with images of the fulfilled promises of childhood.[44] This framework enables us to see in Novalis's rhetoric of nostalgia a dialectics that incorporates regression as a critical moment; the scenes of imaginary fulfillment in *Die Christenheit oder Europa* are always set against images of unimagined lack. Even religion, for Novalis a stage for the blatant erotization of sacred objects, is presented within an economics of loss that implicates both the Marxist and Freudian definitions of fetishism. The sacred relic, by dint of its sheer allegorical force, signifies a lost unity it does not recreate, but relocates—if only through a teleology of death—in the future. Peter Brooks, who reads Freud's theory of the death instinct as a theory of narrative, echoes Lacan in describing desire itself as a narrative impulse, "a forward drive in the signifying chain, an insistence of meaning toward the occulted objects of desire."[45]

As the occulted object of desire in Novalis's novel, the blue flower is the metonymic "link" that identifies the chain of signification as just that: a chain. The flower, which like his mother accompanies Heinrich on his journey, is witness to the vicissitudes of its own fetish. This journey begins with the experience of mistaken identity, the confusion of one thing for another that defines fetishism, of which Narcissus is the supreme casuality. Chapter 3 of this study investigates the relevance of the Freudian category of narcissism for *Heinrich von Ofterdingen:* first, I read the novel in light of Freud's theory; then I explore the discursive origins of the category in the post-Kantian philosophical discussion of subject and object. *Ofterdingen* both narrates and transforms this discussion. The transformation of narcissism from a philosophical allegory into a description of consciousness centered on sexuality points to the lingering effects of Romantic epistemology on psychoanalysis: not only does Freud's language show traces of the post-Kantian vocabulary, but he also defines the function of dream-censorship as perpetuating the illusion that thinkers like Fichte and Schelling described as a Kantian dogma—the illusion that all knowledge is derived from sensory perception.

The first three chapters follow a trajectory along which censorship is removed from the realm of paternal authority (vid. the political context of Goethe's "Erlkönig") and installed as part of an aesthetic and hermeneutic process the aim of which is consciousness, the means to which is a veil that places consciousness on the far side of desire. Chapter 4 is concerned with how stimulus (the aesthetic cipher of censorship) emerges as a formal component in certain nineteenth-century disciplines for which Romanticism laid the metaphorical groundwork. Archaeology in particular, a discipline that preserves the role of quest in the age of its obsolescence, institutionalizes the dilatory space that divides mystery and understanding and ensures the latter by means of the former. Geology, the science that became Novalis's profession, is converted into archaeology through his poet-hero's journey, which projects the vertical excavations of the miner-geologist across a space defined by incomprehensibility (the mystery of ancient fragments inscribed with forgotten languages). Here I contend that archaeology, which provided Freud with the most suggestive metaphor for describing the work of the psychoanalyst, was metaphorical at its very inception, a spatial extension of a Romantic aesthetics that insists upon delay and movement between two moments of identity.

Heinrich's quest for comprehensibility is motivated by the enigma of his initial dream. The formalist categories *fabula* and *sjužet* have been applied to the process of dream-interpretation; the psychoanalysis of dreams can be seen as a search for the principle of interconnectedness according to which the seemingly discontiguous and fragmentary dream-material forms a coherent narrative.[46] The same theoretical concepts have also been used to describe the totalizing direction of the classical *Bildungsroman,* in which the attempt to integrate the individual into the social fabric amounts to the subordination of the intricacies of sjužet to the "superindividual necessity" of fabula.[47] This discussion provides the context for Chapter 5, which treats *Ofterdingen* as a critical reading of Goethe's *Wilhelm Meisters Lehrjahre* in terms of the narrative machinations that make plot a function of surveillance. Not only is the oedipal plot that informs Wilhelm Meister's *Bildung* undermined in Novalis's novel, but the fact that the agencies of surveillance extend into Heinrich's dreams also draws attention to the political implications of dream-interpretation.

This same chapter may suggest that the narratological terms fabula and sjužet were themselves born of an ideological desire to subordinate detail to an integral whole. *Bildung* was a morphological category taken from the study of plants, and Goethe invoked a *Bildungstrieb* to account for apparently recalcitrant formations in terms of an underlying continuity. Continuity was a liberal virtue that the French Revolution, unforeseen by any existing teleology, had disrupted. Chapter 5 concludes by examining the mark this rupture made on the flower imagery in Novalis's *Ofterdingen* and Phillip Otto Runge's engraving, *Fall des Vaterlands* (Fall of the Fatherland, 1809). The context here is political, and while I am not proposing that texts like these are revolutionary as such, I do contend that they bear the indelible traces of the ambivalence that was the legacy of the Revolution and that, furthermore, they help chart the reach of that ambivalence into the deepest fissures of the psyche. The question has rather to do with the political import of a critical tradition that reads these works allegorically, thereby divesting them of their ambivalence and simplifying their overdeterminations. Such readings themselves posit a continuum that begins with an artistic preordination and assumes the kind of subjective autonomy that the very notion of the unconscious undermines. Writing on the "romantic construction of the unconscious," Catherine Belsey suggests that the distinguishing feature of Romantic texts "is that they are composed of irreconcilable discourses, constructed of signifying nonsense which intrudes substantially on sense and remains unmastered by it."[48]

Chapter 6 brings the promised comparison of Novalis's *Ofterdingen* and Coleridge's "Kubla Khan." The Orient, so conspicuous in both works, is displaced by the acknowledgment of the maternal origins it represents; the focus of the comparison is the crisis brought on by such knowledge. Hence the return of family romance. In either text, a visionary experience is located in a subterranean dream-topography where caverns, fountains, and streams evoke the womb and provide the locus of a creative process resembling childbirth. This process is described as hallucinatory, and, in the specific sense, the dreamer experiences his mental imagery as having an objective existence outside the mind. The preface to Coleridge's poem claims it as the product of a dream in which "all the images rose up before [the Author] as *things*."[49] Novalis's poet-hero, while undergoing the erotic baptism of his dream, likewise finds the images of his mind becoming manifest in his vicinity: "neue, niegesehene Bilder entstanden, die . . . zu sichtbaren Wesen um ihn wurden" (images such as he had never seen appeared . . . , turning into visible presences around him, I:197). This last similarity underscores a difference: namely, the dream that gave rise to Coleridge's poem was opium-induced. A connection between hallucinogenic substances and the ritual exaltation of the maternal landscape is explored by Hans Peter Duerr in his book *Traumzeit: Über die Grenze zwischen Wildnis und Zivilisation* (Dreamtime: On the Boundary between Wilderness and Civilization). Duerr's work has a less localized application for a study concerned with describing the Romantic constitution of psychoanalytic discourse, for his larger aim is to implicate Freud in a process of modernization that admits the primitive only to divest it of its proper alterity. Idiosyncratic as Duerr's analysis may be, it is curiously exemplary for an investigation that proceeds from psychoanalysis yet aims at a methodological introversion that would place psychoanalysis well within the hermeneutic field of fire.

# The Politics of Infanticide: Goethe's "Erlkönig"

### THE SLEEP OF REASON

Romanticism and psychoanalysis are dual expressions of disillusionment with a rationalism that had twice failed to make good on its promise of the progressive and pacific betterment of society, the twin specters of bloody revolution (1789–93) and anti-Semitic populism (ca. 1895) having weakened the liberal faith in the capacity of a learned class to avert social chaos through the studied application of reason. At either historical juncture, the waning confidence in liberalism gave way to a growing trust in the perceptions of the fearful and the superstitious. To the degree that Freud's investigation of the phylogenetic origins of neurosis amounted to the redemption of primitive insights, psychoanalysis became the means of remembering the truths that earlier societies had taken for granted. Likewise, the Romantic elevation of *Hausmärchen* (household tales) inverted the Enlightenment domestication of nature by discovering within the home a darker natural order, exposing new sources of terror in the most familiar places.[1] This exaltation of folk culture came in the wake of a late eighteenth-century aesthetics for which the loftiest experience, the Sublime, was linked to the sensation of fear—the rational recollection of a prerational existence. The twentieth-century proposal of a "dialectic of enlightenment" wherein the anxious origins of science would be acknowledged was implicit in a concept with which Romanticism was familiar, but which the Age of Reason could only have regarded as an oxymoron:

rational fear. This linkage is vaguely conscious in Kant's enjoinder to "have the courage" (*Habe Mut*) to make use of one's own intellect because reason leaves one unprotected against the object it violates but subjects one as well to the anger of the authority that autonomous thinking invariably diminishes.[2]

In Goethe's "Erlkönig" (1782), a poem in which a folk idiom asserts its tenacious power in the face of rationalism, such encouragement as Kant's breeds tragedy; that is, fearless reason leads ultimately to the knowledge that both the intimate and the exotic sources of fear, the father and the supernatural, are indistinct. The nocturnal ride into the forest indicates a general trajectory toward the primeval, and the poem suggests itself as a model of the manifold regression Freud ascribed to the apparatus of dreams. As the hallucinatory fulfillment of repressed wishes, dreams present ideas not to the intellect, but to the senses as imagery, and via the senses return the adult to the stage of early childhood in which wishes are met with summary gratification.[3] Corresponding to this ontogenetic return to infancy is a phylogenetic return to the childhood of humankind, the restoration of what Freud regarded as the traumatic beginnings of culture. The latter parallel is a matter of great ambivalence, as the return to the primal position at the mother's breast is simultaneously a return to other archaic origins far less pleasant. This ambivalence is exemplified by the gingerbread house in "Hänsel und Gretel," where the invitation to eat one's fill is combined with the threat of being eaten. In "Erlkönig" as well, a nature that offers both sustenance and pleasure at its ample bosom also harbors the danger of domestic violence.

Seldom has a poem anticipated so brilliantly the resistance a critical tradition would display toward a kind of interpretation the poem would inevitably generate. The vein of this unwelcome reading is psychoanalytic; its opponent is the father, who with the full confidence of Enlightenment rationalism at his back, dismisses the anxiety of his small son, for whom nature is a mysterious, seductive, even murderous presence. It is the father too who makes this reading inevitable, given that psychoanalysis takes shape in opposition to the type of authority he embodies. The oedipal theory itself was born in the shadow of a paternal prohibition against examining the father too closely. In addition, the poem validates the taboo as well as the anxiety, for when the child peers behind nature's menacing forms, he recognizes his father, and this discovery exacts an awful price.

Much of the dream entails a mechanism for subverting its own decipherment—either by scrambling the latent dream-thought or by screening it with another, less threatening interpretation—so does "Erlkönig" censure itself through the father's rejection of his son's elemental sensibilities. What the boy perceives as a nocturnal spirit can be explained rationally as rustling leaves or a tendril of evening mist. And while the father's horror at the final ghastly turn of events suggests a profound attenuation of his view of the world, the child risks being silenced by a tradition bent on replicating the father's natural scientific explanation of the nightside: the child is deathly ill; his father is rushing him to medical care; underway he is subject to hallucinations fostered by his delirium—there is no Erlkönig.[4]

The psychoanalytic understanding of hallucination does not corroborate the simplicity of the above explanation, however. Freud describes the hallucination as the vehicle by which elements of the unconscious can become conscious by passing the censure of preconsciousness (*Vorbewusstsein*), the inward-facing agency charged with shielding consciousness against intrusions from within. To this end, psychic disturbances are converted into sense perceptions so that they appear to originate in the environment rather than beneath consciousness. The hallucination therefore is not a sheer mirage but a genuine perception the source of which has been displaced (*verschoben*). Anxieties and forbidden desires are rendered benign through this outward relocation, which is the guarantor of effective censorship. Preconsciousness fulfills its task by forcing its own circumvention, and the hallucination is a collateral expression of the authority that agency exercises.

Freud uses the analogy of arbitrary political power to illustrate the censorial function of preconsciousness, but he also likens it to subtler forms of repression such as the self-censorship inherent in conventions of social courtesy or that practiced by authors who temper their opinions to make them more palatable (*SA* II:158–59). Freud later elaborated this structure in his theory of the superego, the formation of which he described as the internalization of paternal authority; but even the earlier reference to actual censorship comes in the immediate context of a dream of Freud's own which, by his analysis, is concerned finally with his inability to satisfy the expectations of his father.[5] The father, now deceased, survives in the latent dream-thought, but he also lives on through the mechanism that prevents such thoughts from entering consciousness undistorted. Goethe's poem is revealing in the way it puts the father at the scene of birth of that censoring mechanism. His repeated efforts to assure the frightened child that he has simply misinterpreted harmless sensory information are in keeping with the process just outlined in which inner feelings are disguised as external stimuli.[6] The father's ultimate horror is owing to not only the worsening condition of the boy but also his failure to sustain the illusion—a failure that leads one to suspect that it is the father, of whom the Erlkönig is a projection, who threatens the child.

Freud's description of preconsciousness as an agency that gives inner disturbances the appearance of originating in the environment implicates the Enlightenment, whose subjugation of natural forces depended on their being banished to the outside world. The Enlightenment listed among its aims the control of appetite and base desires (*Begierden*),[7] and this domination of the "nature within us" reinforced a split in the self that was projected as the division of inside and outside. The animation of the surrounding forest in "Erlkönig" is only apparently alien to this undertaking, as the dominion of modern science over nature is heir to a primitive animism that, according to Horkheimer and Adorno, disentangled the subject from nature by locating the source of fear fully within the ambient world.[8] A Freudian reading of Goethe's poem leaves psychoanalysis somewhat unstable by exposing its share in a Romantic project for which the term "narcissism" is key: the recoding of *Angst* as a fear without object,[9] and more generally, the reincorporation of what had been projected outward.[10] In this vein, Novalis speaks of an "outer world within us" (Aussenwelt in uns, III:429); Freud mentions an "internal foreign territory" (inneres Ausland, *SA* I:496).

It has been argued that this cultural withdrawal of cathexis from the surrounding world corresponds to a political reorientation entailing the gradual disappearance of the monarchy as an external power to be reckoned with. Once the bourgeoisie had superseded the nobility as the dominant social class, it grew suspicious of the common people (*Volk*). Likewise, reason had eliminated spirits and demons from its register of threatening external forces only to find itself confronted with the inner demons of the imagination and emotions.[11] By dint of a parallel between the "lower faculties" and the lower classes,[12] the discipline imposed on nature by reason extended to the social stratum whose distance from nature was deemed minimal.[13] The oedipal theory, formulated at a time when the term *Volk* was being invoked in the name of strong, and ultimately successful, populist challenges to the liberal order, is striking as an allegory of political nostalgia: the king is revived in the form of the superego to protect the ego (bourgeoisie) from the id (the nature within us). "Erlkönig," in which "king" and demon coincide, exhibits a subterranean political energy that will continue to haunt the theory that took its name from Oedipus the King. This analysis, therefore, aims to emphasize a continuum between Freud's work and a tradition of (principally German) liberal thought that mourned the loss of the (French) king as much as it celebrated it.

## THE POEM

The first strophe of Goethe's ballad establishes a patriarchal structure, not only along the vertical axis of protective father and dependent child, but also through the horizontal opposition, indeed enmity, between inside and outside. The equation of "safety" and "warmth" aligns all that would threaten the child with the sensation of cold:[14]

> Wer reitet so spät durch Nacht und Wind?
> Es ist der Vater mit seinem Kind;
> Er hat den Knaben wohl in dem Arm,
> Er fasst ihn sicher, er hält ihn warm. (*HA* I:154–55)

> Who rides so late through the night and wind?
> It is the father with his child;
> he has his arm about the boy,
> he holds him safe, he keeps him warm.

What is most obviously missing here is the mother, whose absence is accentuated by the father's apparent usurpation of the maternal role: he protects the child from the elements; he keeps the child safe and warm in his arms.[15] Ensuring the child's safety, however, is less a loving tenderness than a strength of body and mind, the latter of which intervenes now to assure the boy that no apparition exists:

> Mein Sohn, was birgst du so bang dein Gesicht?—
> Siehst, Vater, du den Erlkönig nicht?
> Den Erlenkönig mit Kron' und Schweif?—
> Mein Sohn, es ist ein Nebelstreif.—

> My son—why hide your face in such fear?—
> Father—the Erl-king, don't you see?
> The Erl-king in crown and robes?—
> My son, it is a streak of mist.—

Not until the third strophe is any affection expressed; the source of this affection is the Erlkönig himself. If we are inclined to treat this as a fantasy on the child's part, then we must regard it as a wish for a different kind of family life:

> "Du liebes Kind, komm, geh mit mir!
> Gar schöne Spiele spiel' ich mit dir;

Manch' bunte Blumen sind an dem Strand;
Meine Mutter hat manch' gülden Gewand.''

"Dear child, come, come go with me,
wonderful games will I play with you;
many fair flowers are on the shore,
my mother has many a garment of gold.''

The tenderness of the Erlkönig's ''Du liebes Kind'' isolates the father's more authoritative ''Mein Sohn,'' and the very articulation of ''Kind'' signals an appreciation of the childlike that absolves fatherhood of its patriarchal onus: the Erlkönig is a father who plays children's games. Yet the most remarkable nuance of these lines is the introduction of a mother, the amplitude of flora appearing as the vestment of a maternal nature.[16] The child's reaction to this invitation makes clear that he is impressed by not merely the ''fact'' of the Erlkönig, but the specific ingredients of his promise:

Mein Vater, mein Vater, und hörest du nicht,
Was Erlenkönig mir leise verspricht?—
Sei ruhig, bleibe ruhig, mein Kind!
In dürren Blättern säuselt der Wind.—

My father, my father, don't you hear
what the Erl-king softly promises me?—
Be quiet, stay quiet, my child:
the rustle it is of dry leaves in the wind.—

The rather despotic injunction ''Sei ruhig!'' (Be still!) responds directly to the appearance of a living and loving nature, and the father's explanation, by opposing dry, dead leaves to the brightly colored flowers at water's edge depicted by the Erlkönig, in effect desiccates the bosom of nature. The experience of paternal authority ends the bond of nurture joining mother and child.

This separation from the primordial-maternal determines the Erlkönig's second attempt at enticement, which acquires an erotic flavor not apparent before. The Erlkönig's mother has been superseded by his daughters, who are to serve the child, perform nocturnal dances for him, cradle him, and lull him to sleep:

"Willst, feiner Knabe, du mit mir gehn?
Meine Töchter sollen dich warten schön;

Meine Töchter führen den nächtlichen Reihn
Und wiegen und tanzen und singen dich ein.''

"Will you, fine boy, come with me?
My daughters shall take good care of you;
my daughters lead our nightly dance,
they'll rock and dance and sing you to sleep.''

Because these nymphs retain certain offices of the mother, their appearance underscores the connection between the mother and the love-objects encountered subsequent to separation from her, and this connection further amplifies the erotic attraction the child originally feels toward the mother. The response the child's excitement incurs repeats the father's previous explanation:

Mein Vater, mein Vater, und siehst du nicht dort
Erlkönigs Töchter am düstern Ort?—
Mein Sohn, mein Sohn, ich seh' es genau;
Es scheinen die alten Weiden so grau.—

My father, my father, don't you see
The Erl-king's daughters there in the gloom?—
My son, my son, I see very well:
It is the old willows gleaming so grey.—

The Erlkönig has offered the child a family in which childhood and child-likeness are valued, in which the maternal-feminine plays an active and influential role, in which such aimless activities as dancing, singing, and playing are countenanced and even encouraged, and in which drives are allowed to follow their natural course. One might characterize this vision of the family as pre-oedipal, especially because the father freely offers mother and daughters for the comfort and enjoyment of the son.[17]

This image of an unpossessive and unpatriarchal father is shattered when the Erlkönig makes his last and final bid for the child's affection. Gone now is the preeminence of the maternal, gone the plenitude of natural forms, gone the enticing benevolence. All that remains is naked desire and its corollary, violence:

"Ich liebe dich, mich reizt deine schöne Gestalt;
Und bist du nicht willig, so brauch' ich Gewalt.''—
Mein Vater, mein Vater, jetzt fasst er mich an!
Erlkönig hat mir ein Leids getan!—

> "I love you, your beauty excites me;
> if you're not willing, I'll take you by force."—
> My father, my father, he seizes me!
> The Erl-king has hurt me!—

This development dispels the illusion that the Erlkönig had been working to create—that of a tender and affectionate father. That fantasy seems to have been a screen hiding the father's other nature, which is unveiled now as the Erlkönig sheds his kindly disguise and displays qualities that endanger the boy. The child's exploration of the realm of drive has unearthed an instinctually violent father.

My thesis, should it not yet be clear, is that the father inadvertently kills his own son, who has come dangerously close to speaking a truth the father does not want exposed. In a most extreme way, the child's death satisfies the father's earlier command "Sei ruhig, bleibe ruhig!" (Be still, stay still!), and the threefold repetition of "Mein Vater, mein Vater" (itself already a repetition that suggests a split father image) alerts us to the true subject of the poem and the true object of the boy's terror. The Erlkönig's threat of violence produces not an optical or auditory sensation on the child's part as before, but a direct tactual experience ("jetzt fasst er mich an!"), and one imagines that what he really feels is his father's grip tightening around him, just as the father spurs his horse in fear.[18] The final strophe, which immediately follows the child's exclamation of pain, twice emphasizes the placement of the boy, first groaning, then dead, in his father's arms:

> Dem Vater grauset's, er reitet geschwind,
> Er hält in Armen das ächzende Kind,
> Erreicht den Hof mit Mühe und Not;
> In seinen Armen das Kind war tot.

> The father shudders, swiftly he rides,
> the moaning child he holds in his arms;
> he gains the manor in great distress;
> in his arms the child was dead.

It would be facile to read "Erlkönig" in terms of the familiar opposition of Enlightenment and Romanticism and to see the father's ultimate distress as a de facto acknowledgment of the impotence of reason in the face of the imagination (a figment of which has ostensibly killed the child). If anything, the poem allows for a reappraisal of these categories by showing vividly that an as yet pre-Romantic supernaturalism, so often dismissed by German scholarship as irrational, does not stand opposite the

Enlightenment, but instead shapes the fears lurking close to the heart of rationalism. The terror that eventually passes from the boy to the father is the contagion the latter's explanations are meant to ward off from the start. Certain truths are better left undisclosed, and the poem warns of the consequences of a deep interpretation. The father's efforts to demystify nature are intended less to achieve understanding than to obliterate mystery. Thus, roughly modifying Goya's claim that "the sleep of reason produces monsters" ("El sueño de la razón produce monstruos"),[19] it seems that reason itself is hatched by an incubus to which it remains forever wedded.

The suggestion that reason is born of a moment of primeval dread recalls some familiar theses on the Enlightenment, especially the one set forth by Horkheimer and Adorno describing Enlightenment method as a radical form of mythological anxiety ("die radikal gewordene mythologische Angst").[20] The Age of Reason and myth shared a common aversion to the otherness and unpredictability of natural forces, and much as primitive societies held those forces at bay through ritual reenactment, so did science control nature by subjecting it to the criterion of periodicity. By treating every natural event as the imitation of a constant, immutable law, science deprives that event of its uniqueness and thus its alterity, assimilating it to something already known. In this manner, Enlightenment satisfies a kind of repetition-compulsion (*Wiederholungszwang*), a pattern of behavior by which, according to Freud, a child masters his or her reality by replaying unpleasant experiences symbolically (as in ritual), or even by provoking their actual recurrence (*SA* III:229). A related connection between Enlightenment and myth had already been sketched by Nietzsche, who saw a critique of modern science implicit in the story of Oedipus; its lesson was that to understand nature truly was to expose oneself to its wrath: "Weisheit ist ein Verbrechen an der Natur" (Wisdom is a crime against nature).[21] How else, Nietzsche asks, could one explain the apparent contradiction that the wisest of men—the man who by solving the riddle of the sphinx had pierced the deepest enigmas of nature—had also committed the most egregious sins against the natural order?

## FREUD AND THE FATHER'S SEDUCTION

The abhorrence of piercing insight dramatized by Oedipus' act of self-blinding found its way into psychoanalysis via the theory that bears his name. Freud's work manifests to no small degree the same anxieties it describes, and exhibits the aforementioned dialectic following which unsettling insights are supplanted by less disconcerting explanations. The discovery of the Oedipus complex marks one such substitution because it enabled Freud to abandon, or rather absorb, his controversial seduction theory—a theory that attributed hysteria to actual sexual trauma experienced in early childhood. Many of Freud's patients had in the course of therapy been able to recall being seduced as children, usually by their fathers, and this led Freud to construct a theory that sought the etiology of neurotic disorders in a primal scene of paternal perversion. The assumption of an actual seduction at the hands of the father began to pose a problem for Freud personally, however, once he had diagnosed himself as having hysterical symptoms, for this meant that his own father would now have to be implicated as a seducer. His uneasiness at this possibility is expressed in his letter to Fliess of 21 September 1897, in which he explained his recent renunciation of the seduction theory. There he voiced incredulity that "in every case the *father* had to be accused of being perverse, not excluding my own" (dass in sämtlichen Fällen der *Vater* als pervers beschuldigt werden musste, mein eigener nicht ausgeschlossen).[22] Freud's personal crisis was compounded by feelings of guilt associated with his father's death almost one year earlier, and the Oedipus complex, traces of which he could now freely identify in himself, allowed him to acquit his father and at the same time mitigate his own guilt. The oedipal theory holds that the father's perversion is not real, but a projection of forbidden desires harbored unconsciously by the child: namely, the child wishes to dispose of the father in order to possess the mother completely. Those recollections of seduction by the father are screen memories (*Deckerinnerungen*) that conceal the father's innocence and with it the child's culpability.[23] The appeal of this theory lies in its dual utility, for if it exonerates the father of sexually abusive acts, it also vindicates the child by making those impermissible desires part of a universal condition of childhood. Thus in a single sentence Freud shoulders the blame and disperses it across countless generations: "Ich habe die Verliebtheit in die Mutter und die Eifersucht gegen den Vater auch bei mir gefunden und halte sie jetzt für ein allgemeines Ereignis früher Kindheit" (I have found an amorous disposition toward the mother and jealousy of the father in my own case as well and now consider it to be a general phenomenon of early childhood).[24]

In addition to sharing Oedipus' father-conflict, Freud identified with Oedipus the master solver of riddles. Thus, it may seem paradoxical that he should also have inherited the mythical king's voluntary blindness. Recent investigations of Freud's relationship with his father—studies that make Freud the subject of his own analytical methods—have explained his work in the years following the death of Jakob Freud as an elaborate attempt to shield the deceased from a potential variety of grim accusations. Arguing that Freud's renunciation of the seduction theory was powered by the fear that it would ultimately incriminate his father, Marianne Krüll speculates that Jakob passed on to the young Sigmund an "unspoken taboo" against digging up the father's past.[25] As evidence of his willful blindness to his father's possible sins, she cites a dream Freud reported to Fliess in a letter of 2 November 1896, one week after his father's death, in which he enters an establishment displaying a sign reading "It is requested that the eyes be closed" (Es wird gebeten die Augen zuzudrücken). Freud reads the dream as not only a reminder of obligations owed the dead but also a gesture of self-reproach: he recognizes the establishment as the barber shop where he was delayed on the morning of his father's funeral, making him late for the ceremony.[26] His interpretation seems emblematic of the oedipal strategy of displacing guilt, for while the sign is a veritable image of the censorial mechanism of dreams (and thus of the lingering tenacity of a dead father's authority), Freud reads it instead as a reflection of his own blameworthiness.

Krüll supports her thesis further by noting how arbitrarily Freud treated the Oedipus legend, focusing entirely on Oedipus' own misdeeds while seeming to ignore the important fact that Oedipus' father, Laius, had not only tried to kill his infant son but was also a known pederast. In other words, adherence to the seduction theory would have required Freud to suspect his father of crimes similar to those committed by Laius. Freud's reading of this and other traditions is the focus of a study by Marie Balmary who, much like Krüll, argues that Freud formulated the oedipal theory to protect his father from the charge of perversion. Comparing the variants of the myth available to Freud, Balmary describes how, according to legend, Laius developed a passion for Chrysippus, the young son of King Pelops, forcing the boy into acts that ultimately drove him to suicide.[27] In fact, as Balmary points out, each tragic moment in Oedipus' life recreates one of Laius' faults: the suicide of Jocasta, Oedipus' mother-lover, repeats that of Chrysippus, the victim of Laius' seductions; the sterility of Oedipus' subjects repays Laius' failure to abide by the divine prohibition against having children; and Oedipus' "piercing" of his own eyes corresponds to Laius "transpiercing" the ankles of his newborn son.[28]

Of these various crimes, that of driving a secret lover to suicide links the story of Oedipus to Freud's other master narrative, Virgil's *Aeneid*, the text from which he took the epigraph for *The Interpretation of Dreams: "Flectere si nequeo superos, Acheronta movebo"* (If I cannot bend the

Higher Powers, I will move the Infernal Regions). Balmary points out the extraordinary parallel between Aeneas' journey and Freud's self-analysis: "Through the door of dreams Aeneas proceeds into the underworld to see his father, who [like Jakob Freud] has been dead for a year."[29] The relevance is heightened by the fact that Aeneas' second wife, Dido, to whom he was secretly and briefly married, committed suicide after he left her to found Rome and eventually take a third wife. Balmary contends that the power these two ancient texts exercised over Freud points to an event in the life of Jakob Freud corresponding to the suicides of Jocasta and Dido. Biographers have noted certain discrepancies in records that suggest Jakob may have had not two wives, the official number, but three; he was married briefly to a young woman named Rebecca before his union with Amalie, Sigmund's mother. Balmary extrapolates, based on the textual material, that Freud may have suspected that his father drove the young bride to suicide and for this reason had kept her existence a secret.

It is important to see that the oedipal theory dislodges its predecessor not through outright repudiation, but incorporation, and absorbs into its body the very notion it seeks to discredit. Its strategy is to account for the process of revision that misleads one into drawing conclusions consistent with the original seduction theory. In short, the subject of the oedipal theory is another theory—one that had become as disturbing to Freud as the phenomenon it described. That same phenomenon, the forcible seduction of a child by a father(-figure), is the centerpiece of Goethe's poem, which foretells Freud's crisis in two rather astonishing ways. First, like the oedipal theory, it places the primal scene in full view but represents it as a fantasy of the child's making. Second, it attaches that scene to a conflict between a rationalist and an event he is powerless to explain. Whatever power reason now retains is owing to its association with the paternal, the authority of which is evident in the way it forces that event to be ciphered in a prescientific idiom. The scene of horror in the forest harks back to an age before science had driven a wedge between nature and the supernatural, and to share in the youngster's vision is to recollect a state where nature was at once incomprehensible and intimate. The child's experience assumes the kind of fantastic form the Enlightenment had not yet learned to consider seriously. But the fantasy also manifests the repression that makes it necessary, and an Enlightenment that dares to look more closely runs the risk of finding in itself the sort of arbitrary authority it had, once upon a time, set out to dismantle. The fear that overtakes the father in the end is the fear of one who, like Oedipus, sees too clearly, and the turning point of the poem is signaled by the ambiguity of the father's final exclamation: "Mein Sohn, mein Sohn, ich seh' es genau!"[30] The father shares with Freud the vulnerability that comes from a growing sensitivity to fantastic representations, and one could say that the advent of psychoanalysis proper recapitulates the discovery by the Romantics of the importance of fairy tales: the discovery, namely, that a repressed nature rejoins the supernatural, the monstrous form of which embodies the full force of the repression.

One of Freud's most circuitous forays into the realm of the fantastic is also the work in which the concept of the primal scene (*Urszene*) is elaborated. This is the case study of the Wolfman, a compulsive neurotic for whom fairy tales were a rich source of instruction in sexual matters. This study betrays how the oedipal theory works as a strategem for making the child responsible for the father's unspeakable deeds, and here Freud goes so far as to suggest that the child unconsciously solicits paternal violence as punishment befitting the wish, also unconscious, to be seduced by the father. In the first years of his life, the patient had felt tremendous adulation for his father, often expressing the wish to become "a master like father" (ein Herr wie der Vater). Then at the age of about three and a half, he became the target of the erotic advances of his older sister who took to fondling his genitals, and he soon transferred his passive sexual stance toward his sister to his relationship with his father. His previous identification with his father's mastery was transformed into willing submission to that mastery. But the seduction at his sister's hands also activated the unconscious memory of a much earlier scene of extraordinary nature: it appeared that the patient had, at the age of one and a half, observed his parents having intercourse "in the manner of beasts" (*more ferarum*, the mother positioned on all fours with her husband mounting her from behind). The revival of this event confirmed for the child what various fairy tales (not to mention the remonstrations of his caretakers) had led him to suspect: namely, the prerequisite for being seduced by the father was castration; he had observed the act at very close range and seen the mother's "wound." Castration-anxiety thus intervened to convert the child's tenderness for his father into fear of him, and the father began appearing in the child's nightmares as a hungry wolf, a fairy-tale creature whose iconic upright posture resembled his father's position during coitus and whose voracity recalled the father's one-time habit of expressing affection for his small son with a phrase that ominously intermingles love and brutality: "Ich fress' dich auf" (I'm going to gobble you up). The ensuing animal phobia served to screen the child's fear of the father; that fear in turn disguised his homoerotic feelings for the same person.

An application of Freud's case study to Goethe's poem would yield the reading that the Erlkönig's expression of lust for the boy ("Ich liebe dich, mich reizt deine schöne Gestalt") is a fantasy by means of which the child masks his own desire by inverting subject and object; that is, he makes himself the passive object of an active desire that originates with him, yet he disowns it through projection onto an alien subject. Both Freud's study and Goethe's poem are about forbidden desires that, as they near consciousness, become inseparable from the deadly wrath their satisfaction would presumably incur. Indeed, so closely was violence linked to the Wolfman's fantasies that punishment itself promised pleasure. What counts for Freud is that the father's wolflike ferocity was an undeserved attribution on the child's part, so much so that the boy had to resort to tantrums to provoke the father's anger. In this way, the child became in effect his father's seducer (*SA* VIII:147).

Freud further asks whether the primal scene in the parents' bedroom ever really occurred and concludes that it does not matter because the content of that scene is the property of an inherited phylogeny and could thus be constructed through inference.[31] The child, he says, speaking of primal scenes in general, "fills the gaps of individual truth with prehistoric truth, substitutes the experience of his ancestors for his own" (füllt die Lücken der individuellen Wahrheit mit prähistorischer Wahrheit aus, setzt die Erfahrung der Vorahnen an die Stelle der eigenen Erfahrung ein, *SA* VIII:210). This particular case study, while negotiating a dense tangle of neurotic symptoms, conforms, by dehistoricizing the primal scene, to the general scheme of the oedipal theory, which purports to chart a more normal course of sexual development. With the desertion of the earlier theory deriving neurosis from a specific historical trauma, the discovery of the Oedipus complex marks a decisive move away from the historically unique toward the universal and with it a shift in focus away from the perverse to the normal—a reorientation entirely consistent with Horkheimer and Adorno's thesis according to which modern science works to "normalize" what is initially, and properly, shocking.[32]

## THE FRENCH REVOLUTION AND THE OEDIPAL THEORY

How can one discard the explanatory crutch of influence and still support the claim that a ballad composed by Goethe in the early 1780s could have anticipated the theoretical shift that marked the arrival of psychoanalysis over a century later? I proposed earlier that Freud's discovery recapitulated the Romantic intuition that a repressed nature resurfaces in fantastic or supernatural forms in which both the force and irrationality (vid. arbitrariness) of the repression are manifest. This linkage of repression and representation already points to not only a proto-psychoanalytical component but also political events that demanded a concept of repression be articulated. The violent return of the repressed was precisely how many German observers saw the French Revolution, and Fichte's characterization from 1793 typifies a liberalism that regarded the revolution, however destructive, as the inevitable eruption of natural drives that had been "held back":[33]

> Der zurückgehaltene Gang der Natur bricht gewaltsam durch und vernichtet alles, was ihm im Wege steht, die Menschheit rächt sich auf das grausamste an ihren Unterdrückern, Revolutionen werden nothwendig.

> The suppressed course of nature breaks through violently and annihilates everything that stands in its way; humanity avenges itself most cruelly against its oppressors; revolutions became necessary.

A Freudian adaptation of this anthropological model might hold that revolution results when natural impulses are not adequately "represented," that is, censored so as to defuse the conflict with the repressive agent. Indeed, much of Romanticism seems to consist in the attempt to find alternative cipherings for revolutionary desires. The establishment of the category of *Volk* that lay behind the new fascination with fairy tales amounted to middle-class recognition of the common man (whom it equated with nature) and suggested a vague premonition of the nineteenth-century conflict that seriously destablilized Viennese society at the very moment Freud's theory was entering its most critical and original phase. Romanticism thus prepares for psychoanalysis more specifically in the way it conflates social aspirations with forbidden pleasures. In Ludwig Tieck's *Der blonde Eckbert* (1797), a literary fairy tale so beguiling it mocks interpretation, the heroine's rise from rags to riches coincides with her unwitting entry into an incestuous marriage; this makes her acquisition of wealth strangely akin to the violation of that more universal taboo. In a typically Romantic variation of the oedipal nightmare staged in Goethe's poem, the girl's surrogate *mother,* formerly the tale's moral point of reference, returns to inform Eckbert that his wife, now dead, was his sister, leaving him writhing on the ground in abject madness. Brought to consciousness, the crime becomes its own punishment.[34]

Because Freud tended to relegate politics to an epiphenomenon of the psyche, the oedipal theory itself may be heir to those Romantic strategies for displacing political conflict. Recent commentators, noting Freud's "neutralization" of politics, have wondered at the lack of attention he paid to Oedipus' role as king;[35] it would be just as easy to overlook the fact that the Erlkönig is a king both in name and costume ("mit Kron' und Schweif"), a fact that reminds us that the poem was written shortly before the French Revolution. I am less interested in the possible political thematics of this text, however, than in the political implications of the interpretive models it sets in conflict, for even if Goethe's poem does not allegorize the prerevolutionary milieu, it nonetheless supplies the analytical schemes many soon applied to the events of 1789–93. I have already argued that the poem, by juxtaposing divergent explanations of a supernatural experience, stakes out the parameters of its own critical reception, for while the father's natural-scientific bias logically generates a medical explanation of the child's hallucinations (not to mention his death), the child's view into the substance of fantasy is commensurate with a psychological approach. The collision of perspectives within the poem prophesies a disagreement that was to attend the birth of psychoanalysis much later when Freud's theory of the sexual origins of hysteria inspired the fury of the reigning medical establishment; but it also rehearses a more imminent debate over the causes of the French Revolution, itself supernatural, at least to the degree that its opponents considered it to be, in the words of Edmund Burke, "out of nature."[36] The same categories are compared in the following fragment in which a psychoerotic diagnosis of the revolution is preferred to one grounded in medical pathology. The fragment not only associates an oedipal interpretation with resistance from above, but it also suggests that the threat of castration is more than just the product of a child's guilt-informed fantasy. The fragment is from 1797; its author, Novalis:

> Die meisten Beobachter der Revolution . . . haben sie für eine lebensgefährliche und ansteckende Kranckheit erklärt. . . . Die Genievollsten Gegner drangen auf Castration—Sie merckten wohl— dass diese angebliche Kranckheit nichts, als Krise der eintretenden Pubertät sey. (II:464)

> Most observers of the revolution . . . explained it as a life-threatening and contagious disease. . . . The most ingenious opponents urged castration—they surely noticed—that this alleged disease was nothing other than the crisis of oncoming puberty.

Novalis's fragment is cited by the American Anglist Ronald Paulson in his *Representations of Revolution (1789–1820)*,[37] a deft account of the dynamic that comes into play when artists appropriate existing models from history, myth, and natural science to lend comprehensible form to an experience so novel as to have no precedent in human time. Because representation necessarily gives the new in terms of the old, strangeness and familiarity are enlisted as antithetical factors of a dialectic in which affirmation seems virtually to condition subversion. Whether the revolution in France was depicted as a scene from Roman Republican history or as the opening of Pandora's Box, as a seasonal change or as a geological calamity, that is, whether the figure employed connoted elation or disgust, the effect was to recover for the realm of the familiar something uncompromisingly foreign. The common practice of measuring the revolution against newly established physical principles (e.g., the evaporation cycle) simply emblematizes the link between attempts at representing revolution and the Enlightenment project overall, the thrust of which, according to Horkheimer and Adorno's critique, was to palliate radical insight by treating every occurrence as a recurrence. Even those comparisons of the political upheaval to destructive forces in the earth and atmosphere may be seen as extensions of a scientific Enlightenment that was straining to assimilate those forces to its rational cosmos.

To state the point clearly: a portrayal of the French Revolution as the reenactment of a scene already played mitigates the shock of the new by absorbing it into a tradition of precedents. At the same time, however, the previous scene is made less familiar, catapulted into an alien context by virtue of this new association. Thus, while the historical moment is domesticated, the figurative ground is radicalized. To do as Novalis did, for example, and describe the French Revolution as a post-Enlightenment analogue of the Protestant Reformation was to make explicit the modern political implications of Luther's revolt and, beyond that, to identify a revolutionary tradition on German soil. This by-product of assimilation, this "displacement of an actual revolutionary perception onto something else,"[38] is the subversive twist that redirects the search for radical understanding toward those displaced figurations.

Paulson makes global use of psychoanalysis; he argues both that representations of revolution return the specific historical moment to any number of primal scenes and that these scenes generally correspond to one of two basic Freudian categories: the oedipal and the oral-anal. In the first of these, the revolution is given as a progressive movement wherein the son, after killing and eating the father, internalizes him and assumes the paternal role with its responsibilities. In the second scheme, the revolution is portrayed as an unredeemed regression to sheer appetite: not satisfied by the meal it had made of its father (Louis XVI), the Parisian "horde" now turned on its own, and the image of Saturn devouring his children became a favorite for evoking a tyrant as bad as, or worse than, the one he had replaced (an image, by the way, that resonates of the father of Freud's Wolfman and his affectionate "Ich fress' dich auf").

When Paulson quotes Novalis's fragment, he does so to shield his psychohistory of revolution from the usual charges of anachronism. By demonstrating that the late eighteenth century was in touch with categories that Freud would later isolate, Paulson hopes to justify the historical application of, in his words, "a scientifically valid theory of modern behavior."[39] I cite this in the interest of contradistinction, for the scientific validity of Freudian theory does not interest me as much as the hermeneutic field that involves it with the subject under analysis. I do not, in other words, seek the value of psychoanalysis in its ahistorical objectivity, but precisely in its subjective historicity. Specifically, I am suggesting that the oedipal theory itself is a representation of revolution, one that displaces political conflict onto the familiar (in the narrowest sense of that word) and that, while detracting from the political sphere, politicizes the psyche and makes politics inescapable however far one retreats into the inner reaches of private experience.[40]

One way of conceptualizing the political origins of Freud's theory is to consider his notion of the superego (*Über-Ich*), the agency of conscience and the natural successor to the oedipal stage, as the embodiment of those behavior traits revered by classical European liberalism—what might be called the political ideology of self-restraint. Norman O. Brown begins a famous essay by suggesting that Freud's hypothesis in *Totem and Taboo* of an aboriginal patricide transports into prehistory the English constitutional crisis that culminated in the beheading of Charles I in 1649. One legacy of this event was a variety of liberal philosophies of government that rejected both the revolutionary bloodshed and conservative reactions to it, and these Brown restates in Freudian terms when he notes, for example, how the establishment of the social contract, as the crystallization of a supra-individual will, corresponds to the formation of the superego.[41] This nascent liberalism identifies, as the requisite complement of the rise of civil society, the progressive obsolescence of absolute monarchy and, eventually, of political government as such.

In the teleology of Enlightenment liberalism, the conflict between the people and the law is resolved through internalizing the latter by the former; constraints autocratically imposed give way to restraints society imposes on itself. For Freud, the conflict is resolved through a similar process of internalization wherein the son identifies with the father; the authority represented by the father then resides with the son, and the influence of conscience attests to the continued psychological presence of the father even in his physical absence. In the horde of Freud's primitive scenario, this occurred only after the sons had killed their patriarch and internalized him literally by eating him. In the normal resolution of the oedipal conflict, however, no act of patricide is committed. The liberal scheme of things provides for kings to be outgrown rather than killed, rendered superfluous by the ability of the people to govern themselves peaceably. Both strategies ensure the father's survival, and this is the crux: the Oedipus complex is a representation of patricide (revolution) that substitutes for the actual deed. The answer to the question of whether Oedipus himself had an Oedipus complex is a resounding "no": had he had one, he would not have killed his father and slept with his mother, but only dreamt of these things. His story, in the words of René Girard, "is a simple reflection of unconscious desires that formally excludes any execution of these desires."[42]

The counterrevolutionary charge of the oedipal theory appears to be the legacy not only, as Brown suggests, of a philosophy generated by the English Civil War but also of modifications in the philosophy that the French Revolution made necessary. Even prior to the crucial events in France, the concept of self-domination, which Brown links to that of the superego, had been extensively articulated by the German Enlightenment and incorporated into its notion of education: thinking autonomously (*Selbstdenken*), the goal of that project, was tantamount to policing oneself. In one of the most complex expressions of the German Enlightenment and its limitations, *Die Erziehung des Menschengeschlechts* (The Education of the Human Race, 1777), Lessing explains how developing reason would confirm rather than invalidate natural (revealed) religion; the advance of reason enables us to see retrospectively the wisdom behind those demonstrations of sheer might with which God first alerted humanity to his unique presence. An arbitrary authority physically expressed initiates the development of a faculty that, in its maturity, would at once justify the authority and render it obsolete. The time will come, Lessing predicts, "when man will do good because it is good, not because arbitrary rewards are placed on it" (da er [der Mensch] das Gute tun wird, weil es das Gute ist, nicht weil willkürliche Belohnungen darauf gesetzt sind).[43] Here, as so often elsewhere, Lessing prefers a parable that localizes the process of enlightenment within the familial sphere; the *telos* of growing up is the rational vindication of paternal actions, including the harsh ones:[44]

Als das Kind unter Schlägen und Liebkosungen aufgewachsen und nun zu Jahren des Verstandes gekommen war, stiess es der Vater auf einmal in die Fremde; und hier erkannte es auf einmal das Gute, das es in seines Vaters Hause gehabt und nicht erkannt hatte.

Once the child had grown up amidst beatings and coddlings and had now reached intellectual maturity, the father suddenly forced him out into foreign lands; and here he suddenly recognized the good which he had had in his father's house and not recognized.

The adult's self-mastery through reason replicates the mastery his father exercised over him before that reason had matured. The confidence that the Enlightenment had placed in the certainty of this development was severely shaken by the French Revolution, especially by the *terreur*, in which so many saw nature raising its hand against reason (law). This left German intellectuals at an impasse: reason could not progress in the absence of freedom, yet if the political constraints that kept natural impulses in check were removed before reason had developed, there was nothing to prevent a reversion to a brutal state of nature. Fichte, whose moderate sympathy for the revolution enjoyed the briefest of life spans, stressed more and more the importance of reason's dominion over nature, and he saw in culture the means that would allow the individual to inherit that jurisdiction from his previous masters: "der Zweck aller Bildung der Geschicklichkeit ist der, die Natur . . . der Vernunft zu unterwerfen. . . . Die Erwerbung dieser Geschicklichkeit . . . heisst *Kultur*" (All development of dexterity has the aim of subjugating nature to reason. . . . The acquisition of this dexterity is called *culture*).[45]

This German post-Enlightenment ideology of culture underwent a further adjustment in the hands of Schiller, who criticized Fichte for perpetuating the duality of reason and nature. In his *Über die ästhetische Erziehung des Menschen* (On the Aesthetic Education of Man, 1795), a treatise he revised in the wake of his utter revulsion at the fate of Louis XVI, he rejects Fichte's notion of culture as the rigorous moralization of human sensuality and describes its function instead as that of harmonizing man's physical and rational impulses. There is a relevant distinction here: for Schiller, it is no longer a matter of subordinating the will of the individual to that of the group because aesthetic education renders the two indistinct by effecting the complete internalization of a once alien desire; the individual will becomes the vehicle through which the common will is concretized: "der ästhetische Staat allein kann sie [die Gesellschaft] wirklich machen, weil er den Willen des Ganzen durch die Natur des Individuums vollzieht" (the aesthetic state alone can make society into a reality, because it consummates the will of the whole through the nature of the individual).[46] The decisive term is "nature," for Schiller intends a process whereby ethical behavior, that which formerly had the task of containing natural impulses, is "naturalized," that is, transformed into second nature. Exposure to the aesthetic sphere creates a human being to whom virtue comes naturally—an individual in whom, to quote from another of Schiller's essays, the antagonism of inclination and duty is reconciled as an "inclination to duty" (Neigung zur Pflicht).[47]

The ideology of culture presents the pursuit of aesthetic pleasure as a superior alternative to political revolution in that the cultured individual, rather than being a slave to natural drives, harnesses those drives to civilized ends; culture does not repress nature, but rechannels it. A similar process was described on the eve of the Freudian revolution by Richard von Krafft-Ebing (*Psychopathia sexualis,* 1886) who declared that the highest achievements in science and the arts were the result of what Freud would later term "sublimation"—a redirection of sexual energy into cultural endeavors. While Krafft-Ebing may have inherited his views from the liberalism of Schiller, the implication that natural impulses and culture are inherently at odds smacks less of a liberal legacy than of the conservatism of Thomas Hobbes, who described the innate human drive for self-preservation as the enemy of social progress, even troping the resurgence of that drive, of which the English Civil War seemed to be an expression, as a supernatural beast (*Leviathan,* 1652). The same beast rears its head in the form of a mutiny in the saga of Arion, the first of several tales embedded in the larger narrative of *Heinrich von Ofterdingen* (*Schriften* I:211–13). His life threatened by sailors who consent to ferry him home but then succumb to greed at the sight of the riches he carries, the Orphic poet sings a song that enlists the sympathy of nature, and the taming of a Leviathan-like creature, a monster ("Unthier") that emerges from beneath the waves to rescue the singer, coincides with the frustration of the murderous conspiracy. The outcome seems to confirm the Hobbesian prediction that a society in which all were equal would soon fall victim to human self-interest; when the sailors-turned-pirates set about dividing up the spoils, a bloody struggle ensues, leaving too few survivors to control the vessel, and the ship (of state?) runs aground.

## EVIL MOTHERS

The spectacle of the mighty sea and all its creatures frolicking to Arion's song embodies what Novalis, in a more overtly political context,

45

called the "joy of obedience" (Freude des Gehorsams, III:522). The phrase echoes and amplifies Schiller's "inclination to duty," and the notion of the aesthetic domestication of nature seems a liberal adaptation of an essentially conservative model. The same tale exhibits an opposition of surface and depth that informs the whole of Novalis's work, and indeed Heinrich's quest in part imitates the journey of Virgil's Aeneas, the topography of which Freud used not only to represent the structure of the psyche, but to politicize that structure: Juno's threat to "move the Infernal Regions" if she cannot "bend the Higher Powers," Freud's motto for *The Interpretation of Dreams,* acquires a sharp political edge in 1899, two years after a surge of populism had forced the monarchy to accept an anti-Semite as mayor of Vienna.[48] The danger to the liberal order posed by those forces is represented throughout the work, but one example seems especially relevant in linking liberal aims to conservative fears.

Toward the end of his chapter on dream-distortion (*Traumentstellung*), Freud tells how an acquaintance of his, a jurist who is having an affair with a married woman, dreams that he is arrested one evening while escorting his lover home with him. Infanticide is the charge, but Freud explains that the horrific accusation in fact satisfies a wish by reassuring the anxious dreamer that his mistress has not become pregnant—that his reliance on a particular form of prophylaxis has not been in vain. Freud supports the rapid connection by recalling the fine line traditionally drawn between birth prevention and murder, and he invokes a poem by the late Romantic Nikolaus Lenau entitled "Das tote Glück" (Dead Happiness) which, by his reading, equates contraception with infanticide ("welches Kindermord und Kinderverhütung gleichstellt," *SA* II:171). The dream returns birth control to its phylogenetically prior counterpart, infanticide, but Freud's explication reverses this movement by replacing an act of paternal violence with a practice that epitomizes the much desired quality of self-restraint: *coitus interruptus.* Even within the immediate scope of Freud's discussion, said technique may be a metaphor for the kind of dexterity (*Geschicklich-keit*) Fichte mentioned as the means of subordinating natural impulses to reason. Its delineation of continuity between the primitive and the rational places Freud's analysis within the lineage of Lessing's *Erziehung,* and the rationalist recoding of a potential father's homicidal fantasies may simply be a more extreme form of the "oedipalization" characteristic of that liberal tradition.[49] If the dreamer's being a jurist is not clue enough that Freud has here returned to his tragic master narrative, then one need only remember that Laius' attempted murder of the infant Oedipus was made necessary by the father's failure to obey the oracle's interdiction of having children.[50]

Given the parallel between the jurist's dream and the grand fable of Oedipus, one might wonder at Freud's invocation of so unmonumental a text as Lenau's. An explanation is found in the difference between the two plots, for in the Romantic poem it is the mother who kills the newborn child while the terrified father looks on helplessly. By substituting Lenau's chilling tale for that more venerable text, Freud has managed to displace a father's guilt onto a mother, and it is conspicuous, given his preoccupation with Oedipus, that he should now describe child murder as a "specifically female crime" (spezifisch weiblichen Verbrechens, *SA* II:172). The postulate of female villainy betrays Freud's proximity to the turn-of-the-century cult of the femme fatale, a phenomenon whose regressive aspect links it to the crisis of liberalism with which it coincided. His reference to Lenau's poem further suggests a connection between that cult and Romanticism, in which seductive and demonic women are prevalent. The disfiguration of women in Romantic poetry has itself been explained psychoanalytically as a symptom of pathological narcissism; the inevitable failure of the mother to satisfy all of an infant's needs causes the child to feel ambivalent toward her, and the greater those needs are, the more critical the ambivalence becomes. Images of destructive women are seen as outward projections of deficient mothering that reveal a longing for affection and plenitude somehow refused in childhood.[51] This longing is addressed by the Erlkönig when he promises love and sustenance at the ample bosom of maternal nature, and though a wicked mother is not present, her requisite collaborator, a father, who like the one in Lenau's poem is reduced to an onlooker paralyzed by fear, certainly is. It may well be that the figure of the violent female is an emphatic superfluity, a secondary revision that ensures paternal innocence by creating in the savage mother an inversion of the father's presumed passivity.

In addition to fairy-tale stepmothers, the German tradition harbors Gretchen of Goethe's *Faust,* whose eventual act of infanticide (in response to unwanted pregnancy) constitutes a regression from an earlier period of elective motherhood, when she raised the child of a sister too infirm to breastfeed:

> Und so erzog ich's ganz allein,
> Mit Milch und Wasser; so ward's mein (*HA* III:100).

> And so I raised it all alone,
> With milk and water, as my own.

Inadequate feeding of the kind requiring a surrogate mother appears in Klingsohr's tale, which composes Chapter 9 of *Ofterdingen*. The introduction of the wet nurse, who before long becomes the child's first lover, marks the differentiation of a drive originally directed toward the mother (the child's name, of course, is Eros). As soon as the erotic nature of that drive becomes explicit, the taboo against incest is spoken.[52] In brief, the history of civilization is written from a moment of lack.

If the loss of unity and the concomitant experience of lack does not, in the writings of Novalis, lead to the vilification of the mother, it is perhaps due to an aesthetics that emphasizes the necessity of difference—of distance. The separation that the quest entails is the prerequisite of representation: "Wir verlassen das Identische, um es darzustellen" (We leave the identical in order to represent it, II:104). The philosophy of German idealism saw the aesthetic experience as the means of recovering—as an object within consciousness—a unity of self and world sundered by reflection; the aesthetic reconstitutes an original state of undifferentiation without forfeiting its newfound representability. In the political writings of Novalis, to which we now turn, the inadequacies of present society are described in terms of separation from something all-embracing and maternal (for example, medieval Catholicism). But when Novalis focuses on the remnants and signatures that fill the Church reliquary (or likewise the gold in the Prussian treasury), he foregrounds Catholicism as an institution that mourns and commemorates, and his "politics" is one that ultimately exposes the symbolic unity of subject and object, the purported achievement of aesthetic intuition, as irrevocably allegorical.

# 2

# The Political Novalis

Freud's account of "family romance" charts the movements by which the natural father is replaced by the cultural father, or more accurately, by which the natural father is transformed by a cultural code that renders the limitations of biological origins insignificant. Whereas in *Nathan der Weise* the natural and cultural fathers are two different people, this difference fades as the virtuous Nathan validates the original father, whose eventual reemergence marks the "naturalization" of his cultural (adopted) counterpart. Those writings by Novalis generally termed "political" adhere to the structure of family romance in that they represent the king—an ideal king to be sure—as a figure whose natural claim to the throne is vindicated through acts of cultural fathering. The transparent social order Novalis proclaims runs counter to a tradition of enlightenment that includes the Reformation and the French Revolution and consists in the progressive effacement of the sign. Enlightenment, both as a specific period and overall tendency, is a quest for truths that reason has emptied of historical content. This very trajectory is criticized by Horkheimer and Adorno, for whom enlightenment is a process of abstraction in which the increasing arbitrariness of signs is complemented by the arbitrariness of the power required to enforce a consensus they no longer command. The introduction during the French Revolution of paper money *(assignat)* in place of the *louisdor* provoked a diffidence toward the former inseparable from the doubtful future of the sovereign whose profile adorned the latter.

The linkage between gold and king forms in part the critical latency of Novalis's political writings, in which love is offered as the modern anodyne to the denaturalization of these and other cultural signs, including sacred relics. The term "fetishism" is close at hand, for Novalis's erotic alchemy suggests psychological motivations behind the desire to recover the lost unity of which all such signs are relics. Theories of value and love intersect here to reveal a point of tangency between Marxism and psychoanalysis for which neither tradition had full appreciation until the appearance of Herbert Marcuse's *Eros and Civilization* (1955).

## COIN OF THE REALM

"No state was ever managed more like a factory *(mehr als Fabrik verwaltet)* than Prussia following the death of Friedrich Wilhelm the First" *(Schriften* II:494). At a time when Germany had no factories to speak of, Novalis found in the Prussian administration a governmental counterpart to industrialization, one in which citizens were joined together in a common enterprise by nothing more ennobling than individual self-interest *(Eigennutz)*. To this he holds up the counterimage of selfless love, of which the institution of marriage was the most universal expression. Like many of his contemporaries, Novalis believed that the ascendant king and his new bride, having married for love and not dynastic gain, heralded a new moralization of the public sphere and presented the populace with a concrete basis for identifying with the monarchy in familial terms. Predictably, the suggestion that a royal couple's conjugal bliss would ensure the organic harmony of the state has led critics to accuse Novalis of political naiveté at the very least; they often link him with the regressive desire for outright refeudalization.[1]

The most informed exploration of Novalis's "conservatism" associates it instead with the resistance, inherent in bourgeois society, to its own emancipatory impulses.[2] This ambivalence was addressed by Marx when he likened the bourgeoisie to a sorcerer *(Hexenmeister)*, unable to control the subterranean forces *(unterirdische Mächte)* unleashed by modernization.[3] A similar inner tension is identified by Franco Moretti as the central component of the classical *Bildungsroman*, a genre that celebrates the restlessness of youth but opts finally for the limitations and boundaries that constitute *culture*, subordinating freedom to personality.[4] That the *Bildungsroman* typically ends in matrimony is due to the fact that marriage had come to be seen as the smallest and most commonly accessible manifestation of the social contract, in which the individual's claim to happiness is renounced in favor of a happiness based on reciprocal sacrifice—a happiness Freud might have characterized as "aim-inhibited" *(zielgehemmt)*.[5] The marriage at the close of Goethe's *Wilhelm Meisters Lehrjahre* culminates and crowns Wilhelm's rejection of the spirit of modernity that propelled him into the world several years earlier; he gets rich to be sure, but long after he abandons the mercantilistic project whose exclusive aim is the accumulation of wealth. The good fortune to which he finally attests, entailing marriage, riches, and the discovery of his own patronymy, is located fully outside of the matrix of exchange: " 'Ich kenne den Wert eines Königreichs nicht . . . , aber ich weiss, dass ich ein Glück erlangt habe, das ich nicht verdiene, und das ich mit nichts in der Welt vertauschen möchte' " ("I don't know what a kingdom is worth . . . , but I know that I have acquired a happiness which I don't deserve, and which I would not want to exchange for anything in the world" *HA* VII:610).

Novalis lauded *Wilhelm Meister* for the way it undermined the economic instrumentalism that reduces work to a means to an end, and he likens Wilhelm to alchemists, whose real gains are tangential to, and thus greater than, the intended product of their chemistry (III:639).[6] Moretti too sees a critical moment in the novel's exaltation of precapitalistic, unalienated labor—that is, work that is not there simply to produce commodities whose "meaning" is extraneous to the producer, but contributes to the formation of that person. This closure is exemplified by Wilhelm, whose theatrical pursuits have resulted in a physical stature and poise that radiate a harmonious spirit. By contrast, Werner, Wilhelm's entrepreneurial friend, has pursued a life of commerce at the expense of his other faculties, and his premature decrepitude indicates an ascetic regimen that enlists the body in the achievement of successes in which the body will not share. Like Odysseus' oarsmen, who by numbing their senses become one with their task and different from themselves,[7] Werner has grown to identify with goals so alien that he can detect in himself no outward sign of his own accomplishments. At a time when *Schein* had not yet acquired the suspect connotation of "mere appearance," Werner beholds himself in the mirror and finds nothing that reflects the fruits of his labor (*HA* VII:499). A different discipline is behind Wilhelm's *Bildung,* which defies the teleology that splits the self, forging instead an identity of substance and appearance to which the mirror is entirely adequate—a unity that graces, as presence, every feature, gesture, and turn of phrase.

This internal cohesiveness manifested as an immanence of form, the longing for which drives even Faust to alchemy, is specified through its

51

opposition to the allegorical, which proclaims disintegration and the loss of immanence. If the socially disfigured Werner corresponds to the askesis of allegory,[8] the well-proportioned Wilhelm is commensurate with the *symbolic,* itself the object of Novalis's alchemy of the body politic.[9] Besides describing Natalie, Wilhelm's bride, as an exemplary queen figure (II:498), he implicitly casts Wilhelm as king by literalizing "constitution" as "physique"; the harmonious cooperation of all society's parts finds symbolic expression in the monarch, whose "healthiest of constitutions" (II:499) guarantees a balanced apportionment of power and guards against the poor circulation of "the blood of the state," namely gold and silver ("Gold und Silber sind das Blut des Staats," II:486). The suffusion of every limb with a radiance emanating from the center—the optimum visibility of the whole through each of its parts—distinguishes the symbolic from the device and forced connections of allegory.[10] Hence the distinction between the arbitrary machinations of the state and, to borrow Moretti's formulation, "the flexible and organic bonds of a world where the living sense of authority is still one with everyday life."[11] Novalis's criticism of the "mechanistic administration" (II:494) of Prussia summons the symbol in an argument that points forward to the *homme machine,* of whom, or of which, Werner is a human prototype.[12]

The gist of the foregoing is that the Romantic distinction between symbol and allegory is part of a post-Enlightenment crisis of signification that is also a crisis of value—one developing toward the moment when Marx, in his treatment of fetishism, indicts the most hallowed of precious metals for a counterfeit translucence, asserting that even gold does not embody the value it represents.[13] This analysis marks an advanced stage in a process of demystification that, by focusing on the sundering of sign and signified within the realm of economics, illuminates a more general aspect of the Enlightenment. Once again, Lessing's *Nathan der Weise* proves rich in resonance. Summoned before the Sultan, Nathan, who has just returned from lucrative travels abroad, expects to be extorted, but instead is asked, in his capacity as the sagacious Jew, to determine which of the three major religions is the "true" faith. Surprised by a question that is philosophical rather than financial, Nathan holds forth in a soliloquy that nevertheless implicates money in a debate on truth and exposes the Enlightenment as the progressive abstraction of not only meaning but also *value:*[14]

> —Ich bin
> Auf Geld gefasst; und er will—Wahrheit. Wahrheit!
> Und will sie so, —so bar, so blank, —als ob

Die Wahrheit Münze wäre! — Ja, wenn noch
Uralte Münze, die gewogen ward!—
Das ginge noch! Allein so neue Münze,
Die nur der Stempel macht, die man aufs Brett
Nur zählen darf, das ist die doch nun nicht!

                          —I come
Prepared for money; and he wants—truth. Truth!
And wants it thus, —so bare, so plain, —as if
The truth were coin! —Now, if only
Ancient coin that had been weighed!—
That would be fine! But such new coin,
Made by the stamp, which one might
Count on the table, that isn't it at all!

Nathan's comparison of the two kinds of coin mirrors the distinction Marx would make between use-value and exchange-value, the latter of which represents an abstraction that renders goods interchangeable, however much those goods may differ physically. For Marx, this increase in abstraction leads society to separate the value of a product from the context of human labor that created it. For Nathan as well, this loss of specificity detracts from tradition, history, indeed, from the intimacy of physical intuition: coins that are technically reproduced and need only be counted (*gezählt*) replace those that are weighed (*gewogen*), that is, tested for their tangible properties, and perhaps held and sensed in relation to one's own body. The preference is for the coin that bears the unique imprint of the process that made it, and this orientation toward process distinguishes Nathan from the Sultan (and Wilhelm from Werner). Nathan declines to acknowledge truth that can be extricated from experience; wisdom can be acquired through work but not exchange, and Nathan's storytelling is a strategy for engaging the Sultan in a labor of discovery.

Nathan's "Parable of the Ring," which defines the Enlightenment in terms of an idiom of reproducibility, shows magic to be the first casualty of technical reproduction. Magic in Lessing is a ring that scintillates a thousand colors, its provenance the hand of someone dear ("aus lieber Hand").[15] Its loss heralds an age in which the dream of self-creation is realized, as the unique power of the ring gives way to abilities and talents common to all. But there is also a nostalgia for the ring that marks it as an allegory of alienation brought on by the instrumental reason that endows men with a power over things.[16] Because this power counts the body among its objects, the nostalgia for the ring is at once a longing for a lost wholeness of self. Nathan's parable is a narrative of origins in which the ring is ultimately a metonym for the loving hand that delivered it, which itself is preserved in the tale only as a body fragment. Indirectly, it is a nostalgia for the hand that weighed the coins and thus for an age of "authentic" contact, which serial reproduction has erased, and of which only traces remain.[17]

Such nostalgia soon found a new domain in the collector's cabinet, the miniature utopia in which the bourgeois mounted a private and ritualized resistance to the modern momentum toward sheer equivalency. Walter Benjamin, the theorist of mechanical reproduction who characterized capitalism as the "impulse towards a vanquishment of the unique" (Tendenz einer Überwindung des Einmaligen), described the collector as an allegorist who liberates things from the onus of being useful.[18] As an allegory, the collector's item is a remnant and thus an occasion for a narrative of elusive origins. Because it acquires a value that is not intrinsic to the object, it is a fetish in the Marxist vein; and because the nostalgic myth of presence replaces memories of the body with memories of the thing, it is a fetish in the Freudian sense as well.[19]

In Novalis's *Die Christenheit oder Europa* (Christianity or Europe, 1799), these two senses of fetishism converge on the image of the medieval reliquary, which in addition to personal effects of the saints, often contained remnants of their very bodies or even instruments of their physical agonies. The modern collection, public or private, differs from the Church reliquary in that it lacks the miracle of presence. Between them stands Martin Luther, in whose hands the revealed word became an object of historical reconstruction and whose denial of transubstantiation made the Eucharist into a supreme allegory. Like Novalis, Horkheimer and Adorno situate Luther firmly within a tradition of disenchantment *(Entzauberung)*, of which the Enlightenment proper is only the most rarified expression. Its achievement is the distillation of the sign from imagery, a disembodiment of meaning that substitutes belief for consensus. Abstraction brings a loss of transparency that requires an ever greater degree of intervention to reinforce bonds that have become increasingly tenuous. Novalis is concerned with the same attenuation, but his alignment of the age of Voltaire with that of Luther has the added effect of linking the demise of a sociopolitical translucence with the loss of a more fundamental state of undifferentiation—one to which the mother-bond is analogous. *Die Christenheit* is a discourse on longing that prepares the ground for a psychoanalytical reading of the Reformation (and of its politics) and, just as important, points to the implications of such a reading for the Frankfurt

School, whose understanding of Luther's legacy as an enduring "obedience to the word" (Gehorsam aufs Wort) evokes the Symbolic Order of
the father.[20]


## MEMORY AND THE DIALECTICS OF REGRESSION

The all-encompassing unity of medieval Catholicism is the point from
which, in Novalis's essay of 1799, all history is a falling off. He traces this
fall through Luther's Reformation, the Jesuit militancy of the Counter-
Reformation, the Enlightenment, and the French Revolution. In each of
these developments he discerns both admirable designs and historical necessity, yet each was destined to fail because, unlike the original Church,
it did not minister to the totality of human needs. Thus while Luther
brought changes that were much needed and long overdue, he also fostered
an enmity between learning and spirituality that would inform the Enlightenment and lead ultimately to the slaughter of clergymen during the
French Revolution. In this way, Novalis treats earlier historical periods as
prefigurations of later ones, and he urges his reader to learn to use "the
magic wand of analogy" (den Zauberstab der Analogie, III:518). It is by
means of such magic that he modernizes the Reformation, appropriating
for its description a terminology more adequate to the revolution of 1789:
"Was war natürlicher, als dass endlich ein feuerfangender Kopf öffent-
lichen Aufstand gegen den despotischen Buchstaben der ehemahligen Ver-
fassung predigte" (What was more natural than a volatile character finally
preaching public revolt against the despotic letter of the previous constitution, III:511). But while making Luther into an opponent of despotism,
Novalis also, by virtue of the same analogy, draws the Enlightenment into
a conflict with the primordial-maternal—a struggle already observed in
"Erlkönig."

The relevance of "Erlkönig" for Novalis's essay may be found in the
way the latter historicizes the mythological scene represented in Goethe's
poem: the Protestant Reformation stages the same patriarchal banishment
of the maternal, and the violence of the elements, which in the poem manifests the force with which that separation was achieved, signifies for Novalis the absence of asylum once afforded by the great motherly body of
Catholicism. When Novalis characterizes medieval Church officials as
able steersmen "in whose care one could despise all storms" (in deren
Obhut man alle Stürme geringschätzen . . . durfte, III:507), the metaphor
revives a seminal event in the career of Martin Luther, whose entry into

the monastery at Erfurt fulfilled a desperate vow he made during an electrical storm that nearly took his life. This apocryphal bit of biography has the markings of a primal scene, and the thunderstorm projects fear away from its intimate source and onto something more neutral. His choice of the monastic life came in direct defiance of an ambitious father who envisioned his son prospering as a lawyer in the service of the growing merchant class; and because the young Luther had often felt the sting of his father's fierce and physical temper, he wrote of his decision to become a monk only after gaining the safe custody of the Augustinian brethren. Father and storm become indistinguishable from the vantage point of the monastery, the walls of which lent refuge from both simultaneously.

This father-conflict is the focus of Erik Erikson's psychobiography of Luther, which traces the genesis of Protestant theology back to the great Reformer's efforts to resolve his highly ambivalent feelings toward his father. The radical polarization of Luther's cosmos between God's terrible greatness and man's inexorable depravity represented the sharply bifurcated image Luther held of his father—a split between, on the one hand, a severe moral piety that met every transgression with the whip, and on the other, behavior far too compromising to justify such exacting self-righteousness. Intemperate where his children and, apparently, his alcohol were concerned, Hans Luder was a man of uncertain background which some believed to include a homicide, and Erikson interprets Luther's lifelong contest with Satan as a struggle with those of his father's traits and deeds not consistent with the harsh moralism he so vehemently espoused.[21] The devil functioned for Luther like the Erlkönig for the boy in Goethe's text; it enabled the child to retain a positive father image by investing a figure of the supernatural with menacing features belonging to the father.[22] However, Luther saw in Satan not his father's, but his own depravity, as he could rationalize his father's seemingly arbitrary authority only through the counterpostulate of his own inherent sinfulness, and here one cannot help but recognize the same oedipal maneuver whereby Freud, faced with suspicions of criminal immorality in his father's past, preserved his father's innocence by shifting the blame to himself.

Without recourse to Luther's biography, Novalis manages to extract from the bold silhouette of the Reformation the more finely drawn skeleton of the oedipal conflict detailed by Erikson; and if Novalis had already identified the same conflict as the underlying cause of the French Revolution, his alignment in *Die Christenheit* of that later event with the inception of Protestantism enables him to expose the essentially patriarchal structure of the Enlightenment by isolating the primary casualty of the oedipal crisis—the bond between a child and its mother. Erikson speculates that Luther's father dominated family life to the point of usurping the maternal role altogether, making it impossible for the son to accept the Virgin Mary as divine intermediary.[23] The Protestant creed became an enduring testimony to a paternal authority as unmediated as it was inscrutable, and Luther, as the force behind a movement that institutionalized his own acquiescence to that authority, became himself a father figure who demanded the impossible of his followers while denying them the comforting protection of a gentler parent.

For Novalis, Luther was indeed a strict father who stood between his sons and a happy childhood in which trust was matched by a correspondent trustworthiness; furthermore, by subjecting scripture to the explanatory rigors of philology, Luther effectively purged Christianity of the mystery that nurtured faith by filling the soul with childlike wonder and awe. In this fashion—and this is the critical undercurrent of Novalis's essay—Luther prepares for an Enlightenment that demystified the universe, but in so doing transferred the mystery to those who had the power to explain it. Science is the new sorcery that embroils man and the world in a dynamics of mastery and submission, and Novalis notes that light, the phenomenon from which the Age of Reason took its name, was favored "because of its mathematical obedience" (wegen seines mathematischen Gehorsams, III:516). Novalis's critique resonates of the later assertion by Horkheimer and Adorno that the Enlightenment, by reducing reason to an instrument of domination, reinstalled the mythological component it had presumed to invalidate. An ironic reference to marriage via metaphor strikes at the heart of the bourgeois ideology that naturalizes domination, reproduces it as sacrifice, and defines it as freedom:[24] "Die glückliche Ehe zwischen dem menschlichen Verstand und der Natur der Dinge . . . ist patriarchal; der Verstand, der den Aberglauben besiegt, soll über die entzauberte Natur gebieten" (The happy marriage between the human intellect and the nature of things . . . is patriarchal; the intellect, which vanquishes superstition, is to lord over the disenchanted natural world). Reason is thought to issue from within the natural world it shackles, and marriage too is culture that passes itself off as nature. Novalis seems unaware that love and marriage are contradictory, at least in the sense that marriage is part of the overall oedipal structure that demands renunciation. This represents an inconsistency perhaps more apparent in retrospect. The anti-oedipal impulse in his thinking is more developed in the region of theology, where his rejection of Protestantism amounts to a revolt against the patriarchal interference with the mother-bond. Within the eroticized framework of Catholicism he idealizes marriage. When he praises early Christianity for "the inviolability of its marriages" (die

57

Unverbrüchlichkeit seiner Ehen, III:523), he sounds rather like a child dreading the separation of his parents; and even though the essay begins as a paean to the church fathers, what ultimately fetches them praise is their deference to the Holy Virgin, whom Novalis describes as every young child must see its own mother, possessed of extraordinary beauty and god-like powers, an ever-reliable source of comfort and protection: "Sie predigten nichts als Liebe zu der heiligen, wunderschönen Frau der Christenheit, die mit göttlichen Kräften versehen, jeden Gläubigen aus den schrecklichsten Gefahren zu retten bereit war" (They preached nothing but love for the holy, wondrously beautiful lady of Christianity who, endowed with divine powers, was poised to rescue every believer from the most frightful dangers, 507).

The tension between external peril and the family configuration in which the father endorses the intervention of a mother who protects and provides once more suggests a kinship between the pre-oedipal vision found in "Erlkönig" and Novalis's image of medieval Catholicism. The same opposition appears in the dedication of *Heinrich von Ofterdingen* where Novalis exalts an unspecified female benefactor:

> Mit deiner Hand ergriff mich ein Vertrauen
> Das sicher mich durch alle Stürme trägt (I:193).

> With your hand a trust took hold of me
> Which bears me safely through all storms.

Of the same person, he says "at her full bosom I drank of life" (An ihrem vollen Busen trank ich Leben), and in terms of this longing for oral gratification Novalis, for whom early Catholicism represents the historical concretization of childhood, describes the needs to which a revived church would minister: "Sie muss das alte Füllhorn des Seegens wieder über die Völker ausgiessen" (It must once again pour the old cornucopia of blessing over all peoples, III:524).

But beyond the promise of luxuriance, the new church offers the prospect of total physical reunion with the mother; hence the religion to come is described as one "which receives all thirsty souls into its bosom" (die alle . . . durstige Seelen in ihren Schooss aufnimmt, 524). The longing for a return to the church is couched in imagery suggestive of what Freud termed "secondary narcissism," a desire for refusion with the body of the mother. And indeed Novalis's prophecy of the imminence of that return bespeaks an identification with the female reproductive function: "Wer fühlt sich nicht mit süsser Schaam guter Hoffnung?" (Who does not, with sweet shame, feel themselves of good hope? ["guter Hoffnung" is a polite equivalent of "pregnant"], 519). Novalis seeks in his visionary church what Luther originally found in the monastery: refuge from a storm. The storm enabled Luther to project outward and thus camouflage his father-crisis, yet the disguise ultimately becomes an interpretation of the thing it serves to hide. Novalis argues that the consequences of the Reformation are fully realized in the Enlightenment, whose desire it is to dominate the natural world; to experience the rage of the elements is to become acquainted with the opposition of inside and outside unknown to the small child, who finds in its mother a unity of self and environment.

Novalis's effusively nostalgic evocation of the childlike trust that medieval Christianity instilled in its flock has prompted a generation of critics to treat *Die Christenheit oder Europa* as a prototypical expression of the restorative inclinations of Romanticism. Georg Lukács's polemical *Reaktion und Fortschritt in der deutschen Literatur* (Reaction and Progress in German Literature, 1945) is a textbook example of the once widely held view of Romanticism as a longing for feudal stability in the face of irresistible social change or, more generally, as an attempt to find refuge from present realities in fantasies of the past. This sharp opposition of reality and fantasy recalls the literal-minded father of the Enlightenment for whom a child's vision of the supernatural is but a simple hallucination rather than a shrewd distortion informed by a keen perception. The principal achievement of Novalis's piece is found in the way it foregrounds the *analyzability* of such visions by describing the conditions under which they arise—conditions inferred from symptoms that emerge when the fantasies disappear. The following lines make evident that Novalis's approach to religion is anthropological; the reality of faith is to be sought in the human needs it satisfies:

> Erst durch genauere Kenntniss der Religion wird man jene fürchterlichen Erzeugnisse eines Religionsschlafs, jene Träume und Deliria des heiligen Organs besser beurtheilen und dann erst die Wichtigkeit jenes Geschenks recht einsehn lernen. Wo keine Götter sind, walten Gespenster. (520)

> Only by means of more exact knowledge of religion will one learn to better judge those frightful products of the dormancy of religion, those dreams and deliria of the holy organ and only then to understand truly the importance of that gift. Where there are no gods, ghosts prevail.

This condensation of religion, dreams, and deliria suggests the psychoanalytic account either of religion as the collective dream of society or conversely of dreams as the ontogenetic internalization of religion; the implication that those "frightful products" are symptomatic of the disintegration of an all-embracing structure of belief anticipates the Freudian logic that holds that repressed desires—and Novalis in effect portrays the rise of Protestantism as the repression of these wishes—return in the form of neuroses. The contiguous reference to ghosts *(Gespenster)* recalls further Freud's explanation of such phenomena as the disembodied projections of the neurotic's inner demons.[25] The same reference also haunts of the foreboding announcement made some fifty years later by Marx and Engels of a specter moving about ("Ein Gespenst geht um")—a figure in which "all the powers of old Europe" (alle Mächte des alten Europa) saw the reflection of their own declining strength.[26] Truly Novalis's essay contains the elements of a more overtly radical tradition that, like psychoanalysis, is concerned with a dynamics of repression and disguise.

The contention implicit in the foregoing is not that Novalis and Marx share a common political vision but that they describe the same struggle and in quite similar terms. It is the struggle between a wholly rationalized, dehumanized world and a prior stage wherein a felicitous innocence was nurtured by an overwhelming sense of mystery. The ascendancy of the rational and functional entails a gradual demystification, and the rhetoric of both texts gives this process as an unveiling. For Marx and Engels, the failure of the bourgeois economy is owing to its inability to represent itself as anything other than what it actually is: sheer greed is denuded of its "sentimental veil" (sentimentalen Schleier).[27] Although religion plays no role in the Marxist vision of the future, its desecration at the hands of the middle class nonetheless highlights the brutality with which capitalism destroys the illusory happiness of that earlier stage:[28] "alles Heilige wird entweiht, und die Menschen sind endlich gezwungen, ihre Lebensstellung, ihre gegenseitigen Beziehungen mit nüchternen Augen anzusehen" (everything sacred is profaned, and people are finally compelled to gaze with sober eyes upon their position in life, their relationships to each other).

Novalis shares with Marx and Engels a view of this struggle as one for domination over nature and thus over the natural drives of human beings; the uninhibited gratification of instincts is incompatible with productivity in the workplace. Novalis is uncannily specific in his diagnosis of the destructive schism ("Spaltung") that results when the erotic life is repressed ("verdrängt") by the self-interested life of commerce ("Geschäftleben"). Of early Christianity, he declares:

> Es war eine erste Liebe, die im Drucke des Geschäftlebens entschlummerte, deren Andenken durch eigennützige Sorgen ver-

drängt, und deren Band nachher als Trug und Wahn ausgeschrien
und nach spätern Erfahrungen beurtheilt. . . . Diese innere grosse
Spaltung, die zerstörende Kriege begleiteten, war ein merkwürdiges
Zeichen der Schädlichkeit der Kultur, für den Sinn des Unsicht-
baren, wenigstens einer temporellen Schädlichkeit der Kultur einer
gewissen Stufe. (509)

It was a first love, which fell dormant under the pressure of commercial life, whose memory was repressed by selfish concerns, and
whose bond was later decried as deceit and madness and judged according to subsequent experiences. . . . This great inner schism,
which was accompanied by destructive wars, was a conspicuous
sign of civilization's harmfulness toward the sense of the invisible,
at least of a temporary harmfulness of civilization at a certain stage.

Certainly this passage, with its erotization of religion and politics and its
psychological explanation of war, reads less like *Das Kapital* than Freud's
*Das Unbehagen in der Kultur* (Civilization and its Discontents). Its primitive anticapitalism aside, Novalis's essay tends toward a mode of thinking
with which an orthodox Marxism would have little sympathy. The genu-
inely radical implications of Romanticism could not be realized until the
historical distance from both Marxism and psychoanalysis was sufficient
for their similarities to emerge. The true grandchildren of *Die Christenheit*
may be critical works like Herbert Marcuse's *Eros and Civilization,* an
essay that, by exploring the political ramifications of Freudian concepts,
exposes the political origins of psychoanalysis, not to mention the Frankfurt School's own debt to Romanticism, attributable in part to the common ambivalence toward the Enlightenment. Novalis's reference in the
above lines to the repression of memory provides a case in point: the same
problem is discussed by Marcuse in a passage in which the orthodox dichotomy of regression and progress is negated—and in which Novalis's
rhetoric of nostalgia finds vindication:

the *truth value* of memory . . . lies in the specific function of memory to preserve promises and potentialities which are betrayed and
even outlawed by the mature, civilized individual, but which had
once been fulfilled in his dim past and which are never entirely forgotten. . . . The psychoanalytic liberation of memory explodes the
rationality of the repressed individual. As cognition gives way to recognition, the forbidden images and impulses of childhood begin to
tell the truth that reason denies. Regression assumes a progressive
function.[29]

When Novalis comments on the self-consciously regressive character of his vision, he links memory with need and restates the important connection between medieval Catholicism and a child's dreams, suggesting that both reflect a longing for plenitude: "Man gedenkt des Frühlings im Spätherbst, wie eines kindischen Traums und hofft mit kindischer Einfalt, die vollen Speicher sollen auf immer aushalten" (One remembers spring in late autumn like a dream of childhood, hoping with childish simplicity that the granaries should forever be full, 510).

## MAGIC AND THE VEIL OF CENSORSHIP

*Ananke*, the scarcity that necessitates the renunciations that make up civilization (*SA* IX:186),[30] is also the experience that ends the stage of early childhood Freud termed "primary narcissism." It is prior to the experience of deferred gratification, which instills in the child a sense of a world that, unlike the nursing mother, is radically separate from the self. During this stage all needs are satisfied with minimal delay and because no wish has yet gone unfulfilled, the child develops a belief in the magical power of thoughts (*SA* III:43). The equation that Novalis implies between empty granaries and the empty sign indicates that the disenchantment stemming from the Reformation is akin to the demise of primary narcissism—the experience of lack where before none was felt. Aesthetics in Novalis is a play of desire that inhabits this lacuna without rushing to close it. Magic is a veil whose infinite play of folds lends a new sensuality to the object it only partially conceals. Alluding to Schleiermacher, whose speeches on religion had just appeared, and whose name means "veilmaker," Novalis displays the erotic economy of an aesthetics that facilitates the reacquaintance with the lost mother under new circumstances: "Dieser Bruder . . . hat einen neuen Schleier für die Heilige gemacht, der ihren himmlischen Gliederbau anschmiegend verräth, und doch sie züchtiger, als ein Andrer verhüllt" (This brother . . . has made a new veil for the Holy Virgin which caressingly betrays her heavenly frame, and yet conceals it more modestly than any other, III:521).

Informing these lines is a dialectic of revelation and concealment that is at the core of Novalis's poetics. This dialectic ascribes to poetic language the power to foster knowledge by rendering the familiar strange, where unfamiliarity acts as a stimulus to understanding. The desire to know is hereby alloyed with a more fundamental drive *(eros)*; Luther's demystification of religion was simultaneously a de-erotization, a movement counteracted not only by the return of the erotic through Mary, but also by "attempts at mystifying the sciences" (Mystifikationsversuche der Wissenschaften, 521).

This alliance of mystery with understanding betrays the crucial insight that concealment forces associations that in turn facilitate analysis. As a response to repression, disguise is itself already an interpretation waiting to be made explicit. Hence the critical power of analogy: the nonidentity of comparative terms defines the space in which analysis occurs. Novalis builds his essay by pairing historical moments that are as different as they are similar; the differences are as essential to the comparison as the similarities. Indeed, the nonidentity of the terms must be asserted, for only within the context of difference do the similarities afford a critical focus. Should I wish to insult someone, I would do better to use an epithet that is only partially accurate.

Doubly relevant here is the category of fetishism: not only did both Marx and Freud employ it as an analogy for describing the phenomenon of confusing nonidentical elements; but they also borrowed the concept from, in Marx's words, "the nebulous region of the religious world" (die Nebelregion der religiösen Welt).[31] Marx describes commodity-fetishism as the habit of confusing things for work, that is, of ascribing an intrinsic value to things, the true worth of which is a function of the human labor that produced them. Whereas the inordinate value of precious metals is tied to the unusual difficulty involved in locating, extracting, and refining them, societies have long believed that value to inhere in the metal itself. For Freud, fetishism occurs when a nonerogenous part of the body, or even an inanimate object, is invested with a sexual attraction proper only to the reproductive organs; a foot, or even a shoe, might become a substitute for an appropriate sexual object with which it is associated. The example of the inanimate object supplies the better analogy with Marx's commodity-fetishism, for in both cases value is displaced from a human being to a lifeless thing. Implicit in Freud's notion of "sexual over-evaluation" (Sexualüberschätzung, SA V:63) is an economical infrastructure of the psyche that became explicit when Walter Benjamin, in his discussion of fetishism in the fashion industry, referred to the "Sex-Appeal of the Anorganic" (Sex-Appeal des Anorganischen).[32] This merger of the Marxist and Freudian concepts of fetishism illuminates the way desire, as a response to the discrepancy between need and satisfaction, forges identities between nonidentical elements.

These various aspects of fetishism coalesce insidiously in "Blumen" ("Flowers"), the poem with which Novalis prefaced *Glauben und Liebe* (Faith and Love). Written a year before *Die Christenheit* and published in the *Jahrbücher der Preussischen Monarchie* (Annals of the Prussian Monarchy), this collection of fragments heralds the arrival of Friedrich Wilhelm III, who took the throne in November 1797. Novalis joined the ranks of many Berlin intellectuals who saw in the new regent the dawning of a new political era. The inspiration behind this optimism was the king's young wife, Princess Luise von Mecklenburg-Strelitz, whose love—so they believed—would have a moralizing influence on her husband and ensure that his rule be compassionate and virtuous. It was thought that their mutual love and the integrity of their family life would engender new hope and trust in the monarchy, making Friedrich Wilhelm and Luise the ideal couple to head the larger household of the nation. Luise thus becomes the political analogue of Mary, a feminine corrective to a rigid patriarchy, and Novalis even uses the figure of the veil, now familiar from *Die Christenheit,* to endow the queen with the same sensuality he lent the Holy Virgin. In the final strophe of the prefatory poem, the exalted Luise becomes the source of erotic appeal heightened by a piece of clothing that retains the scent of its cherished wearer:

> Der Duft des Schleyers, der mich vor dem umgab,
> Sinkt dann vergoldet über die Ebenen,
> > Und wer ihn athmet, schwört begeistert
> > Ewige Liebe der schönen Fürstinn. (II:484)

> The fragrance of the veil, which enveloped me before,
> Sinks gilded over the planes,
> > And whoever breathes it pledges with passion
> > eternal love to the beautiful queen.

Smell, Freud observed, was the sense most likely to inspire the associations that underlie fetishism because the most common objects of fetish, in particular the feet and hair, emit odors similar to those given off by the genitals. He recalls Faust's suggestion that his lust for Gretchen would invest an innocent neckerchief from her bosom with the erotic value of a garter ("Strumpfband") by moving it closer to more exciting regions of her body (*SA* V:64–65). Luise's veil acts here as a similar trophy, acquiring the quality of a more intimate garment, and the description of its scent as "gilded" (vergoldet) links the erotic object to that most fetishized of all substances. (One is reminded too of the "garment of gold" worn by the Erlkönig's mother.)

The linkage is not surprising, for gold, the color as well as the metal, had come to symbolize the undifferentiation that is always the inversion of desire. The unity of spirit and matter assigned this substance by alchemy had evolved into the broader semiotic unity of sign and signified, and Romantic aesthetics found in the color gold the immanence or presence that distinguished symbol from allegory. The color appropriate to the latter form was thought to be blue, which suggested intangibility: blue was not a property of the object, but of the atmosphere between the object and its beholder. Goethe reflected a more general attitude of the period when he characterized blue as "an enticing nothingness" (ein reizendes Nichts), a color that, while drawing us ever toward itself, recedes indefinitely from us (*HA* XIII:498).[33] If the famous blue flower of Heinrich von Ofterdingen's dream is a symbol of longing, then its color represents the separation that conditions longing; the resolution of this condition is foretold when the youth awakens from the dream to his mother's embrace in a room "gilded" by the morning sun ("die schon die Morgensonne vergoldete," I:197). The unity, or presence, that gold seems to embody corresponds to the oneness of self and world Heinrich finds in his mother's arms.

This correspondence suggests that the state of fusion with the mother is an aboriginal moment of which all other unities, actual or desired, are imitations, and it can be said that the longing for those unities, as a response to the loss of the mother, is closely akin to grief. It is consistent that Novalis's nostalgia for the cult of Mary also extends to the symbolic practices of the church aimed at making what is absent present, such as the use of saintly relics—physical remains or clothing of venerated dead that, not unlike the primitive fetish, provide a tangible link with the spiritual. When Novalis relates the tending of the church reliquary to the secular phenomenon of bereaved lovers clinging to vestiges of their deceased companions, he not only draws out the erotic aspect of the religious practice, but he also places death, as that which occasions ultimate reunion, at the opposite end of desire: "So bewahren liebende Seelen, Locken oder Schriftzüge ihrer verstorbenen Geliebten, und nähren die süsse Glut damit, bis an den wiedervereinigenden Tod" (Thus loving souls carefully save locks of hair or handwriting of their departed darlings, and with these nourish their sweet ardor, until death comes to reunite them, III:508). In *Glauben und Liebe* as well as *Die Christenheit*, Novalis states his political, religious, artistic, social, and ethical concerns in terms of a basic dynamics of wish fulfillment, and it is only superficially surprising that in the earlier text he should interrupt his discussion of the royal court's moral leadership with the following one-sentence fragment: "Nichts ist erquickender als von unsern Wünschen zu reden, wenn sie schon in Erfüllung gehn" (There is nothing more invigorating than to speak of our wishes when they are already being fulfilled, II:494). Inscribed in every desire is the memory of a time when satisfactions were never deferred, but were simultaneous with their needs—a simultaneity known briefly at the mother's breast and available subsequently only as dream-hallucinations.

This returns us to Marcuse's statement about the "psychoanalytic liberation of memory" and his claim that "the forbidden images and impulses of childhood begin to tell the truth that reason denies." The suggestion that there is a kind of truth that reason suppresses undercuts the rationalist opposition of knowledge and impulse, and the implication that the desire to know and desire per se have as their common object a lost state of undifferentiation clears a path through Freud back to the philosophical erotics of Novalis: "Was man liebt, findet man überall, und sieht überall Ähnlichkeiten" (Whatever one loves, one finds everywhere, seeing similarities in everything, II:485). As an impulse to restore an aboriginal identity, love, like faith, becomes a mode of understanding in which knowledge and memory are one. Novalis contradicts the Enlightenment view of history as the progressive movement away from ignorance toward truth; he characterizes it instead as the recollection of truths once known but now forgotten. The quest for knowledge—and this applies most directly to *Heinrich von Ofterdingen*—is a journey home, one for which the *Odyssey* is paradigmatic and to which the related concept of *anagnorisis* ("re-recognition") is essential.[34] Each new insight recapitulates an ancient wisdom, the return to which is erotically motivated, fostered by the stimulus of disguise. Every representation is inherently nonidentical with the thing represented, and the greater that discrepancy, the more powerful the stimulus to overcome it. In this same context Paul Ricoeur declares that "enigma does not block understanding but provokes it."[35] By means of this very dialectic, Novalis, stating that the pleasure of re-recognition increases in proportion to the degree of concealment, functionalizes mystery in the interest of ultimate understanding:

> Der mystische Ausdruck ist ein Gedankenreiz mehr. *Alle Wahrheit ist uralt*. Der Reiz der Neuheit liegt nur in den Variationen des Ausdrucks. Je contrastirender die Erscheinung, desto grösser die Freude des Wiedererkennens. (II:485, emphasis added)

> The mystical expression is one further stimulus to thought. *All truth is primordially ancient*. The stimulus of novelty lies only in the variations of the expression. The more contrasting the appearance, the greater the joy of re-recognition.

This is one of several introductory fragments to *Glauben und Liebe* that broach the issue of public secrecy by asserting the need to create "a language of tropes and riddles'' (eine Tropen- und Räthselsprache, 485), the deeper sense of which would evade all but the initiated. Here Novalis follows the eighteenth-century debate over esoteric and exoteric speech, yet he assumes a stance counter to the Enlightenment through both his declaration, just emphasized, that the discovery of truth is always actually a *re*covery and through his vindication of concealment as the prerogative of parenthood. These two aspects collaborate in response to a rhetorical question that sets Novalis in direct dialogue with Enlightenment rationalism: ''Aber fordert nicht die Vernunft, dass Jeder sein eigener Gesetzgeber sei?'' (But does reason not demand that every individual be his own lawgiver? II:501). Very much in the tradition of Lessing's *Die Erziehung des Menschengeschlechts,* a text that promotes reason while asserting its limitations, Novalis argues that the source from which the great lawgivers of antiquity gleaned their laws, namely a profound feeling for humanity, is no different from that in which every mature individual would find the principles of self-governance. Thus, no valid law is truly arbitrary, yet the provisional necessity of written laws bears witness to the present impenetrability of their source. The proper function of authority is not to deny access to that source, but to protect it from the probes of inadequate reason.

Censorship, or the custodianship of certain knowledge, is hereby placed within the legitimate purview of parental responsibility. Such had been the role of the pope, whom Novalis believed to be justified in protecting the mysteries of creation from ''untimely, dangerous discoveries in the realm of knowledge'' (unzeitigen gefährlichen Entdeckungen, im Gebiete des Wissens, III:508). Seen dynamically, the pope's resistence to premature discoveries carries the authority of subsequent experience of the effects of science on the world. It is not altogether anachronistic, therefore, to project a critique of instrumental reason onto earlier periods. Freud held that when seventeenth-century peoples attributed certain patterns of behavior to demonic possession, they were not simply misguided by superstition, for the language of possession supplied a preliminary framework for describing neurosis. On the same principle, Native Americans who planted a fish along with corn knew nothing of the fertilizing properties of nitrogen, yet the discovery of the latter only verified the wisdom implicit in the traditional practice.

This second example is offered by the American poet and critic Wendell Berry in an essay that represents a recent expression of impulses common to Romanticism, psychoanalysis, and Critical Theory. The general object of Berry's attack is the immodest belief in the adequacy of our intellectual powers to make informed decisions. Focusing on the problem of

land use, he emphasizes how traditional communities free of this rationalist ''superstition''—that is, people who accept ignorance as both an inevitable and tolerable condition of life—tend to make better decisions
about the treatment of their natural habitat than a technological society
fired by scientific optimism. Developing the classical apposition of culture
and agriculture, Berry argues that what mediates the acquired wisdom of
generations is not clear consciousness but cultural tradition, the latter of
which compensates for the deficiencies of reason. Berry uses marriage as
an example of a cultural institution the inherent reasonableness of which
experience bears out, yet which few people enter into rationally. In the
passage that follows, Berry points out that the true justification for getting
married often becomes clear only in retrospect, and he seems to echo
Lessing's assertion that revealed truths may not have been rational at the
moment of their revelation, but would evolve into rational truths in time.
Concluding with an allusion to Oedipus, Berry suggests that culture en-
compasses the restraint and self-limitation the story teaches and that culture reproduces itself ontogenetically as ''character.'' He thus echoes not
only the later Lessing's reassessment of reason but also Nietzsche's view,
quoted earlier, that to know nature too well is to sin against it.[36] We are
left then with the stance of parents vis-à-vis the desires of their children:

> What parent, faced with a child who is in love and going to get mar-
> ried, has not been filled with mistrust and fear—and justly so. We
> who were lovers before we were parents know what a fraudulent jus-
> tifier love can be. We know that people stay married for different
> reasons than those for which they get married and that the later rea-
> sons will have to be discovered. Which, of course, is not to say only
> that the earlier ones must wait for confirmation.
>
> But our decisions can also be informed—our loves both limited
> and strengthened—by those patterns of value and restraint, principle
> and expectation, memory, familiarity, and understanding that, in-
> wardly, add up to *character* and, outwardly, to *culture*. Because of
> these patterns, and only because of them, we are not alone in the
> bewilderments of the human condition and human love, but have the
> company and the comfort of the best of our kind, living and dead.
> These patterns constitute a knowledge . . . that includes informa-
> tion, but is never the same as information. Indeed, if we study the
> paramount documents of our culture, we will see that this second
> kind of knowledge invariably implies, and often explicitly imposes,
> limits upon the first kind: some possibilities must not be explored,
> some things must not be learned. If we want to get safely home,
> there are certain seductive songs we must not turn aside for, some
> sacred things we must not meddle with.[37]

In reading these last lines, it is difficult not to overhear the "seductive song" of the Erlkönig, yet Berry's essay, by rediscovering a rationale for paternal censorship, does not allow us to exonerate the father in Goethe's poem, but rather to examine his guilt from another perspective. Harm comes to the child not as a result of direct violence, but through the father's attempt to disabuse him of fear: "Mein Sohn, was birgst du so bang dein Gesicht?" (My son—why hide your face in such fear?). In a fascinating passage from his autobiography, Goethe recalls how his father subscribed to the practice of using terror to wean children of fear: he forced his sons to sleep alone and masqueraded as a phantom to frighten them back to their beds if they tried to escape.[38] Both Goethe's father and the father in his poem become the source of the fear they compel their children to confront, and the autobiographer's rhetorical question summarizes the confusion of a child whose very cries for help ("Mein Vater, mein Vater") name the object of his fear: "Wie soll derjenige die Furcht los werden, den man zwischen ein doppeltes Furchtbare einklemmt?" (How is one to get rid of fear when one has been wedged between a twofold terror? *HA* IX:14).

If the father in "Erlkönig" fails his son by entreating him not to avert his gaze from whatever frightens him, then he presents an interesting foil against which Freud's father might be reappraised, a father whose taboo (whether real or imagined) against probing family secrets too carefully surfaces in the barber shop sign of Freud's dream reading, "Es wird gebeten die Augen zuzudrücken" (It is requested that the eyes be closed).[39] Much of Freud's work consists in the attempt to locate such censorship within a process of enlightenment that aims at the child's eventual identification with the authority behind the obfuscation. If one looks at the displacements and distortions of dream-work *(Traumarbeit)* as devices meant less to confound the dreamer than to ensure that only a mature intellect solve the enigma, then dream-distortion acquires the same "pedagogical" function as biblical parables that, in Lessing's view, had the function of delaying the discovery of their hidden truth, at the same time preparing the mind for that moment of eventual comprehension. It is important to emphasize (though it seems tautological once stated) that the mechanism working to foil interpretation reckons with the human capacity to do just that—to interpret and decipher. Viewed within a strictly anthropological framework, this process of second-guessing the movements of the rational mind seems reasonable as a stratagem for protecting reason from itself by preventing it from interfering with the proper and necessary function of the instincts. But Freud's rationalization of an authority that seeks to mystify coincides with political events that were leading him to fear those "infernal regions" *(Acheronta)*—events marking the enfeeblement of the rational, liberal order that should have guaranteed him a secure position within Vienna's professional hierarchy.

The classical *Bildungsroman* works to avoid revolution by moderating the tension between the middle and upper classes, and this is also the residual political force of the oedipal theory.[40] Freud noted that family romance typically begins when a child is left envious by chance encounters with the nobility (*SA* IV:224). The apparent probability of such encounters suggests that certain political vestiges of romance proper were still in place at the turn of the century. These circumstances are restored in *Heinrich von Ofterdingen,* an alternative *Bildungsroman* of sorts, though Novalis recreates feudal society in specific contradistinction to the age of the rising bourgeoisie. It is a retroactive construct that translates "feudalism" as "pre-capitalism," and what endears the Middle Ages to the narrator is not politics per se, but object-relations. The society he describes is characterized by a stance toward the surrounding world governed by receptivity, not intervention. This aesthetic stance invests even the most common objects with charm, mystery, beauty, life. According to Marcuse, this is an attitude for which Narcissus and Orpheus have been the traditional mythopoetic harbingers and to which Freud's own concept of narcissism is potentially appropriate. Marcuse sees in narcissism the possibility of creating a new reality-principle—of establishing a fundamental relatedness to the world not based on domination. He draws a tentative and cautious analogy to the aesthetics of Kant, at the heart of which is the concept of disinterestedness, and he theorizes a context beyond Kant in which the Kantian terms of the "aesthetic dimension" circumscribe a nonrepressive order.[41] The following chapter brings a sustained reading of *Heinrich von Ofterdingen* in light of Freud's theory of narcissism and, rather less cautiously than Marcuse, explores that theory as an elaboration of a Romantic problem.

# 3

# The Philosophical Unconscious

### THE ANXIETY OF INFLUENCE

"The anxiety of influence" is a critical model introduced by Harold Bloom, the American scholar of English Romanticism, for describing what we might call the dream of poetical self-determination. The agon that for Bloom is the energy behind creative genius is a family romance in which poets gain control over their own origins to insulate themselves against the influence of their forebears. This is not simply a matter of choosing one's parents, but of making oneself more original than one's originators by enveloping their visions within one's own—by creating the illusion of having fathered one's own fathers.[1] The creative/defensive moment is thus poised between introjection (of a foreign originality) and projection (of a native belatedness), an interchange of displacements akin to that described by Freud in his discussion of "instincts and their vicissitudes."[2] Bloom's theory is itself perched at the point where Romanticism and psychoanalysis converge in a common effort to circumnavigate the limitations that foiled the Enlightenment's promise of autonomy. The Romantic poet's longing for self-origination through genius coincides with the bourgeois desire for self-disinheritance through "talent,"[3] also a factor in the constitution of psychoanalysis: "Family romance" itself maps a process in which the father is reborn through the reason of his children.

The anxiety of influence is appropriate to the Enlightenment desire of which Romanticism is a radicalization—the desire to shape one's life, in Kant's words, "without the ordination of another" (ohne Bestimmung

71

eines Andern).[4] The latent insight of Bloom's formulation is that influence and fear are coeval. The same apposition is of concern to Fichte, whose project of a *Wissenschaftslehre* (Theory of Knowledge) is that of grounding "the condition of the possibility of such foreign influence in the ego itself" (die Bedingung der Möglichkeit eines solchen fremden Einflusses im Ich selbst).[5] Fear arises with the awareness of an Other and its common boundary with the self. Introjection and projection violate this boundary; its undecidability is the source of *abjection*.[6] The infant's recognition of its mother's breast, or even its own excrement, as something apart from the self brings an end to the "oceanic" or "all-encompassing feeling" (eines allumfassenden Gefühls) associated by Freud with primary narcissism (*SA* IX:199–200). It is as if Fichte, in his philosophy of identity, were trying to restore this state of primary undifferentiation by exposing the *Nicht-Ich,* the Other that limits and defines the *Ich,* as a misperception.[7]

To say that the philosophy of German idealism is in some sense "narcissistic" is to soften the hegemony that a critical tradition has long granted this philosophy over poetical works in which patterns of narcissism are commonplace. Although texts like *Heinrich von Ofterdingen* have often been treated as figurative elaborations or translations of philosophical structures, it may be more accurate to see them as a medium through which the latent needs and motivations of post-Kantian philosophy became manifest—a philosophical unconscious as it were. In her study of narcissism in English Romantic poetry, Barbara Schapiro speculates that "the Romantics were open to the deeper layers of the psyche and were in touch with those earliest, formative stages of personality development in which external reality and one's own identity are first being realized."[8] My claim is rather less universal. Let us say that what Schapiro calls the "psyche" was available to the Romantics as discourse and that what these writers were "in touch with" were the more localized crises that post-Kantian philosophy was trying to absorb—crises that pertain to the French Revolution, the ascendancy of the middle class, the fight for political and moral autonomy, and so on.

Not that all of this is reducible to an infrastructure of sociopolitical circumstances. My suggestion has been that Romanticism and psychoanalysis have in common the elaboration of the metaphorical implications of desires that were initially social. If these desires are submerged beneath the rational structures of post-Enlightenment philosophy, they reemerge in the poetical works of Romanticism, no longer as exclusively social desires, but in the form of images that associate political conflict with a more fundamental narcissistic drama, which that very philosophy was working through.[9] Literary Romanticism already constitutes an analytical moment that mediates between Fichte and Schelling on the one hand and Freud on the other. The following segments represent two separate and mutually relativizing phases in this mediation: the first, a psychoanalytic interpretation of *Heinrich von Ofterdingen,* applies Freud's theory of narcissism to the crisis of "first separation" with which Heinrich's journey begins; the second turns this analysis around by examining the concept of narcissism in light of Fichte's and Schelling's philosophy. I intend neither to anchor Freud in Romanticism nor to ground Romanticism in the psyche, but to treat psychoanalysis as a renewed attempt to neutralize the crises ignited by the search for autonomy. This quest continues to inform Bloom's allegedly post-New Critical model and contributes to the reading of Romantic texts in terms of their own commonplaces.[10]

### CRITICAL SEPARATION: HEINRICH AND NARCISSISM

In his letter of 24 July, Goethe's Werther observes how his nascent love for Lotte has left him unable to draw; his overwhelming passion has inhibited the capacity of his eye to apprehend sharp outlines. Yet he speculates that he could achieve a form of expression adequate to his feelings if only he had some plastic substance to mould in his hands. He concludes resolutely: "Ich werde auch Ton nehmen . . . und kneten, und sollten's Kuchen werden!" (I shall take clay . . . and knead it, even if it should come out cakes! *HA* VI:41). This renunciation of sight—for the Enlightenment the sensory analogue of reason—in favor of touch indicates a psychological regression reinforced by the verbal association of haptical and oral desire. Corresponding to this regressive turn is a gradual withdrawal from the ambient world, and Werther's failure to find an appropriate love-object leads finally to a death which is both autoerotic and homoerotic: he dies literally by his own hand, even kissing the fatal pistol, and his last breath is drawn during a lingering kiss on the lips from Lotte's eldest brother.[11]

This regression is also marked by a shift in Werther's preference in literary landscape, as he abandons the beneficent presence of Homeric nature for the precipitous heights of the Ossianic sublime. It has been theorized that the sublime landscape, as a figure of absence or loss, represents a projection of deprivation anxiety,[12] and the following lines from Goethe's Swiss diary (1775) show how just such a landscape emerges at the first hint of separation from the womb and bosom of mother-nature:

Ich saug' an meiner Nabelschnur
Nun Nahrung aus der Welt.
Und herrlich rings ist die Natur,
Die mich am Busen hält.
Die Welle wieget unsern Kahn
Im Rudertakt hinauf,
Und Berge wolkenangetan
Entgegnen unserm Lauf. (*HA* I:102)

I suck nutrition from the world
Through my umbilical string.
And nature splendrous all around
The breast to which I cling.
The current rocks our boat along
At the rhythm of a row,
And mountains reaching to the clouds
Loom larger as we go.

After a nostalgic pause the landscape returns, but here nature has been drawn close and particularized, and the final trope of the poem, ripening fruit mirrored in the water's surface, employs reflection to transform a potential source of oral gratification into a purely visual image. The initial narcissism is resolved, and the prevalence of sight represents a successful separation from the mother. Indeed, the trajectory of the poem runs contrary to the attempt by the mythological Narcissus to touch his own reflection, an object that exists for the eye alone. Such resolution evades Werther, however, whose willful death culminates a desire for physical union with the mother. Death holds for him the promise of Lotte's "eternal embraces" (ewigen Umarmungen), and he identifies Lotte as a maternal figure when he describes her deceased mother, whom he longs to meet in the afterlife, as "your very likeness" (Deine Mutter, dein Ebenbild, *HA* VI:117).

If Werther achieves the immortality he desires, then it is because his death sets the stage for a generation of post-adolescent literary protagonists who in effect work through the same complex of emotional problems that embroil Goethe's tragic hero.[13] The fact that many of these later figures are artists points to a link between Werther's death and his artistic failings; this implies that Werther's suicide is a substitute for a creative talent he either lacks or cannot express, and one is tempted to regard the Romantic *Künstlerroman* as a therapeutic project. *Heinrich von Ofterdingen* is a novel devoted to working out the consequences of the mother-bond;

and while Novalis's treatment of object-relations is compatible with Freud's description of narcissism, he presents narcissism as an alternative that recalls the emancipatory potential described by Marcuse.[14]

Werther seems numinously present through much of *Ofterdingen,* and the difference between him and Heinrich can be measured in the narrator's attitude toward the compulsion, exhibited by Werther, to consume the surrounding world. Although Heinrich's original relationship to the world is altogether oral ("An ihrem vollen Busen trank ich Leben" [At her full bosom I drank of life], 193), the tendency of his development is toward a less ingestive and more reflective posture, one enabling him to register nature's gentlest intimations. In the initial state of enchantment that precedes his first dream, Heinrich finds himself, much like the impassioned Werther, unable to comprehend fully the world around him; but while he too seeks a remedy in an alternate form of expression, he does not display the same regressive impulses: "Es muss noch viele Worte geben, die ich nicht weiss: wüsste ich mehr, so könnte ich viel besser alles begreifen. Sonst tanzte ich gern; jetzt denke ich lieber nach der Musik" (There must be many words I don't yet know; if I knew more, I'd be able to grasp everything much better. Once I liked to dance; now I prefer to think musically, 195–96).

Heinrich's inability to "grasp" (begreifen), that is, to understand the world, does not, as it did with Werther, result in the childlike urge to grasp it literally. His renunciation of conceptual language in favor of the language of music is wholly commensurate with the Romantic program of restoring to language its primordial musical character; the text, however, demonstrates that this is not a matter of poetic technique, but an aesthetics in the broadest sense—an overall stance toward the world that allows the world free play. This is evident at the beginning of Chapter 6 when the narrator distinguishes between poets and those for whom the world is but an object to be mastered, used, and devoured. This distinction is cast in terms that invite a psychoanalytical reading, for while the tireless intervention of these men of action is equated with the infantile urge to touch and consume everything in sight ("Sie müssen überall selbst Hand anlegen" [They always have to touch everything themselves], 266), the poet's calm receptivity is couched in imagery that suggests a stilling of such drives:

> Es sind die Dichter . . . , die schon hier im Besitz der himmlischen Ruhe sind, und von keinen thörichten Begierden umhergetrieben, nur den Duft der irdischen Früchte einathmen, ohne sie zu verzehren und dann unwiderruflich an die Unterwelt gekettet zu seyn. (267)

It is poets . . . who, already in possession of heavenly tranquility here on earth, and not driven about by foolish desires, merely inhale the scent of earthly fruits instead of consuming them and thus being irrevocably chained to the underworld.

This passage is especially important because of the connection it draws between eating and death, and the voracity of those interventive individuals appears as a breast-fixation and as such a desire for refusion with the mother.[15] Their heroic mastery of the world does not stand in opposition to narcissism; on the contrary, it has the insulary function of "hardening their inner world somewhat against . . . the distractions of many and multifarious objects" (ihr Gemüth . . . gegen die Zerstreuungen vieler und mannichfaltiger Gegenstände gewissermassen abhärten, 266). The need to protect oneself against the onslaught of external stimuli becomes ultimately a wish to return to the original inundation of the womb and thus constitutes a longing for death. Womb and death are associated through the reference to the "underworld" (Unterwelt), an allusion to not only the mythical land of the dead but also the subterranean cavern of Heinrich's first dream, the veiled light and fluid enclosure of which evoke the womb. To be "irrevocably chained" to that world is to be fixed to the prenatal environment, and Heinrich's development as a poet requires that he relinquish his desire for infantile bliss and adopt a stance that leaves things in the world free to fulfill their essence. His maturation resembles the structure of the poem by Goethe discussed above in which the earthly fruits become aesthetic objects only after the subject has grown detached from the mother and adopted a more tranquil stance.

The separation from mother-nature that reflection incurs is represented spatially in *Ofterdingen* as landscape, and Heinrich's evolving relationship to the world is paralleled by structural changes in the landscapes he traverses in the course of his quest. The first waking landscape seems to appear in response to the melancholy he feels at leaving the "city of his birth" (Geburtstadt, 204), and his expressed wish for inundation tempts one to regard the vista before him as an image of both deprivation and narcissistic desire: "Er war im Begriff, sich in [die] blaue Flut [der Ferne] zu tauchen" (He was about to submerge himself in the blue flood of the distance, 205). The semantic structure of Novalis's landscape consists in the opposition of distance and proximity and their respective cognates, blue and gold, and the increasing prevalence of the latter in subsequent landscapes reflects Heinrich's growing intimacy with the world around him. This polarity is suspended when he arrives at his grandfather's home in Augsburg (the initial destination of his journey) and finds the now familiar topography of landscape recreated in miniature on the feast table. The distant flood of blue, mediating between the viewers and the prospect, has here been replaced by a golden river of spilled wine flowing around flowers and food:

> Blumenkörbe dufteten in voller Pracht auf dem Tische, und der Wein schlich zwischen den Schüsseln und Blumen umher, schüttelte seine goldnen Flügel und stellte bunte Tapeten zwischen die Welt und die Gäste. (272)

> The table was resplendent with baskets of fragrant flowers, and the wine meandered between the flowers and dishes, shook its golden wings and laid colorful tapestries between the world and the dinner guests.

Heinrich's enjoyment of food and drink at Schwaning's house satisfies the earlier counsel of his mother who, noting her son's lingering state of reverie following his dream, had urged him, "Iss und trink, dass du munter wirst" (Eat and drink, so that you may awake more fully, 198). A continuum emerges here between Heinrich's first truly positive social experience and that original stirring from an autoerotic dream to his mother's voice—between Heinrich's feasting at his grandfather's house and the act of nursing that his mother's offer of sustenance evokes. This contiguity extends to Mathilde, the maiden Heinrich meets and falls in love with at the banquet; their eventual betrothal culminates the efforts of Heinrich's mother to make her son more extroverted by introducing him to new experiences and, in particular, exposing him to the charms of women. In psychoanalytic terms, this development demonstrates how the mother, as the child's first object of desire, activates the libido, makes the child receptive to the surrounding world, and thereby facilitates the gradual detachment from the mother. But the appetite Heinrich exhibits at his grandfather's table reveals that his bond with his mother is still strong, and the passage quoted above describing poets as those content but to savor the fragrance of earthly fruits suggests that Heinrich, himself destined to become a poet, is on the verge of a critical separation.

This crisis unfolds in Heinrich's second dream, in which Mathilde's death by drowning is prefigured—a dream remarkable in the degree to which it explicates its own mechanism. The first image to appear, a channel of deep blue water, hints of the desire for inundation and as such represents a projection of deprivation anxiety. The compensatory nature of this initial vision is underscored when Heinrich is struck by the enormous incongruity between his anxious heart and the serene setting: "Seine Brust war beklommen. Er wusste nicht warum. Der Himmel war heiter, die Flut ruhig" (His breast was uneasy. He knew not why. The sky was clear, the water calm, 278). Suddenly, the placid surface of the stream is broken by a whirlpool that begins to pull Mathilde's boat downward; that is, the repressed source of anxiety becomes conscious, in response to which Heinrich plunges himself into the rushing current, losing consciousness altogether. The verbal correlation between fear and loss of consciousness ("Die entsetzliche Angst raubte ihm das Bewusstseyn" [Terrible fear dispossessed him of consciousness]) betrays the insulary function of the unconscious, and Heinrich's action seems motivated by a longing to return to the womblike enclosure of the dream in Chapter 1. In fact, Heinrich, still dreaming, comes to himself in a waterscape resembling that of his earlier dream, and here he and Mathilde are joined for eternity in passionate embrace.

In light of the foregoing, Heinrich's first and second dreams appear to conform respectively to the psychological states Freud termed primary and secondary narcissism. The normal condition of very early childhood, primary narcissism is a stage of development at which the sexual drive is as yet indistinct from the drive for self-preservation, allowing for the simultaneous gratification of hunger and erotic desire through feeding. The child's only sexual objects at this point are itself and its mother, and because the mother is also a part of the child, the self is at once source and sole receptacle of libidinal energy.[16] Only when the energy is invested in objects other than the self does this aboriginal condition end. Freud later specified primary narcissism as the state of undifferentiation of the ego and the id; that is, the experience of the outer world necessary to the development of the ego had not yet taken place (*SA* III:329). Secondary narcissism, described by Freud as a regression caused by a failure to resolve the Oedipus complex, results in the libido being retracted from external objects and reinvested in the self or its surrogates: the infant self, the mother, and the ego-ideal (*SA* III:56). In the extreme, secondary narcissism is an impulse to escape the differentiation of the ego and return to the oneness of self and environment of which life in the womb is the purest expression (and for which, it may be added, death is the only attainable substitute).

The topography of the dream-cave in Chapter 1 mimics the shape of the womb, and the manner of Heinrich's entry and exit—he climbs in through a manmade opening and is carried out into daylight by a fluid—is mildly suggestive of conception and birth. But his experience deep within the cave is one of explicitly erotic self-encounter. A winding passageway leads him to a spacious cavern containing a basin fed by a luminescent fountain. Tasting of the shimmering liquid, he succumbs to an irresistible urge to bathe:

> Es dünkte ihn, als umflösse ihn eine Wolke des Abendroths; eine himmlische Empfindung überströmte sein Inneres; mit inniger Wollust strebten unzählbare Gedanken in ihm sich zu vermischen; neue, niegesehene Bilder entstanden, die auch in einander flossen und zu sichtbaren Wesen um ihn wurden, und jede Welle des lieblichen Elements schmiegte sich wie ein zarter Busen an ihn. Die Flut schien eine Auflösung reizender Mädchen, die an dem Jünglinge sich augenblicklich verkörperten. (196–97)

> He felt as if immersed in a cloud reddened by the sunset; a heavenly sensation poured over his inner being; countless thoughts strove lustfully to intermix within him; images such as he had never seen appeared, flowing into each other and turning into visible presences around him, and each wave of the delightful element caressed him like a soft breast. The flood was like a solution of voluptuous maidens who momentarily incarnated themselves at the youth's touch.

Heinrich emerges from the cave and spies a blue flower, to which he finds himself strangely attracted. As he approaches, the blossom undergoes a metamorphosis, displaying a maidenly visage, which is displaced by that of Heinrich's mother as he awakens.[17] The flower establishes a metonymic relationship between the mother and other erotic objects (Heinrich later interprets the face in the flower as Mathilde's); but it also reveals one of those objects to be the self, for the appearance of the face in the blossom is precipitated by something resembling onanism: "die Blätter wurden glänzender und schmiegten sich an den wachsenden Stengel" (the leaves grew shinier and rubbed up against the growing stem, 197).

The second dream differs from the first not only in the anxiety that produces it but also in Heinrich's gesture upon awakening: this time Mathilde's father, the poet Klingsohr, receives Heinrich's spontaneous embrace, despite the presence of his mother at his bedside. Heinrich soon redirects his affection toward his mother, but only after Schwaning, in a remark that illuminates the fluidity with which libidinal objects are exchanged, tells Klingsohr, "Das gilt euch nicht" (That is not meant for you, 279).

The coincidence of Mathilde's death (or dream thereof) and this sign of momentary separation from the mother clarifies Heinrich's love for Mathilde as part of a prolonged attachment to his mother, and it is only appropriate from a psychoanalytic standpoint that Klingsohr, who as Heinrich's ego-ideal manifests the superego, should interfere in Heinrich's expression of tenderness toward his mother. Mathilde's departed spirit later appears in a vision as the Holy Virgin, in whom mother and maiden are one, and the two figures remain indistinguishable in a question Heinrich poses to Sylvester not long afterward: "Aber musste die Mutter sterben, dass die Kinder gedeihen können?" (But did the mother have to die in order for the children to prosper? 327). Heinrich continues his epic journey without his mother, and whether she dies symbolically or actually is never clear. Yet this lack of clarity is commensurate with the minimal distinction between the experience of the death of a loved one and the detachment from the mother. Part Two of the novel finds a grief-stricken Heinrich making his way through a rugged mountain terrain, while he is absorbed in thought to the point of being impervious to his surroundings.[18] A similar oblivion had been apparent when Heinrich first left home, and his wish then to "submerge himself in the blue flood of the distance" (sich in [die] blaue Flut [der Ferne] zu tauchen) is echoed now by a longing for the utter dissipation of the self: "Er wollte sich in die Ferne verweinen, dass auch keine Spur seines Daseyns übrig bliebe" (He wanted to cry himself into the distance, so that no trace of his being would remain, 320). The parallel of these two passages reflects the kinship between narcissism and grief, illustrates the withdrawal of cathexis symptomatic of both, and shows furthermore that these two events—leaving home and the death of the mother(-figure)—constitute different stages of the same crisis.

The vicissitudes of first separation are clarified at the time of Heinrich's departure when the narrator pauses to reflect on the pain the youth feels at having "his familiar world torn from him" (seine bisherige Welt von ihm gerissen, 204). The experience of separation is described in terms of bereavement: Heinrich leaves home "in melancholic mood" (In wehmüthiger Stimmung), and the sense of loss casts him into a state of "adolescent mourning" (jugendliche Trauer). Heinrich's reaction to this experience is narcissistic, but the ensuing withdrawal of cathexis and concomitant longing for a permanent and secure environment are associated with dying, making first separation an unforgettable monument along a psychic journey the final destination of which is death:

> Eine erste Ankündigung des Todes, bleibt die erste Trennung unvergesslich, und wird, nachdem sie lange wie ein nächtliches Gesicht den Menschen beängstigt hat, endlich bey abnehmender Freude an den Erscheinungen des Tages, und zunehmender Sehnsucht nach

einer bleibenden sichern Welt, zu einem freundlichen Wegweiser und einer tröstenden Bekanntschaft. (205)

As the earliest premonition of death, first separation remains unforgettable, and after long having haunted one like a nocturnal visage, it becomes in the end a friendly guide and comforting companion, as the joy in daytime phenomena diminishes and a longing for a more secure and abiding world increases. (*PH* 26)

Death is here redefined as a heightened state of the security one knew in infancy, and narcissism is revealed as the precondition of mourning; the latter is a reactivation of the original separation-crisis. The transformation of that "nocturnal visage" into a "comforting companion" would seem a variant on the metamorphosis of the face in the blue flower into that of Heinrich's mother, and it is significant that this presentiment of death brings about a regressive gesture that can best be described as secondary narcissism—as a longing for a time when "mother" and "world" were one and the same: "Die Nähe seiner Mutter tröstete den Jüngling sehr. Die alte Welt schien noch nicht ganz verlohren, und er umfasste sie mit verdoppelter Innigkeit" (The proximity of his mother comforted the lad. The old world did not yet seem totally lost, and he embraced it with doubled passion, 205). These passages expose a correlation between the self's identification with the mother and the retraction of the libido from surrounding objects ("bey abnehmender Freude an den Erscheinungen des Tages" [as the joy in daytime phenomena diminishes]), hereby establishing the parameters of a development in which Heinrich's stance toward the object-world is revised as his relationship with his mother evolves. The desire for refusion with his mother indicates a lack of self-identity that precludes the realization of an integrated whole of self and environment. Such a relationship is prevented first by narcissism, then later by the recrudescence of narcissism as mourning, and only when his grief subsides is Heinrich able to experience the things around him as individual presences: "der Tod [erschien ihm] wie eine höhere Offenbarung des Lebens. . . . Jeder Stein, jeder Baum, jede Anhöhe wollte wiedergekannt seyn" (death appeared to him as a higher revelation of life. . . . Every stone, every tree, every rise in the landscape wanted to be recognized anew, 322).

Heinrich is developing then toward a stage where surrounding phenomena will be more than simply substitutes for lost objects. It has already been suggested that the various love-objects Heinrich encounters are but surrogates for his mother, and because his love for her is essentially a love of self, these figures function as narcissistic objects—mere vehicles in the service of instincts. Mathilde's prominence as the ultimate narcissistic object is betrayed by the imagery Heinrich employs to describe their affinity: "bin ich der Glückliche, dessen Wesen das Echo, der Spiegel des ihrigen seyn darf?" (am I the fortunate one whose being is the echo, the mirror of her being? 277). A significant inversion is to be noted here in that Heinrich has placed himself in the position not of Narcissus, but of his reflection—a reversal that simply underscores the view that confusion of the self for an Other is the essence of narcissism.

This exchange of the desiring subject for the desired object calls to mind the essay in which Freud analyzes the pairs sadism-masochism and voyeurism-exhibitionism in terms of a disposition of the ego, in emulation of the primary state of narcissism, to redirect its instincts away from external objects and back toward itself.[19] He describes masochism and exhibitionism as deformations of sadism and voyeurism respectively: masochism satisfies the same instinctual aim as sadism, that is, that of inflicting pain; the difference is that the masochist makes himself or herself the object of that aim. Similarly, Freud explains exhibitionism as voyeurism directed toward the self. The exhibitionist, he argues, is a voyeur who makes himself or herself the passive object of his or her own active scoptophilia (*Schaulust*); the subject of voyeurism is projected as an alien "I," and the exhibitionist imagines that he or she is the object of a desire other than his or her own. This projection recalls an archaic stage of primary narcissism at which the self, having not yet found an object beyond its own body, practices an autoerotic voyeurism (*SA* III:95). The psychic ambivalence of this experience is suggested by the way Heinrich splits himself in two; he identifies with not solely the reflection in the pool but also Echo, the nymph whose unreciprocated passion for Narcissus left her to bewail her fate amidst the trees until nothing remained but her voice. Heinrich assumes the role of the object both desired and rejected; in so doing he renders explicit the separation that narcissism only implies, and he eventually wishes to make Echo's fate his own when grief instills in him the longing to "cry himself into the distance" (sich in die Ferne verweinen).

## SCHELLING, FREUD AND THE UNCONSCIOUS

The introduction into this discussion of Freud's "metapsychological" papers on the economic distribution of instincts marks a juncture at which the psychoanalytic reading of a Romantic literary text may be converted to a Romantic interpretation of Freud, for the discovery of the narcissistic object and the concomitant demotion of the object-world in these writings afford an especially clear association between psychoanalysis and the Romantic enterprise. Freud describes exhibitionism and masochism, forms of desire wherein the self replaces something other than the self as the invested object, as returns to narcissism, and the drives underlying such behavior are shown to exist prior to the subject-object split and thus prior to consciousness itself. The Kantian implications of this aspect of Freud's thinking are pointed out by Paul Ricoeur who declares that "the exchange of roles between the self and another . . . forces us to question all the so-called self-evidences concerning the relation between a subject-pole and its objective counterpart."[20] This parallel between the psychoanalytic concept of narcissism and Kantian epistemology prompts speculation that the myth of Narcissus achieved its original significance for Romanticism as a philosophical allegory: Narcissus's failure to recognize the face in the pool as his own reflection represents the epistemological dogma that fell prey to Kant's critique, in terms of which Narcissus's error corresponds to the assumption that one can actually know "things in themselves" (*Dinge an sich*).

In post-Kantian terms, Narcissus's "mistaken identity" is tantamount to the fallacious belief in an autonomous non-ego (*Nicht-Ich*). Schelling describes a stage in ego development in which the self, through the act of reflection, divides itself into subject and object and projects the nonobjective part of the self as an Other. Although this stage entails a misconception, it is nonetheless the prerequisite of full consciousness, because only through objectivication can the original, unconscious identity of subject and object be placed before consciousness. Freud argues similarly that elements buried in the unconscious cannot enter consciousness unless they acquire the appearance of sense perceptions owing to external stimuli. Freud's argument is fascinating because he describes this process of representation as a way of circumventing or even subverting a principle we cannot but recognize as Kantian. In his *Kritik der reinen Vernunft* (Critique of Pure Reason, 1781), Kant contended that all human knowledge was "deduced" (*abgeleitet*) from sensory experience and that extrasensory knowledge, or "intellectual intuition" (*intellektuelle Anschauung*), was a faculty reserved for God alone ("allein dem Urwesen").[21] In Freud's account, the preconscious (*Vorbewusstsein*) performs the Kantian censure by accepting nothing as real (and allowing nothing into consciousness) that does not seem to originate as a perception from without:

Es ist, als sollte der Satz erwiesen werden: Alles Wissen stammt aus der äusseren Wahrnehmung. Bei einer Überbesetzung des Denkens werden die Gedanken wirklich—wie von aussen—wahrgenommen und darum für wahr gehalten. (*Das Ich und das Es, SA* III:292)

It is as if the proposition were to be proved: All knowledge stems from external perception. Whenever thinking is over-cathected, thoughts are actually perceived—as if from without—and are therefore held to be real. (*The Ego and the Id*)

When Heinrich undergoes the erotic immersion of his dream, his thoughts become images that then turn into "visible presences around him" (zu sichtbaren Wesen um ihn wurden), and the dream, in keeping with its regressive movement, works to convert thoughts into perceptions—a process that foretells Heinrich's eventual task as a poet. His special talent for rendering his inner world as imagery is noted at several points in the narrative: following his arrival in Augsburg, for example, his hosts marvel at "the plenitude of his visual thoughts" (die Fülle seiner bildlichen Gedanken, 276).

This process whereby sense perceptions originate from within rather than without resembles intellectual intuition, that *intuitus originarius* Kant had denied to humankind; to know something other than by mediation of the senses was tantamount to creating it, and only God, wrote Kant, produces what he thinks.[22] The post-Kantians did not directly contradict Kant's assertion that extrasensory knowledge of the world was unavailable to human cognition; instead they accounted for the possibility of intellectual intuition by redefining it. Although one may not have spontaneous knowledge of things, one did have such knowledge of one's own intelligence. According to Fichte, the ego has immediate knowledge of that "pure act" or *Tathandlung* wherein it "simply posits originarily its own being" (Das Ich setzt ursprünglich schlechthin sein eignes Seyn).[23] Because in every intellectual act the ego has an immediate intuition of its own intellect, all knowledge implies the unity of subject and object. Schelling, for whom the task of philosophy was that of describing "the continuous history of self-consciousness" (die fortgehende Geschichte des Selbstbewusstseyns, *SW* III:331), defined intellectual intuition as the original unity of subject and object—a unity negated in reflection and only conscious if represented objectively through art. He therefore characterized art as "intellectual intuition made objective" (die objektiv gewordene intellektuelle [Anschauung], *SW* III:625).

Although the Romantics did not directly challenge the Kantian tenet that extrasensory knowledge of things was the exclusive province of God, they nonetheless entertained the analogy between art, now understood as the objectification of intellectual intuition, and divine creation. To create artistically was to bring forth oneself; hence, Fichte's act of self-positing becomes that of self-creation. This principle is given lyrical expression by Clemens Brentano in his cycle *Nachklänge Beethovenscher Musik* (1815) in which the famous composer's deafness underscores the creative genius's independence of sense perception ("Selig, wer ohne Sinne schwebt" [Blessed, whoever hovers without senses]).[24] Just as God's creation was brought forth out of nothing, so too does the artist create things not previously given unto his senses. In both cases, the subject mirrors itself in its objective form; the creation is identical with its creator:

> Nein, ohne Sinne, dem Gott gleich,
> Selbst sich nur wissend und dichtend,
> Schafft er die Welt, die er selbst ist

> No, without senses, like God,
> Knowing and creating only himself,
> He makes the world, which he himself is

This association of knowing and creating echoes the view that extrasensory knowledge is a kind of cognition that engenders its own object, and the same apposition is present in the opening lines of *Ofterdingen* where Heinrich, in reference to the blue flower, exclaims: "ich kann nichts anders dichten und denken" (I can create or think of nothing else, 195).[25] This is soon followed by the dream, which gives the first sensuous form to an apparently innate idea Heinrich has never seen, but yearns to see: "die blaue Blume sehn' ich mich zu erblicken" (I long to catch a glimpse of the blue flower, 195). This passage effectively establishes a parallel between intellectual intuition and dreaming and thus between art and the transposition of the dream into waking reality. This is not only a critical commonplace, but as Brentano's poem illustrates, a Romantic one as well:

> Und den Traum, den Mitternacht gesponnen,
> Üb ich tönend, um den Tag zu grüssen.

> And the dream by midnight spun,
> I set to song to greet the day.

The entertainment of such commonplaces brings us dangerously close to the established habit of trying to understand Romantic literature by isolating its philosophical infrastructure. The proximity of Early German Romanticism to the epicenter of post-Kantian thought has made that literature uniquely susceptible to the kind of reading that would translate poetical texts into—ostensibly *back* into—a discursive, nonfigural vocabulary. My point here is not to deny an influence. Instead, I am interested in how the philosophy of idealism may have been transformed by the literature it influenced. My more specific, if tentative, suggestion is that works like *Ofterdingen* tapped and amplified the anthropological implications of the philosophy of identity and thus enabled that philosophy to become, as it were, psychoanalysis. The concept of identity is not only central to both transcendental idealism and psychoanalysis, but it also represents a phase that both "disciplines" locate at the beginning of the history of the ego. Freud adopted the term "narcissism" to refer to that stage as well as to the problems that obtain after its demise, and while Schelling did not, the myth of Narcissus became his generation's preferred fable for ciphering the various problems of self-consciousness that concerned him. That myth aptly represents the phenomenon both Schelling and Freud describe—namely, that every perception is simultaneously a self-perception. For Schelling, the ego exists only insofar as it knows itself; it is an act of cognition that produces itself as its own object: "Das Ich ist nichts anderes, als ein sich selbst zum Objekt werdendes Produciren, d.h. ein intellektuelles Anschauen" (The ego is nothing other than a producing that becomes its own object, i.e. an intellectual intuition, *SW* III:370). The ego of psychoanalysis too is not a subject vis-à-vis an object, but the place where inner and outer world meet. Freud describes the ego as a surface phenomenon from which both internal and external perceptions may arise; one could say it represents the point at which the id is refracted by external reality. It is a projection of the body's surface; hence, the body becomes an object unto itself: "Der eigene Körper . . . wird wie ein anderes Objekt gesehen" (One's own body . . . is seen as another object, *SA* III:294).

Freud's statement that in the formation of the ego one's own body comes to be perceived as a foreign object takes us back to his analysis of the mode of deviance wherein the body becomes the object of an *apparently* alien desire: exhibitionism. That discussion is important in the way it affirms the primordiality of narcissism, as exhibitionism recalls the autoerotic stage of infancy in which the child derives enjoyment from looking at its own genitals. It is important because it appears at the heart of Freud's redefinition of the ego as existing prior to consciousness.[26] And not only does this new understanding of the ego jibe with Schelling's in the sense that both thinkers describe the ego as existing prior to the subject-object split, Freud even employs the vocabulary of German idealism to name one polarity that governs this aspect of the psyche: *Ich* and *Nicht-Ich* (*SA* III:96). His claim that the non-ego is in fact a projection *of* the ego *by* the ego onto an imagined Other provides a parallel with Schelling that transcends mere vocabulary. Schelling too understands the *Nicht-Ich* as a projection, one issuing from intellectual intuition, that is, from that moment of spontaneous self-apprehension in which the ego posits its own being. This results in a rupture in the unity of the ego, which in the act of reflection becomes its own object. Because the ego cannot think of itself as its own object, it posits a subject outside of itself. Put differently, the ego necessarily posits itself as finite, and because it cannot conceive of itself as both finite and self-defining, it believes itself defined by an autonomous non-ego:

> Das Ich findet [das Begrenztseyn] gesetzt durch ein dem Ich Entgegengesetztes, d.h. das Nicht-Ich. Das Ich kann also sich nicht anschauen als begrenzt, ohne dieses Begrenztseyn als Affektion eines Nicht-Ichs anzuschauen. (*SW* III:403)

> The ego finds its limitedness posited by something opposed to the ego, that is, the non-ego. The ego cannot conceive of itself as limited without seeing that limitation as the effect of a non-ego.

Like Freud's exhibitionist, who makes an outside agency the source of his or her own self-directed voyeurism, and like Novalis's Heinrich, who describes himself as Mathilde's mirror-image, the ego in Schelling's system is descended from Narcissus, the "infinite tendency toward self-contemplation" (unendliche Tendenz zur Selbstanschauung) which, because the subject and object of reflection are indistinguishable, "discovers within itself something alien to the ego" (findet . . . in sich etwas ihm [dem Ich] Fremdartiges, *SW* III:405). Novalis writes in the same vein that transcendental philosophy helps us to realize that there is such a thing as "an outer world within us" (eine Aussenwelt in uns, III:429); that is, the non-ego is part of the ego.[27] Later Freud used the same terminology—excusing his choice of words all the while—to explain the repressed as something the ego could only experience as a strange land within itself: "das Verdrängte ist aber für das Ich Ausland, inneres Ausland, so wie die Realität—gestatten Sie den ungewohnten Ausdruck—äusseres Ausland ist" (*SA* I:496) (the repressed is for the ego a foreign territory, an internal foreign territory, just as reality—if you will permit the uncustomary expression—is an external foreign territory).

Earlier instances can be found in which the language of idealism is used to describe phenomena of the kind that interested Freud. In his *Confessions of an English Opium-Eater* (1821), Thomas De Quincey, an English Romantic who like Coleridge was well versed in contemporary German philosophy, fits his own dream-experiences to a post-Kantian framework.

Like Freud, he foregrounds that conceptual vocabulary by qualifying it parenthetically: "To my architecture succeeded dreams of lakes—and silvery expanses of water;—these haunted me so much that I feared lest some dropsical state or tendency of the brain might thus be making itself (to use a metaphysical word) *objective;* and the sentient organ might be projecting itself as its own object."[28] This usage of "projection" is emblematic of a more general transference that seems to have taken place in Romanticism whereby a philosophical schema devised to suit the rarified concerns of a Fichte or Schelling was activated through a figural context of poetical works so that the sexuality implicit in the imagery of those texts became centered within a systematic description of consciousness. This transfer may represent a subversion of that metaphysics, and De Quincey's suspicion that his dream might be a visual projection of the body appropriates that language for the realm of the utterly physical, pointing toward Freud's eventual derivation of the ego from the body. In this context it would seem fruitful to consider Heinrich's dream not simply in idealistic terms as the objectification of the self through reflection, but also in psychoanalytic terms as the symbolic representation of the body to the mind: the dream converts Heinrich's instincts into imagery, and the rapture he experiences on finding the blue flower suggests that archaic stage of autoerotic voyeurism in which the child revels in the visual contemplation of its own sexual organs.

Freud's discussion of voyeurism and exhibitionism in relation to the economic distribution of libido affords a unique point of comparison between Romanticism and psychoanalysis, largely because it falls at the center of that phase of Freud's thought in which, as in the philosophy of German idealism a century earlier, the problem of subject and object was being radically rethought. In addition, Freud's view of the importance of looking (*Beschauen*) for sexual development recalls the connection, fundamental to late eighteenth-century aesthetics, between erotic experience and sight, the sense to which that aesthetics accorded special priority. Freud's statement that optical impressions are the condition under which the process of natural selection transforms the sexual object into something beautiful (*SA* V:66) indicates that the very concept of beauty may be erotic in origin and compel one to reconsider the original meaning of "aesthetics." Indeed, Freud's claim that the sense of sight was derived from that of touch has its corollary in the eighteenth century. In an essay on the sister-arts controversy entitled *Plastik* (1778), Herder argues that sight (*Gesicht*) amounts to the visual extension of the tactile sense,—that is, when we contemplate a statue, we do not apprehend it visually but run our hands over it mentally instead.[29] Herder traces the capacity for such sensations back to the primordial "plastic" experience at the mother's breast, a moment he describes, in terms that anticipate Freud's account of primary narcissism, as the unity of erotic desire (*Wollust*) and nutritional need (*Nothdurft*).[30] Surprisingly, not the plastic form of sculpture but painting evokes a voluptuous response; the difference is that the former combines visual and tactile experience while the latter is strictly visual. Because it is limited to the representation of surfaces, painting has the effect of clothing, at once concealing what lies beneath and arousing curiosity about what is hidden: "so öfnet sie [die Mahlerei] auch der Phantasie ein weites Feld und lockt sie in ihre gefärbte, duftende Wollustgärten" (thus painting exposes fantasy to a broad spectrum and entices it into its colorful, redolent gardens of lust).[31]

Herder is speaking exclusively of painterly and sculptural renderings of the human form, but his inference that the erotic attraction of the painted body is due to an incomplete mimesis raises some general issues regarding the analytical project and shows the nonidentity inherent in representation to be the prerequisite of analysis. Herder associates vision with dreams ("Im Gesicht ist Traum"),[32] an obvious connection perhaps, but one that points to the related association of dreams and surface appearances. We have already witnessed this linkage in Heinrich's second dream where the placid surface of the water (consciousness) is broken to reveal a more anxious state of affairs underneath. Following Freud, the ego itself is a projection of the body's surface—and as such a representation of the body; hence, the difference between the body and the ego is that between touch and sight. The ego is that aspect of the body that can be seen or, more accurately, translated into imagery, and it is the separation implicit in seeing that creates the condition for analysis.

In Herder's framework, a strictly visual perception signals a rupture in the totality of the plastic experience in which not only hunger and lust, but also desire and gratification, are indistinct—an identity that disappears along with primary narcissism; yet the dream, as the fulfillment of a wish, recreates the identity visually in the form of an hallucination. To awaken from a dream and experience a need that the dream had shown satisfied, say thirst, is to awaken to the inadequacy of sight to such needs, and it is not without a certain irony that the narrator in Novalis's novel observes that Heinrich, beholding a particular spectacle during his journey, "could not feast his eyes enough" (konnte sich nicht satt sehen [literally, could not satisfy his hunger with his eyes], 264).[33] Much as in Schelling's system art functions to represent objectively the identity of subject and object sundered by reflection, so does the dream, by depicting all desires as satisfied, confer symbolic form upon a lost identity of self and environment—of infant and mother. And just as the restoration of that unity is a libidinal aim, so too is the loss of identity that symbolization represents the precondition of dream-analysis. In other words, desire and analysis are two kindred responses to the nonidentity inherent in representation. Heinrich's most explicit attempt at interpreting his dream occurs when his erotic passion is most intense; he is virtually in heat ("erhitzt," 278) when he concludes that the face he had seen in the blue flower belonged to his darling Mathilde: "Jenes Gesicht, das aus dem Kelche [der blauen Blume] sich mir entgegenneigte, es war Mathildens himmlisches Gesicht" (That face that leaned toward me out of the calyx of the blue flower, it was Mathilde's heavenly face, 277). Mathilde embodies the identity that Heinrich has lost, for in contemplating her he experiences an "undivided existence" (ungetheiltes Daseyn).

The possible kinship between Eros and Hermes is in part the subject of this study's next chapter, which explores how Novalis constructed a broad hermeneutics around a rudimentary, organological model of stimulus. For the present, I wish to restrict this discussion to specific parallels between Schelling and Freud by focusing on the role they ascribe to representation in the movement toward greater self-consciousness. Both agree that the unconscious must be placed before the senses for it to enter into consciousness; both contend with a split in the self caused by separation from a preconscious totality. For Schelling, that totality is nature, which he described as "the absolute unconscious" (das absolut Unbewusste, *SW* III:351); for Freud, it is the mother. Odo Marquard, who understands psychoanalysis as the continuation of transcendental idealism in demystified form, argues that what Schelling and Freud have in common is a *définition noire* of nature—a post-Enlightenment conception of nature as a potentially destructive force that stands beyond the purview of rational consciousness and domination. The service of art for Schelling, like that of therapy for Freud, was to facilitate the "harmless presence of nature" (unriskante Präsenz der Natur).[34] This apposition of the unconscious and a threatening nature sheds light on a possible therapeutic need behind late eighteenth- and early nineteenth-century artistic renderings of nature's most dangerous and awesome manifestations—images commonly associated with the Sublime such as tempestuous seas, electrical storms, and foreboding alpine landscapes. Fear is mitigated through the aesthetic representation of its source.

On the surface, the Enlightenment and its children had less to fear from nature, having subjected the more hazardous of its forms to scientific scrutiny. But even as the objects of fear were rationalized, the human capacity to experience it grew all the more mysterious. To shield oneself from the dangers of the outside world was to become exposed to the influence of the unconscious, and it seems likely that the fascination with thunderstorms and precipices—the desire of many to "taste" the danger posed by such phenomena—amounted to a descent into the hidden folds of the psyche.[35] This "aesthetics of anxiety" might be attributed to the discovery of a nonobjective nature, one that does not confront the subject as a separate entity "outside," but is recognized, in Schelling's words, as what is most basic within us ("das Letzte in uns," *SW* III:616). The post-Enlightenment began to relive the primitive experience of nature as a force that, though strange and unfathomable, entailed—indeed entangled—humanity. A connection between preanimism and the Enlightenment was drawn by Horkheimer and Adorno, who even as they sought to refute "psychologizing" explanations described the fear of nonobjective nature, which the primitives ciphered as Mana, as "the actual superior power of nature echoing in the savage's feeble soul" (das Echo der realen Übermacht der Natur in den schwachen Seelen der Wilden).[36] In German Romanticism, especially in that later variation known as *Schauerromantik* ("Romanticism of Chills"), the voice of nature issues from below, often beckoning some nocturnal subject to plunge himself into a deep well or rushing current. The return to nature is a return to that which subsumes man and nature: the unconscious. This (re-)discovery of an ominous nature beneath consciousness is chronicled beautifully in a seven-line poem published in 1826 by Joseph von Eichendorff. Its economy allows its insertion here as an example of how, when the lights go out, nature's murmur is heard from within:

> "Der Abend"
> Schweigt der Menschen laute Lust:
> Rauscht die Erde wie in Träumen
> Wunderbar mit allen Bäumen,
> Was dem Herzen kaum bewusst,
> Alte Zeiten, linde Trauer,
> Und es schweifen leise Schauer
> Wetterleuchtend durch die Brust.[37]

> Evening
> A hush befalls man's loud desire:
> The earth it rustles dreamily
> With every tree, a mystery,
> Of which the heart is scarce aware,

Times of old, sadness deep,
And through the breast soft shudders sweep,
Like flashes in the summer air.

As eventide approaches, pleasure ("Lust") gives way to mild forms of un-
pleasure ("linde Trauer," "leise Schauer"), and with this movement, the
human subject and natural surroundings seem to exchange roles: nature
appears to dream, and it dreams things of which the subject is barely conscious ("kaum bewusst"). And just as the inner life of the human individual is projected onto nature, so too is the sublime object internalized.
When the ingredients of the unconscious are brought before consciousness, they appear as one of nature's threatening forms. Yet the actual threat
has been removed altogether: "Wetterleuchten" denotes heat lightning or
lightning seen from afar, both of them harmless. The "safe presence of
nature" is achieved when forces appearing to belong to the outer world are
discovered hidden within, and Heinrich, now well underway in his travels,
experiences this same phenomenon as a figure of an internal distance:
"die Blume seines Herzens liess sich zuweilen, wie ein Wetterleuchten in
ihm sehn" (the flower of his heart could be seen from time to time like a
distant flash of lightning within him, 234).

## STORMY ROMANCES

As a systematic attempt to ground the possibility of moral autonomy in
the individual self, Fichte's thought is a philosophical complement to a
tradition of poetics that looks backward to Lessing, who defined genius as
that which creates its own laws, and forward to Harold Bloom, who ascribes to the "labor" of poetry an autonomy he denies the individual
text.[38] Bloom's theoretical model, in which even the illusion of self-
fathering is reserved for genius, tropes the affiliation between the bourgeois claim to self-governance and the abject terror that fuels the most
violent male fantasies: the "anxiety of influence" has its phylogenetic analogue in the fear of the flood.[39] The threat of inundation and the abhorrence of the maternal-feminine coincide in *Ofterdingen* when the crusaders
tell Heinrich of their intended conquest of Jerusalem. As the song of one
of their captives testifies, the soldiers' fear of the Saracen masses transforms them into the very flash-flood they so dread (lending a certain historical texture to the phrase "storm-trooper"):

Fürchterlich, wie Meereswogen
Kam ein rauhes Heer gezogen,
Und das Paradies verschwand (235)

Terrible, like waves in storm
A brutal horde of men did swarm
And my paradise was gone.

This is the contrastive moment that foregrounds Heinrich's narcissism; the experience the crusaders abhor is welcomed by the dreaming Heinrich, who revels in a flood that produces a female element as yet indistinct from himself: "Die Flut schien eine Auflösung reizender Mädchen, die an dem Jünglinge sich augenblicklich verkörperten" (The flood was like a solution of voluptuous maidens who momentarily incarnated themselves at the youth's touch, 197).

Inaugurated under the sign of "first separation" (erste Trennung, 205), Heinrich's journey initiates the gradual loss of the state of undifferentiation represented by the dream. It is a division of self and world addressed by the philosophers of the day, but it also coincides with another, obliquely political separation. Prior to his departure Heinrich bids a fond goodbye to the countess (*Landgräfin*), who is also his godmother (*Patin*). This leave-taking hints of the residual political crisis of Freud's family romance, in which the imagined bonds of kinship of a past feudal order are reproduced in the soul of the bourgeois (*SA* IV:224). The social juncture marked by Heinrich's appearance at court reemerges more forcefully in the *Atlantismärchen*, the second tale told by the merchants traveling with Heinrich. It is a tale of revolution, at least in the sense that revolution transforms a repressed nature into a radical presence; yet the social changes that eventually come about, most notably the dissolution of strict class boundaries, are made peacefully, and the potential for political upheaval is "sublimated" in the form of sexual liberation.

This too is a tale of first separation, though here the protagonist is a princess whose father, a widower-king, has stubbornly opposed any marriage not worthy of his daughter's noble ancestry. When one day she ventures out into the forest alone, leaving for the first time the insulary walls of her father's court, the nature that envelops her answers a need represented by the motherless, patriarchal world she has left behind: "Die Frische des hohen Waldes lockte sie immer tiefer in seine Schatten. . . . Es kam ihr die Lust an, Milch zu trinken" (The refreshing coolness of the tall forest tempted her ever deeper into its shadows. . . . She was overcome by the urge to drink milk, 216). Her thirst draws her to a secluded cottage where a young commoner lives with his father, and the encounter leaves her pleasantly confused by inner sensations she had never before known. Equally unfamiliar is the "timid reverence" (scheue Ehrfurcht) with which she regards her father upon returning to court. The stirring of natural desires leads her to recognize him as an enemy of those desires, and through an act of self-censorship she duplicates the repression he exercises: "Es schien ihr eine unabänderliche Nothwendigkeit, nichts von ihrem Abentheuer zu erwähnen" (She thought it absolutely imperative that she mention nothing of her adventure, 218).

The return of the repressed takes the shape of a sudden thunderstorm that besieges the princess and her new companion during a walk that had taken them deep into the forest. The foul weather actually seems triggered by their first kiss, as the storm manifests not only the mounting passion of the lovers-to-be, but also the royal and paternal rage its consummation would likely incur: "Die Prinzessin dachte an das Schrecken des Königs und des Hofes; eine unnennbare Ängstlichkeit fuhr zuweilen, wie ein zerstörender Strahl, durch ihre Seele" (221) (The princess thought of the fears of the king and court; a nameless anxiety shot at times through her soul like a shattering lightning bolt [*PH* 44]). The frightened pair find a cave that affords refuge from the wind and crashing boughs, and a precarious situation gives way to a *locus amoenus* reminiscent of Gottfried von Strassburg's *Minnegrotte* (likewise a safe haven from a king's wrath). It also recalls the narcissistic unity of Heinrich's dream-cave, for this too is a world without lack: "Ein wilder Mandelstrauch hing mit Früchten beladen in die Höhle hinein, und ein nahes Rieseln liess sie frisches Wasser zur Stillung ihres Durstes finden" (A wild almond branch laden with fruit hung into the cave, and a nearby trickling sound helped them find fresh water to quench their thirst, 221). Once the princess and her companion are safely inside, the continuing turbulence without heightens their erotic inclinations, which they satisfy to the fullest "amid the bridal hymn of the tempest and the wedding torches of the lightning strokes" (unter dem Brautgesange des Sturms und den Hochzeitfackeln der Blitze, 222).

An "other" nature, replete with outsidedness and full of danger, is now framed by the portal of the cave, a transformation explicable perhaps in terms of late eighteenth-century theories of the Sublime, which attributed the aesthetic experience of overwhelming natural forces to human moral superiority.[40] It is difficult, however, to reconcile the inherent moralism of these theories with the fact that the princess and the youth succumb to natural impulse and even conceive a child in this setting. The aesthetics operating here is not one that demands distance and mediation as the condition of beauty: this is a libidinal nature in the absence of repression. Thus, instead of reading this text back through Kant, we may read it forward to Marcuse, who seeks to emancipate Kantian aesthetics from the requirements of its moralism by reacquainting "sensuousness" with "sensuality," both of which are rendered by the German *Sinnlichkeit*.[41] The plenitude of the nature inside the cave is compatible with freedom, which is the absence of lack; scarcity (*Ananke*) is that which necessitates the renunciation of pleasure in favor of work and productivity. The aesthetic play of the imagination does not transfigure nature as a mere image of human autonomy, but taps nature's own potential for freedom by means of a "narcissistic" reciprocity that suspends the dichotomy of inside and out, of domination and submission. The couple's erotic union corresponds to the order of abundance they discover in the cave; their passion augments the storm, itself an instinctual nature that, in Marcuse's words, has been "liberated from its own brutality."[42]

Jean Baudrillard, who has criticized Marx for equating man with labor and thereby perpetuating the metaphysics inherent in bourgeois political economy, routes his indictment of Marxist anthropology through Marcuse, whom he accuses of subjecting play—the aesthetic dimension—to the rationality of labor.[43] Baudrillard faults Marx for locating the essence of human beings in production (of the material conditions of their own lives). Marx inherited this idea from eighteenth-century bourgeois thought, namely "the *idea* of man *producing* himself in his infinite determinism."[44] The formulation returns our attention to philosophy and especially to Schelling's definition of the *Ich* as "a producing that becomes its own object" (ein sich selbst zum Objekt werdendes Produciren, *SW* III:370).

If we regard Schelling's aesthetics as a philosophy of productivity (i.e., aesthetic intuition completes the process in which the ego produces itself as its own object), we may begin to discern a current in Novalis's tale that runs counter to its overt trajectory—one roughly compatible with Baudrillard's critique of Marcuse. The *Atlantismärchen*, told by merchants whose eagerness for material gain is not hidden and whose understanding of art is largely instrumentalist,[45] reinstates the teleology of (re)production as a corrective to the barrenness of the aesthetic realm over which the king of Atlantis reigns. The cave in the forest is a remote philosophical unconscious where the desire for social self-creation is realized; it is an ideal locus where the king's interdiction of a *mésalliance* is circumvented by a commoner who fathers an heir to the throne and thus "becomes the king's son'' (wird des Königs Sohn, 227). It is the point at which the middle-class desire for upward mobility is reunited with that of ascertaining paternal identity; it recalls the moment when Heinrich's father invokes the night of his son's conception (not to mention Freud's personal family romance, in which virulent anti-Semitism rendered the desire for social ascendancy inseparable from the wish to choose one's own father).[46] The *Atlantismärchen* recovers the princess for the ethos of productivity from which her father had removed her. She is for him a truly narcissistic object in which beauty and death coincide, a ''tender song'' (''zartes Lied'') and visible reminder of the wife for whom he still grieves. Her singing is enough to draw him into a state of narcissistic contemplation that ''repels all other activity in the erotic surrender to beauty'' (Marcuse):[47] ''Er . . . vergass oft die wichtigsten Angelegenheiten, ja die Bedürfnisse des Lebens über einem neuen, hinreissenden Gesange'' (He . . . often forgot the most important matters, even the basic needs of life at the sound of a new, spell-binding song, 214).

In the psychoanalytic sense *Heinrich von Ofterdingen* is narcissistic; it situates its narrative movement between two points of undifferentiation and even aligns itself with the drive toward the second of those moments, which is death. It is narcissistic in the modernist sense by virtue of its self-referentiality—its tendency to reflect upon its own status as fiction.[48] The next two chapters of this study are concerned with these two senses of narcissism respectively. The following chapter examines Novalis's novel in light of an aesthetics grounded in the deferral of gratification; it also implicates certain nineteenth-century disciplines in this aesthetics—specifically geology, archaeology, and philology—each of which, as a modern form of quest inscribed with distance, is a discipline of romance.

# 4

# The Stones Speak!
# The Romantic Archaeology of the Psyche

The usefulness of archaeology as a metaphor describing the recovery of hidden or forgotten associations is apparent to those familiar with the work of Sigmund Freud and Michel Foucault, both of whom found in that discipline a means of conceptualizing the stratified and contiguous arrangements that structure mental life. Archaeology suggested to Freud an interplay of surface and depth that corresponded to that between consciousness and the unconscious, promising further a prehistorical substratum at which the ontogenetic and phylogenetic origins of neurosis would coincide.[1] What archaeology offered Foucault was access to, in his (translator's) words, "a *positive unconscious* of knowledge,"[2] a body of rules that, though never formulated in the mind of the practitioner, conditioned the discourse of a wide range of disciplines. Foucault's definition of the library—the site of his excavations—as a space that collapses temporal distance by rendering all historical epochs copresent,[3] is not unlike Freud's account of the process whereby sense perceptions, as they work their way into the more complex folds of the psychic apparatus, proceed from temporal to spatial configurations (*SA* II:515).

A departure is marked by Foucault's juxtapositions of the *archive* and the *archaic;* the former he understood as an inescapable interior of language that refuses all access to origins.[4] Yet by characterizing languages as "the locus . . . of what lies hidden in a people's mind,"[5] and by thus privileging philology as the means of penetrating the deeper layers of discourse, Foucault not only recalls how Freud probed the surface of a patient's speech for traces of the unconscious, but he also points to an implication of that practice made explicit by Lacan, who held that the unconscious is linguistic in structure.[6] The post-Freudian focus on language, by modifying Freud largely from within, revives certain impulses that as part of Freud's intellectual heritage may have contributed to the possibility of psychoanalysis. A dissociation of language from the realm of conscious intention was crucial to the work of Wilhelm von Humboldt, who regarded language not as the product of consciousness, but as its formative agent.[7] His concept of linguistic relativity built upon the historicist view that language, rather than being an analogue of universal human reason (as the Enlightenment believed), was part of the cultural-geographical matrix within which the thinking of a particular people took its unique shape. Hence Jacob Grimm's equation of language and history: "Unsere Sprache ist auch unsere Geschichte" (Our language is also our history).[8] Grimm conceived of Germanic philology as a form of historical self-analysis, a means of recovering origins that the historical process had obscured (*getrübt*).[9] A parallel emerges between Foucault's emphasis on the library and its idiom of proximity and the shift in attention, marked by Grimm, away from Oriental tongues to older German languages that were exotic by virtue of time alone, not space.

This literal reorientation brings to light a second spatial extension performed by the metaphor of archaeology, for in addition to providing an architectonics based on depth, it also isolates, as a virtual necessity, the element of distance: the archaeological site is one that must be gained by journey, the more arduous the better.[10] The suggestion of an enduring impulse to travel fosters the proposal that archaeology did not simply *become* a metaphor for disciplines that appeared later, but was metaphorical at its very inception, an attempt by a nostalgic era to preserve a role for quest in the face of its social and institutional obsolescence. Archaeology shows that Romanticism did more to compensate for the loss of adventure than merely exalt that pseudo-nomadic survivor of a less sedentary age, the traveling merchant. The "fernhinsinnender Kaufmann," the "tradesman in thought far-wandering" blessed by the gods in Hölderlin's *Archipelagus*,[11] found his modern incarnation in Heinrich Schliemann, whose explorations so captivated Freud that he likened his own discovery of the Oedipus complex to the former's excavation of Troy.[12] Schliemann's "conversion" from magnate to explorer is emblematic of how the advent of archaeology in effect replaced commercial venture, the modern form of romance, with adventure proper. Freud himself identified the importance of that substitution when he wrote that Schliemann achieved through archaeology a happiness wealth alone would have denied him;[13] Freud generalized elsewhere that money lacks the power to bring true happiness because it does not satisfy a childhood wish.[14] By placing Schliemann's discovery of Priam's treasure within a basic economics of wish fulfillment, Freud prepares the ground for the hypothesis that archaeology constitutes a formal imitation of regression and as such represents the desire to return to primary positions long since abandoned.

### THE ROMANCE OF PHILOLOGY

That Germanic philology too was inspired by a nostalgia for quest is suggested by the imagery Jacob Grimm used when he located the birth of that discipline in the library of his teacher, the legal scholar Friedrich Carl von Savigny, where as a young law student he caught his first glimpse of medieval German poetry. At a ceremony honoring Savigny years later, Grimm recalled how the sight of the strange language instilled in him a fascination that presaged his eventual commitment to the study of older German texts. What distinguishes Grimm's account is its stylization; the visit to Savigny's home is represented as a meanderous pilgrimage through the medieval city of Marburg where narrow streets and winding stairways take him through churchyards and towers to heights that afford Romantic vistas of the surrounding countryside. His immediate destination is the house in which the professor leads a reclusive existence, and once inside the visitor continues inward to the sanctum of the library. Grimm's prose, halting and winding, pausing for detail before continuing upward, recreates the breathlessness the "climb" itself must have produced:

> Zu Marburg muss man seine Beine rühren und Treppe auf, Treppe ab steigen. Aus einem kleinen Hause der Barfüsser Strasse führte mich durch ein schmales Gässchen und den Wendelstieg eines alten Turms der tägliche Weg auf den Kirchhof, von dem sichs über die Dächer und Blütenbäume sehnsüchtig in die Weite schaut, da war gut auf und ab wandeln, dann stieg man an der Mauerwand wieder in eine höherliegende Gasse vorwärts zum Forsthoff. . . . Zwischen dessen Bereich und dem Hoftor unten, mitten an der Treppe, klebte wie ein Nest ein Nebenhaus, in dem Sie Ihr heiteres, sorgenfreies und nur der Wissenschaft gewidmetes Leben lebten. Ein Diener . . . öffnete und man trat in ein nicht grosses Zimmer, von dem eine Tür in ein noch kleineres Gemach mit Sopha führte. Hell und sonnig waren die Räume, . . . die Fenster gaben ins Giesser Tal, auf

Wiesen, Lahn und Gebirg duftige Aussicht, die sich zauberhafter Wirkung näherte, in den Fensterecken hingen eingerahmt Kupferstiche . . . , an denen ich mich nicht satt sehen konnte, so freute ich mich deren scharfe und zarte Sauberkeit.

In Marburg one must really move one's legs, climbing up stairs and down stairs. From a small house in the Barfüsser Strasse, my daily walk led me along a narrow alley and up the spiral staircase of an old tower to the churchyard, from which one gazed longingly beyond roof tops and flowering trees into the distance, that was quite an up-and-down hike, then one climbed along the wall up to an even higher lane and onward to the Forsthof. . . . Between its realm and the gate below, perched midway on the stairs like a nest, was the side house in which you led a happy and carefree life devoted only to learning. A servant . . . answered, and one stepped into a small room, from which a door led to an even smaller chamber with sofa. The rooms were bright and sunny, . . . and the fragrant view that the windows afforded of meadows, the river Lahn, and the mountains beyond bordered on magic; in the windows hung framed copper engravings . . . on which I could not feast my eyes enough, so did I delight in their sharp and delicate clarity.

The copper engravings, intelligible to the eye and placed in full view of the natural landscape, are monuments to the Enlightenment cult of visibility, an attitude interrupted when Grimm's attention is diverted by old books altogether lacking in the clarity of those pictures. Replacing intelligibility with mystery, Grimm's discovery demarcates an historical watershed, sealing once and for all the end of the Enlightenment:

Doch noch viel grösseren Reiz für mich hatten die im Zimmer aufstrebenden Schränke und in ihnen aufgestellten Bücher. . . . Ich entsinne mich, von der Tür eintretend an der Wand zur rechten Hand ganz hinten fand sich auch ein Quartant, Bodmers Sammlung der Minnelieder . . . mit Gedichten in seltsamem, halb unverständlichem Deutsch, das erfüllte mich mit eigner Ahnung. . . . Solche Anblicke hielten die grösste Lust in mir wach, unsere alten Dichter genau zu lesen und verstehen zu lernen.[15]

Yet I found an even greater attraction in the room's towering cabinets and the books displayed in them. . . . I remember how on the right hand side in the back as one entered there lay a quarto, Bodmer's anthology of medieval songs . . . with poems in strange, half incomprehensible German, and I was filled with a peculiar premonition. . . . Such impressions kept awake in me the tremendous desire to study and understand our older poets.

One reader of this tale, pointing out the intentional arrangement of Grimm's narrative, has discussed this account as the "primal scene" of German philology, that is, as an attempt to locate the origins of that discipline in a single apocryphal moment.[16] But if Grimm's tale seems contrived, it is as much an imitation as an invention. His trek to the private center of his teacher's monastic world retraces the steps of the poet-hero in Novalis's *Heinrich von Ofterdingen,* whose quest leads him deep into the cave of Friedrich von Hohenzollern, a former crusader now pursuing scholastic interests in subterranean isolation. The journey to the cave bears a topical similarity to the route Grimm followed to Savigny's house, and like Grimm, Heinrich ends up in a library, a veritable archive of illuminated manuscripts:

> Der Einsiedler zeigte ihnen seine Bücher. Es waren alte Historien und Gedichte. Heinrich blätterte in den grossen, schöngemahlten Schriften; die kurzen Zeilen der Verse, die Überschriften, einzelne Stellen, und die saubern Bilder . . . reizten mächtig seine Neugierde. (264)

> The hermit showed them his books. They were old histories and poems. Heinrich leafed through the large, beautifully painted writings; the short verse lines, the titles, individual passages, and the clear pictures . . . greatly aroused his curiosity.

The essential similarity between these two experiences is that the desire to understand the books is fostered by their strangeness and incomprehensibility. Grimm's discovery of poems in difficult medieval German ("in seltsamem, halb unverständlichem Deutsch") kindles in him the desire to study older German poets. Heinrich finds himself likewise drawn to a manuscript whose language, Provençal, is completely unfamiliar to him: "Er hätte sehnlichst gewünscht, die Sprache zu kennen, denn das Buch gefiel ihm vorzüglich ohne dass er eine Sylbe davon verstand" (He yearned to know the language, for the book pleased him immensely even though he understood not a single syllable, 264).

Heinrich's descent into the cave mirrors the dream at the beginning of the novel in which he enters an opening in a mountainside and follows a dark passageway to a luminescent fountain. But his discovery of the old manuscript, described by Hohenzollern as a romance about the life and adventures of a poet (265)—and as such a mirror-image of the novel itself—replays a philological find responsible in part for the genesis of *Ofterdingen.* In 1799, Novalis explored a historian friend's library where he discovered a manuscript of Johannes Rothe's fifteenth-century chronicle of Thuringia (*Düringsche Chronik*). In this work Novalis encountered the historical Heinrich von Ofterdingen, a courtly poet none of whose works survive, though some Romantics wrongly thought him the author of the *Nibelungenlied*. Rothe's history tells of how in the year 1206, Heinrich won the Wartburg song-competition, an event in which Novalis's novel would, if completed, have culminated.[17]

In pointing out this library experience, my aim is not to reduce Novalis's work to a particular historical antecedent. Instead, I want to argue that the novel in question attests to a functional affinity between philology and romance. Philology appears in *Ofterdingen* disguised as romance, and the quest becomes an expression of the same needs and desires that cause one to delve into old and strange texts. Grimm's apparent fashioning of his conversion to philology on a literary model suggests a science born of poetry, and his characterization of his new interest as the fascination for the unfamiliar exposes the Romantic aspect of that discipline. Heinrich's pilgrimage, as a quest for the self in the unknown, constitutes the narrative spatialization of philological inquiry. As an undertaking Novalis could only know vicariously, the journey is an attempt to supersede philology— to substitute the text with a more immediate experience. In representing Rothe's history as the Provençal romance, the novel introjects its own source; yet at the same time it subordinates that find to another, more primal event. The structural counterpart of the manuscript in Hohenzollern's cave is the spring at the heart of Heinrich's dream-cave; both are sources (*Quellen*), and the association of written text and dream contradicts Heinrich's skeptical father who declares that old texts are the only "sources" of true revelation: "Die alten Geschichten und Schriften sind jetzt die einzigen Quellen, durch die uns eine Kenntniss von der überirdischen Welt . . . zu Theil wird" (Old histories and manuscripts are now the only sources through which we may gain knowledge of the spiritual world, 198).

The same opposition of natural and verbal sources pervades no less influential a work than Goethe's *Faust,* the action of which proceeds from the hero's desire to abandon the enclosure of his library in favor of a more immediate experience of nature and society. Goethe represents this tension repeatedly as that between text and spring or breast, as illustrated in a rhetorical question Faust puts to the bibliophile Wagner: "Das Pergament, ist das der heil'ge Bronnen, / Woraus ein Trunk den Durst auf ewig stillt?" (The parchment, is that the sacred fount, / a drink from which would still this thirst forever? *HA* III:25). Faust's drama begins as a search for a privileged kind of text that, rather than confining him to his library, would lead him out of it. His lament of being "confined by this heap of books"

(Beschränkt von diesem Bücherhauf, 21) represents the modern condition Foucault attributed to the loss of faith in the revelatory sign and the ensuing realization that, ultimately, language can only represent itself.[18] This nascent understanding of language as nonmimetic would necessitate the advent of a science that studies language as an object unto itself, namely philology. The awareness that our knowledge of the world is indissociable from the texts that represent it makes philology the dominant mode of discourse, and the library, as the space in which texts are gathered and organized, defines the outer limits of human vision.[19] This lesson is lost on Wagner, whose faith in the revelatory power of texts is unshaken: "entrollst du gar ein würdig Pergamen, / so steigt der ganze Himmel zu dir nieder!" (if you just unroll a worthy parchment, / all the heavens will descend to you, *HA* III:40). This is a far cry from the elder Ofterdingen's assertion that, in an age in which the gods no longer speak to man, the most we can do is read ancient accounts of the revelatory experiences of others. His claim that revelation is available only through texts *as history* represents a modernist insight that Romanticism at once acknowledges and resists. And it is worth considering whether Novalis, by giving Heinrich's dream chronological priority over Hohenzollern's manuscript, is not attempting to reinstate the primacy of vision by literally burying the philological origins of his novel.

The presence of history is felt throughout *Ofterdingen*—so much so that even the fairy-tale world, described elsewhere by Novalis as a state of natural anarchy thoroughly opposed to the world of history (III:281), contains various harbingers of historicism. The most conspicuous of these is Sylvester, whose house Heinrich's father had visited in Rome and who appeared in the dream the father recounts for Heinrich. While the novel is set in the Middle Ages, Sylvester's "parlor" (*Stube*) resembles that of the middle-class professor of history who transforms his private dwelling into a reflection of his antiquarian fancies—a monument to what Nietzsche called the pious historian's "fanaticism for collecting" ("Sammelwut"):[20] "Die Stube war voll Bücher und Alterthümer . . . ; er erzählte mir viel von alten Zeiten, von Mahlern, Bildhauern und Dichtern. . . . Er wies mir Siegelsteine und andre alte Kunstarbeiten" (200) (The parlor was full of books and antiquities . . . ; he told me much about ancient times, of painters, sculptors and poets. . . . He showed me seals and other antique works of art). Sylvester appears in the dream as a guide, leading Heinrich's father by the hand through long corridors and into an open space where, like his son twenty years later, he is enchanted by the sight of a blue flower. It is striking that the dream entails the agency of its own analysis: Sylvester tells Heinrich's dreaming father that a great fortune will be his if he returns within the year and bids God reveal to him the meaning of his dream ("wenn du . . . Gott herzlich um das Verständniss dieses Traumes bittest," 202). The problem of understanding dreams is a recurrent theme in this novel; Heinrich and his father have already debated the meaning and function of dreams, and at several stations in his journey the youth is faced with making sense of his own dream-imagery. What makes Sylvester crucial is the relation between his role as dream-patron and his other pursuits. As a doctor, ardent lover of literature, and collector of antique figures he reminds us of Freud, who was all of these— reminds us, in other words, that Freud's investigation of the human psyche in general and of dreams in particular was at base an excavation of pre-history. Freud's overriding view that the meaning of the present was informed by the past finds ample representation here, and Sylvester's nostalgia, which his numerous collectibles are meant to satisfy, suggests the historicism of a Grimm or Ranke: "[er] sehnte sich mit unglaublicher Inbrunst in dies graue Alterthum zurück" (he yearned with incredible fervor to return to that grey antiquity, 200; *PH* 21).

## ARCHAEOLOGY, GEOLOGY, AND THE IMAGES OF KNOWLEDGE

That Sylvester's various interests in old texts, archaeological finds, history, and art converge on the site of the father's dream and recommend themselves to its interpretation exemplifies how Novalis's novel, by concocting a kind of *allgemeines Brouillon* of the sciences, uses existing disciplines metaphorically to ground others that had yet to emerge. The thesis here is that Heinrich's quest is a scientific fable and that the places he visits or dreams and hears about—caves, old archives, mythic landscapes, ancient civilizations, the Orient—are *topoi* of the fields of natural history, philology, comparative religion, archaeology, and Orientalism. To the extent that metaphor has the power to transform what it transfigures, the metaphorical grounding of one discipline in another effects certain important transfers; for example, the relocation of an exotic culture in an underground dream-text suggests the hidden presence of the past and with it the possibility of an archaeology of the mind. Hence the prophecy of a science that would not appear for many years, but the need for which was being produced by a new understanding of dreams and myths.

Freud's most vivid application of the archaeological metaphor occurs in his controversial treatise on the sexual aetiology of hysteria that, when delivered as a lecture to colleagues in 1896, was ill received, characterized by one of the more distinguished auditors as "a scientific fairy tale" (ein wissenschaftliches Märchen, *SA* VI:52). The label betrays what the user did not intend: namely, Freudian theory is part of a post-Enlightenment discourse that redeemed the folk tale by exposing the reason at the core of what was manifestly irrational; beyond that, Freud's reliance on the imagery of romance bears witness to his inability to detach himself from the narratives, epic or otherwise, of which psychoanalysis is a retelling. The passage in which Freud compares his method with the uncovering and deciphering of ancient inscriptions is, like Grimm's account discussed earlier, striking in its attempt at sustained narration. One is left with a sense of generic, if not novelistic, purpose, as both texts are retarded by an unexpected opulence of minor detail—particulars which in turn are transfigured by the unifying trajectory of quest.[21] Freud's paragraph is here reproduced in full:

Nehmen Sie an, ein reisender Forscher käme in eine wenig bekannte Gegend, in welcher ein Trümmerfeld mit Mauerresten, Bruchstücken von Säulen, von Tafeln mit verwischten und unlesbaren Schriftzeichen sein Interesse erweckte. Er kann sich damit begnügen zu beschauen, was frei zutage liegt, dann die in der Nähe hausenden, etwa halbbarbarischen Einwohner ausfragen, was ihnen die Tradition über die Geschichte und Bedeutung jener monumentalen Reste kundgegeben hat, ihre Auskünfte aufzeichnen und—weiterreisen. Er kann aber auch anders vorgehen; er kann Hacken, Schaufeln und Spaten mitgebracht haben, die Anwohner für die Arbeit mit diesen Werkzeugen bestimmen, mit ihnen das Trümmerfeld in Angriff nehmen, den Schutt wegschaffen und von den sichtbaren Resten aus das Vergrabene aufdecken. Lohnt der Erfolg seine Arbeit, so erläutern die Funde sich selbst; die Mauerreste gehören zur Umwallung eines Palastes oder Schatzhauses, aus den Säulentrümmern ergänzt sich ein Tempel, die zahlreich gefundenen, im glücklichen Falle bilinguen Inschriften enthüllen ein Alphabet und eine Sprache, und deren Entzifferung und Übersetzung ergibt ungeahnte Aufschlüsse über die Ereignisse der Vorzeit, zu deren Gedächtnis jene Monumente erbaut worden sind. *Saxa loquuntur!* (*SA* VI:54)

Imagine that a traveling explorer came to a little-known region where his interest is aroused by an expanse of ruins, with remains of walls, fragments of columns, and tablets with faded and illegible inscriptions. He may content himself with examining what is already visible, then interrogate the semi-barbaric inhabitants dwelling nearby about what tradition has told them regarding the history and meaning of those monumental remains, record the information and—journey onward. But he can also proceed differently. He may have brought picks, shovels, and spades with him, and he may set the inhabitants to work with these implements, together with them start upon the ruins, remove the rubble and from the visible remains uncover what is buried. Should this work meet with success, then the findings will clarify themselves; the fallen walls belong to the fortification of a palace or a treasure-trove, out of the column-fragments a temple is constructed, the numerous inscriptions, which, if fortune prevails, are bilingual, reveal an alphabet and a language, whose decipherment and translation yields unsuspected clues of events from the remote past, in commemoration of which these monuments were built. *The stones speak!*

The Latin exclamation with which Freud concludes his story becomes one of the found inscriptions, performing the same *ekphrasis* or "speaking out" it proclaims and awakening multiple resonances, one of which is the opening line of Goethe's *Roman Elegies:* "Saget, Steine, mir an, o sprecht, ihr hohen Paläste!" (Declare to me, stones, speak ye tall palaces!" *HA* I:57).[22] The allusion to the elegiac supplies an intimation of death that reinforces the formal closure the epigram provides, suggesting further a connection, theorized by Walter Benjamin, between mortality and "The End" of narrative.[23]

While Freud's reference to "bilingual" inscriptions shadows the concept of overdetermination developed in *The Interpretation of Dreams,* it also invokes what for Romanticism became the essence of indecipherability—the Egyptian hieroglyphs. The hieroglyphs of Isis and the complex of theoretical problems they represent are central to Norvalis's novel-fragment of 1798, *Die Lehrlinge zu Sais.* The following passage, describing travelers who have come from afar to learn about the forgotten language and the people who spoke it, contributes to the impression that Freud, as well as Grimm, was subject to the dictates of a Romantic genre:

> Die Trümmer dieser Sprache, wenigstens alle Nachrichten von ihr, aufzusuchen, war ein Hauptzweck ihrer Reise gewesen, und der Ruf des Alterthums hatte sie auch nach Sais gezogen. Sie hofften hier von den erfahrnen Vorstehern des Tempelarchivs wichtige Nachrichten zu erhalten, und vielleicht in den grossen Sammlungen aller Art Aufschlüsse Selbst zu finden. (I:107)

> To search for the remains of this language, or at least word of it, had been the principal purpose of their journey, and the call of antiquity had drawn them to Isis. They hoped to get important information

from the experienced custodians of the temple archive and perhaps to find clues of all kinds in the large collections.

This hieroglyphic language, as the object of an archaeological expedition, is a metaphor representing the language of nature, a "script of ciphers" (Chiffernschrift, I:79) that was everywhere legible, yet that had become unintelligible to a society grown alienated from the natural world. Underscoring the metaphorical role of archaeology is the ease with which Novalis, in the course of his writing, replaces it with geology, the discipline he practiced professionally during the last four years of his life, and which, as a natural science which is also an archaeology, casts the study of language as a form of natural history.

That the study of nature becomes a kind of source-work through language is apparent in the case of the old miner Heinrich meets whose boyhood interest in mineralogy is characterized as a search for hidden origins: "Von Jugend auf habe er eine heftige Neugierde gehabt zu wissen, . . . wo das Wasser in den Quellen herkomme" (From the days of his youth he had felt a powerful curiosity to know . . . where the water in the springs came from, 239). This describes a program already realized by Heinrich in his first dream in which he follows a stream from its source deep within the earth to a spring above ground. Much as Heinrich seeks the words that would help him understand his dreams, so too did the miner wish as a boy that the glittering stones he collected could speak so as to reveal their secret origin: "Er habe . . . nur gewünscht, dass sie zu ihm reden könnten, um ihm von ihrer geheimnissvollen Herkunft zu erzählen" (He only wished they could speak to him and reveal their mysterious provenance, 239–40). Novalis's novel thus makes the earth into a *tertium comparationis* of manifold relevance, and geology appears as a sibling to those humanistic disciplines that seek to uncover the archaic strata of consciousness that have disappeared from view. It is significant in this context that Novalis's mentor, Abraham Gottlob Werner, a preeminent geologist who saw his field as a foundational science in which other disciplines could be grounded, was also planning a universal etymological encyclopedia in accordance with classificatory principles he had developed for mineralogy.[24]

The analogy by which the study of the earth becomes a discipline of memory is compressed brilliantly into a few lines in the Tale of Atlantis, one of the shorter narratives embedded in *Ofterdingen,* when a love-struck youth finds a ruby engraved with "incomprehensible ciphers" (unverständliche Chiffern, 218). Believing the gem to belong to his new beloved, he spontaneously scribbles down a poem, the meaning of which evades even him, and wraps it around the tiny treasure. The image of a precious stone bearing mysterious inscriptions enfolded by a cryptic poem poses the problematic nature of writing that has other writing as its subject— that is, translation in the broad sense. The poem itself describes a parallel between sign (*Zeichen*) and image (*Bild*), invoking the familiar Romantic distinction between a script of letters and one of visual images, between *Buchstabenschrift* and *Bilderschrift*,[25] and making writing in stone an analogue of memory:

> Es ist dem Stein ein räthselhaftes Zeichen
> Tief eingegraben in sein glühend Blut,
> Er ist mit einem Herzen zu vergleichen,
> In dem das Bild der Unbekannten ruht. (218–19)

> There is engraved an enigmatic token
> Full deep into the jewel's glowing blood;
> Of likeness to a heart may well be spoken
> Which holds the stranger's image like a bud. (*PH* 41)

The poem has certain methodological implications in that it suggests, through its analogy, that the study of cryptic languages might have something to teach us about how the psyche represents itself. Freud once offered that psychoanalysis could benefit from an understanding of the philologist's procedure; he maintained that dreams, like the Egyptian hieroglyphs, were not informed by a universal grammar but had to be understood in terms of their own internal syntax, that certain elements of dreams determined other elements but themselves possessed no translatable content. Here the possibility of always finding a verbal equivalent of the image is denied. The object of psychoanalysis is not the dream-image, nor is it the narrative told by the analysand about the dream; rather it is the juncture at which the narrative falters to reveal a resistance—the trace of a repression.[26]

The problem of translating dream-imagery into a verbal narrative becomes explicit when Heinrich finds the mysterious Provençal manuscript in Hohenzollern's underground library. Not only does the old romance correspond topographically to the fountain at the center of the original dream-cave, but it also contains figures from that dream, which appear at the point where the images are the most obscure. Heinrich's reaction to the book is as to a dream:

> [Einige Bilder] dünkten ihm ganz wunderbar bekannt, und wie er recht zusah entdeckte er seine eigene Gestalt ziemlich kenntlich

unter den Figuren. Er erschrack und glaubte zu träumen. . . . Die letzten Bilder waren dunkel und unverständlich; doch überraschten ihn einige Gestalten seines Traumes mit dem innigsten Entzücken. (264–65)

Some of the pictures seemed oddly familiar to him, and as he looked closely he discovered his own form rather distinct among the figures. He started and thought he was dreaming. . . . The final pictures were dark and incomprehensible; yet several shapes from his dream surprised him with the innermost delight.

Heinrich's longing to know the language of the manuscript is premised on the belief that a narrative would lend the imagery coherence and intelligibility, a premise Heinrich voices at the outset of the novel when, estranged by his own excited emotional state, he asserts that a greater command of words would give him a better grasp of things: "Dass ich auch nicht einmal von meinem wunderlichen Zustande reden kann! . . . wüsste ich mehr [Worte], so könnte ich viel besser alles begreifen" (That I can't even speak about my peculiar condition! . . . If I knew more words, I could grasp everything much better, 195). This is the assumption the poem interrogates; enshrouding the inscribed talisman, it is little more than a commentary on the incomprehensibility of those inscriptions, and the analogy the poem constructs merely uses one form of puzzlement to represent another.

A kind of dream-book, the manuscript represents the dream as a text of words that defy comprehension. The resistance dreams pose to translation is exemplified by Heinrich's second dream (Chap. 7), which foretells the death by drowning of Mathilde, his future fiancée. After reuniting in an aquatic underworld reminiscent of the waterscape in which he first saw the blue flower, Heinrich and Mathilde share a lingering kiss during which she imparts a mysterious word directly to his soul—a word he cannot recollect upon awakening:

Sie sagte ihm ein wunderbares geheimes Wort in den Mund, was sein ganzes Wesen durchklang. Er wollte es wiederholen, als sein Grossvater rief und er aufwachte. Er hätte sein Leben darum geben mögen, das Wort noch zu wissen. (279)

She spoke a wonderful, secret word into his mouth which resonated through his whole being. He wanted to repeat it just as his grandfather called, and he awoke. He would have given his life to remember that word.

The kerygmatic word of the second dream corresponds to the elusive blue flower of the first, and Heinrich's quest for self-knowledge is clarified as a search for a lost word. The claim that Heinrich would have sacrificed his very life to exhume that word makes death the condition of full understanding, and the equation of life with the absence of clarity places interpretation itself within a curious relationship with human mortality. Aesthetics, which the Enlightenment had opposed to philosophy and designated as the "science of confused perception,"[27] now begins to acquire the function of sustaining life by confounding clarity. Incomplete almost by definition, the German Romantic novel is shaped by the wish to exclude that moment at which things become irreducibly clear, and *The Arabian Nights,* for Novalis and others a standard for narrative, describes the perpetual delay of an ending equal to the desire to stay alive.[28]

## THE DEATH-INSTINCT AND THE HERMENEUTICS OF STIMULUS

The structure of Novalis's novel would thus indicate that death is more than an ending that confers meaning on all that has come before: death is the inevitable end of which even the beginning is an anticipation and of which every intermediate station is but a deferral. Upon awakening from a dream that simulates his own birth, Heinrich defines life itself as a "pilgrimage to the holy grave" (Wallfahrt zum heiligen Grab, 199), thus casting death as the *telos* of life, the result of internal momentum rather than external circumstance. The "grave" Heinrich mentions refers simultaneously to what is to become his geographical destination, the Holy Sepulchre of Jerusalem, and this double reference establishes a parallel between instinct and quest, identifying the economy of *Todestrieb* (death instinct) as a narrative economy.[29] Indeed quest romance, as the tale of an epic hero who is by nature *fey* ("feig")—that is, fated to die ("dem Tode bestimmt")[30]—now becomes a paradigm for a development in which death is the object of tireless striving. The journey charts a temporal expanse between two moments of undifferentiation: the latter is death; the former is the unity of self and world known to the infant at the mother's breast. In between lies a state of excitation, a general experience of nonidentity, and the movement toward death is conceived as a drive to eliminate stimulus. As the pertinent myth reveals, the death instinct satisfies a narcissistic aim, and Heinrich's path can readily be described in terms of narcissism. The narrative is replete with images of inundation and orality, as the youth wavers between a gradual separation from his mother and a lingering attachment to her. Equally interesting, however, is the way Novalis represents the middle ground of that development in terms of its epistemological counterpart: incomprehensibility. Novalis would elsewhere characterize philosophy itself as an odyssey of instinct, as the "drive to be at home everywhere" (Trieb überall zu Hause zu seyn, III:434). That the enigmatic word of Heinrich's second dream is delivered with a deep kiss suggests a connection between mystery and desire, and just as his journey amounts to the repeated encounter with the incomprehensible, so might one define his movement toward epiphany as a periodic deferral of understanding. Consider in this context that the only inscription Heinrich sees is at once both immanently legible and literally cryptic: the epitaph of the hermit's wife, who lies buried within the cave.

The equation of stimulus with incomprehensibility is apparent in Grimm's narrative as well as Novalis's. In either case, the relative opacity of the language engenders the desire to understand it, an act that would in turn neutralize the incitement. So defined, understanding constitutes a kind of stimulus-reduction, the quelling of the disturbance that attends any contact between a life-form and its environment. In a fragment that restates a familiar philosophical problem in anthropological, if not biological, terms, Novalis argues that the elimination of stimulus is the basis of all mediation between subject and object: "Der Geist strebt den Reitz zu absorbiren. Ihn reizt das Fremdartige. Verwandlungen des *Fremden* in ein *Eignes*. . . . Einst soll kein *Reitz* und nichts *Fremdes* mehr seyn" (The mind strives to absorb stimulus. It is stimulated by strangeness. Transformations of the *strange* into the *familiar*. . . . Eventually there shall be no more *stimulus* and no more *strangeness*, II:646). The transformation described here is commensurate with the reduction of stimulus Freud held to be the originary function of the unconscious and the principal task of living organisms. Organic life resulted from the disturbance of inorganic matter, an event that instilled in the organism the drive to restore the original hypostasis. Freud defined "drive" as the impulse on the part of the organism to recover the state of inertia or nonlife that external stimuli had interrupted (*SA* III:246). Put differently, the goal of a drive is the satisfaction that can be attained only by undoing the stimulus at the source of that drive.[31] This notion of *Trieb* seems an elaboration of *Bildungstrieb*, a morphological concept introduced by the anthropologist Johann Blumenbach and adopted by Goethe, the latter of whom described organic development as the progressive manifestation of previously latent stages leading ultimately to the reproduction of the original stage. It seems only appropriate that Novalis's *Bildungsroman*, which was developing toward its own elegiac culmination in "Das Lied der Toten" (The Song of the Dead), should spring to life through excitation from without: "'Du hast in mir den edlen Trieb erregt'' (You have aroused in me the noble drive, 193)—so reads the first line of the novel's dedication, a moment soon to be repeated when Heinrich encounters a stranger whose uncanny tales activate in him an ''inner drive'' (inniges Treiben, 195).

The notes for the continuation of this novel indicate that Heinrich's route to Jerusalem was to be anything but direct, a circuitous journey leading first to Loreto and Rome, then to North Africa, Egypt, and Greece, each of these the setting of an adventure, insubordinate as it were—a sojourn in its own right (I:335–48). In light of the above discussion of the death instinct, it will seem less paradoxical that a journey should have the purpose of forstalling arrival instead of accelerating it: the journey as end in itself, as opposed to the end of the journey. The ''pilgrimage to the Holy Grave'' is a veritable allegory of instinctual gratification, the deferral of which is the ground whereupon Novalis founds his aesthetics. The so-called ''Orient-chapter'' of *Ofterdingen* (Chap. 4) presents two versions of that pilgrimage: one is aligned with the Christian crusades, the other with the mystery and beauty of the Middle East. At the beginning of this chapter, Heinrich and his companions are received for the night by an aging nobleman who that same evening is hosting a feast for his fellow crusaders—men of whom it is said that they knew no other pastime than ''the full [wine-]tumbler'' (den gefüllten Becher, 230). Heinrich is allowed to attend the drunken affair and is there encouraged to participate in the next campaign, and the warriors promise more libation at the other end of the journey, predicting that within the year they would meet in Jerusalem to celebrate victory ''with wine from the fatherland'' (bey vaterländischem Wein, 231). They represent the goal of their quest as the expeditious return to an earlier state of minimal excitability, and the assimilatory aims of their military mission are reproduced at a more basic level by the desire to suspend any difference between the self and the world around it.[32] Zulima, the young Saracen captive Heinrich meets after leaving the crusaders to their pleasures, characterizes the murderous zeal of her captors (they have slain her husband) in terms of a ''dark impulse,'' activated by the experience of strange surroundings, to return to ancestral origins:

> und vielleicht ist es dieser dunkle Zug, der die Menschen aus neuen Gegenden, sobald eine gewisse Zeit ihres Erwachens kömmt, mit so zerstörender Ungeduld nach der alten Heymath ihres Geschlechts *treibt*. (237, my emphasis)

> and it is perhaps this dark impulse which, with the coming of an age of awakening, *drives* men with destructive impatience from new regions back to the homeland of their ancestors.

The crusaders' instinctual urge to forge an identity out of difference is close to what Freud defined as secondary narcissism, the desire to recover the undifferentiation of infancy (*SA* III:329). Novalis's text emphasizes that the narcissistic tendency to avert or absorb stimulus runs contrary to aesthetic experience. Music itself is described as the mediation of *Reize*—the plucking of the strings of a lute and the receptivity of the ear to those vibrations[33]—and it is Zulima's song that transforms the German countryside into a fantastic Oriental landscape (in contrast to the crusaders' alcohol, which transforms the Other into the Same).

The organological model of stimulus furnishes Novalis with a framework for describing an aesthetics that opposes, not necessarily the natural propensities of the organism, but certainly a notion of philosophy that follows that model. The deferral of understanding mentioned earlier defines the space of aesthetics as the domain of *Reiz;* the "anaesthetic" tendency is embodied by the heavy drinking crusaders and their inability to tolerate stimulus (and the difference it represents) or, less crudely, their subordination of stimulus as an instrument of its own undoing. They appeal to Heinrich's sense of the exotic to enlist him in their cause, and his momentary enthusiasm corresponds to a sexual awakening. His host presents him with a sword, which he takes in his hand and kisses passionately (231), an onanistic gesture later replicated in even greater caricature by the Scribe of Klingsohr's tale—an act of self-stimulation that underscores the narcissistic character of his endeavor: "Er kitzelte sich, um zu lachen" (He tickled himself in order to laugh, 304). In analogy to the hermeneutic principle discussed earlier according to which "enigma does not block understanding but provokes it,"[34] it can be said that radical cultural difference does not deter assimilation but ensures it. Stimulus becomes incompatible with the end to which it is the means, and the context of colonialism shades Novalis's fragment with an ominous hue: "Einst soll kein *Reitz* und nichts *Fremdes* mehr seyn." The narcissistic aversion to prolonged excitation provides the counterpoint to Heinrich's poetic apprenticeship, which entails the cultivation of a stance toward the world that allows the world free play. The critique of narcissism is pronounced in a passage contrasting poets to "men of action" who devour earthly fruits instead of contenting themselves with their fragrance (267). The aesthetic experience for Novalis is one of *sustained difference,* as becomes explicit in a fragment defining Romantic poetics as "the art of making an object foreign and yet familiar and compelling" (die Kunst . . . , einen Gegenstand fremd zu machen und doch bekannt und anziehend, III:685). What is most damning in Zulima's characterization of the crusaders is the impatience with which they seek to nullify the difference that is the source of excitation and thus to collapse the distance wherein narrative takes shape. Zulima's legacy to Heinrich is, most appropriately, a hair-band bearing her name in "unfamiliar letters" (unbekannten Buchstaben, 239).

One might conclude by reconsidering Freud's observation that Schliemann, through his discovery of the lost city of Troy, fulfilled a wish born in childhood when his father told him stories from the *Iliad*.[35] It now seems possible to read Novalis's novel as a commentary on that interpretation, at least to the extent that Heinrich, whose own longing to travel is induced by a stranger's tales of afar, and whose initial journey is tethered to the enterprise of the merchants he and his mother accompany to Augsburg, articulates a distinction crucial to psychoanalysis generally and underlying Freud's remarks on Schliemann. Freud's implicit denial that the large cache of gold the archaeologist found was anything more than an indirect source of gratification echoes Heinrich's own disavowal of greed; his first utterance of the novel, contrasting the legendary riches with the inauspicious blue flower, expresses surprise at a bewildering cathexis: "Nicht die Schätze sind es, die ein so unaussprechliches Verlangen in mir geweckt haben . . . , aber die blaue Blume sehn' ich mich zu erblicken" (Tis not the treasures which have awakened in me such unpronounceable desire . . . , but I yearn to glimpse the blue flower, 195). Heinrich betrays an awareness that the flower, unlike the precious metals and gems, is not self-representing—that is, not a symbol in the idealist vein, but a metonymy that facilitates connections between the hero and the various love-objects he encounters, himself included. The flower's attraction (*Reiz*) lies in its nonidentity; inscribed in its very color is the "romantic distance" (romantische Ferne) that adorns the commonplace with an aura of mystery by transforming even the most mundane household utensils into "sacred relics" (geweihten Pfändern, 203).[36] The journey, that essential component of the archaeological venture, is the spatial extention of this nonidentity. Heinrich's words warn against the confusion of value that is intrinsic with that imputed on the basis of contiguity.

In a paper from 1899 entitled "Screen-Memories" (Deckerinnerungen), Freud discussed the role of contiguous associations in such confusion, and his analogy seems tailored for Schliemann: he declares that a particular childhood memory may acquire a certain value because of its proximity to another, more deeply submerged experience; that is, "not because it is itself gold, but because it has lain next to gold" (nicht etwa weil es selbst Gold ist, sondern weil es bei Gold gelegen ist).[37] The same distinction informs Freud's analysis of the sexual fetish, and the importance of gold for the Schliemann episode only makes it easier to relate Freud's concept of fetishism to that of Marx. Both describe a similar logic of dis-

114

placement, and both borrow their metaphor from the theological domain, Marx to emphasize the mechanism of mystification, Freud to implicate the very origins of religion. But the analogy itself implicates these respective disciplines as part of an archaeology, a search for not only sacred objects and their modern surrogates, but also what lies beneath the historical sedimentation of language. This new sensitivity to the "enigmatic density" of language made philology the modern form of criticism—this according to Foucault, who characterized the first book of *Das Kapital* as an "exegesis of 'value.' "[38] The following passage from that book (indeed, from the discussion of commodity fetishism) suggests that Marx, contemporary of Grimm and successor to Novalis, found in the archaeology of language a metaphorical foundation for his own critical project:[39]

> Der Wert verwandelt vielmehr jedes Arbeitsprodukt in eine gesellschaftliche Hieroglyphe. Später suchen die Menschen den Sinn der Hieroglyphe zu entziffern, hinter das Geheimnis ihres eigenen gesellschaftlichen Produktes zu kommen; denn die Bestimmung der Gebrauchsgegenstände *als* Werte ist *ihr* gesellschaftliches Produkt so gut wie die Sprache.

> Value actually transforms every product of labor into a social hieroglyph. People try later to decipher the meaning of the hieroglyph, to penetrate the mystery of their own social product; for the determination of use-objects *as* values is *their* social product just as much as language.

By the time Marx had written his chapter on fetishism and certainly by the time Freud began interpreting dreams, the recalcitrant hieroglyphs of the famous Rosetta stone had been decoded, and the feat well publicized; the stone had spoken, and the powers of philology been confirmed. This meant that the discourse of Marxism, as well as of psychoanalysis, is predicated on the ultimate possibility of decipherment. By contrast, Novalis lived and died in an age that had come to accept the apparent indecipherability of the hieroglyphs. In a lecture Novalis probably attended, Schiller speculated that the first Egyptian priests of monotheism, in an effort "to employ this device of deception to the advantage of truth" (von diesem Kunstgriffe des Betrugs auch zum Vorteil der Wahrheit Gebrauch zu machen), developed a system of highly codified pictograms to disguise and thereby preserve their forbidden teachings while simultaneously through the appeal of their imagery to fire the imagination of the novices and make them receptive to truths they would only later comprehend.[40] Schiller suggested that the key to the code had been lost, and the images themselves became mistaken for the truths they were meant to veil.[41]

This account is stark in its anticipation of the link, of great concern to the later Freud, between the censorial mechanism of preconsciousness and the calculations of an ancient monotheistic priesthood (*Der Mann Moses und die monotheistische Religion*). It also reveals a tension between psychoanalysis and Romantic aesthetics. Schiller's account of how the hieroglyphs assumed an attraction independent of their meaning describes an untranslatability that conditions this aesthetics.[42] This same condition is what psychoanalysis undertakes to relieve. Romanticism had made the lure of the untranslatable the basis for a quest not subordinate to its destination but extant for the sake of the journey, an allegorical pilgrimage as it were,[43] and it is worth considering whether archaeology, once associated with a realizable goal (once the possibility of translation was secured), did not become dislodged from its metaphorical beginnings. In any case, the Romantic narrative of deferred arrival is resituated, inscribed by Freud as a process that portends death for anyone who succeeds in lifting the veil of Isis.[44]

# 5

# Allegories of Plot

The psychoanalytic interpretation of dreams has been explained in terms of the distinction between *fabula* and *sjužet*, narratological concepts introduced by Russian formalism to describe different levels of organization in narrative. The opposition of these terms corresponds to an inter-relationship between surface and depth, whereby fabula acquires the privilege and authority of the latter.[1] Sjužet refers to the order in which the events of a story are told (as opposed to the order of their occurrence), though disruptions in temporal sequence are only part of the individual enunciation that characterizes sjužet and brands it a distortion.[2] True to an "original" chronology and thus anterior to the intervention of narrative, fabula denotes an underlying coherence to which sjužet alludes but does not manifest. Fabula is therefore understood as a construction, inferred from the surface particulars of narrative and as such produced in the act of reading.

Tzvetan Todorov has suggested that this process of gleaning the order of fabula from the chaos of sjužet is exemplified schematically by detective fiction, in which the sleuth has the explicit task of doing what the reader otherwise does: interrogating seemingly unrelated and discontinuous bits of information according to the laws of causal sequence. The *telos* of the detective story is the revelation of fabula in the detective's formal reconstruction of the crime.[3] Sherlock Holmes's notorious gift for coaxing an extensive biography from the most inert clue (for example, the hat in

"The Adventure of the Blue Carbuncle")[4] indicates that this teleology has more at stake than sequential propriety: it aims to create a world replete with meaning by purging details of their presumed insignificance. What Walter Benjamin says of the collector is valid for the detective as well: namely, in each particular object the world is not only fully present but also ordered, and this "according to an unexpected set of interconnections that elude the uninitiated" (nach einem überraschenden, dem Profanen unverständlichen Zusammenhange).[5] Benjamin observes that collections resemble dreams in their ability to invest the most neutral and innocuous things with meaning,[6] a comparison that indirectly implicates both psychoanalyst and detective in the collector's campaign against the dispersal of modern society. For the aim of the collection is an arrangement commensurate with the order and sequence of fabula: "Der Sammler . . . vereint das Zusammengehörige; es kann ihm derart gelingen, über die Dinge durch ihre Verwandtschaften oder durch ihre Abfolge in der Zeit zu belehren" (The collector . . . unites what belongs together; he may succeed in this by illuminating things via their affinities or their succession in time).[7]

For Freud, similarity and succession represent different moments in the process by which associations are formed in the psychical apparatus. Sequence enjoys a certain primacy in interpretation, which works to unpack the simultaneities created in this process; analysis follows the path of regressive representation, which corresponds to "a fixed chronology" (eine feste Reihenfolge, *SA* II:513). As a search for the continuum purported to lie beneath the fractured surface of the dream-narrative, psychoanalysis repeats the detective story's "syntactic regression . . . from *sjužet* to *fabula.*"[8] Nowhere in Freud's writings is this regression more apparent than in the final footnote to the "Wolfman," in which the particulars of Freud's most circuitous case history are retold in chronological order (*SA* VIII:230–31).

Freud himself acknowledged the similarity between psychoanalysis and criminology by offering the murder investigation as a metaphor for describing the psychoanalytic habit of excusing nothing from suspicion, not even the most innocent and minor slip of the tongue (*SA* I:52). But Freud seems also to have suspected that his quest for transparency signaled an ambivalence toward modernity similar to that exhibited by the collector, for the practice of investing everything with sense suggests not only the methodical scrutiny of the detective but also the totalizing determinism of the shaman, whose universe is devoid of chance (*SA* I:46).[9] Such ambivalence also informs the classical *Bildungsroman,* itself poised on the verge of modernity, which compensates for increasing social complexity and fragmentation with an ideal of total scrutability. In his criticism of *Wilhelm Meisters Lehrjahre,* Novalis isolated as "ridiculous" the "secret surveillance" (geheime Oberaufsicht, III:646) of the Society of the Tower, whose invisibility allows conspiracy to disguise itself as fortune and whose eventual self-revelation coincides with a retelling that suffuses Wilhelm's diverse experiences with the wisdom of preordination. In a vaguely ironic citation of Goethe's novel, the narrator of *Heinrich von Ofterdingen* invokes *Bildung* at a juncture where the variegated particulars of Heinrich's journey are inscribed with the necessity of a plot that precludes chance: "Mannichfaltige Zufälle schienen sich zu seiner Bildung zu vereinigen, und noch hatte nichts seine innere Regsamkeit gestört" (Many various coincidences seemed to unite in his formation, and yet nothing had disturbed his inner responsiveness, 267–68).

In Goethe's novel as well, *Bildung* represents a hegemony of destiny over chance and as such corresponds to the authority of fabula over sjužet. This authority is affirmed during Wilhelm's initiation into the Society of the Tower, when he learns that the propitious encounters of the past several years have in fact been part of a plan (a benevolent masterplot that makes a mockery of his name), and that his actions have been the object of surveillance and manipulation. The authority of fabula is clinched when Wilhelm, having gained the innermost sanctum of Lothario's castle, discovers a parchment scroll, the title of which is roughly that of Goethe's novel ("[Wilhelms] Lehrjahre," *HA* VII:497). In this moment of retrospective illumination the first five hundred pages can be recounted from the standpoint of the secret agency that has masterminded Wilhelm's maturation. Natalie, who is part of the society's plan, shows herself to be an agent of its rationality when she extracts, from disparate fragments, the continuous thread of Mignon's life story, which she plots backwards to an original "crime" of incest. Her negotiation of Mignon's reticence is worthy of detective and psychoanalyst alike: "unsere werte Freundin hat es aus einzelnen Äusserungen, aus Liedern und kindlichen Unbesonnenheiten, die gerade das verraten, was sie verschweigen wollen, zusammengereiht" (our dear friend pieced it together from individual utterances, from songs and childlike lapses in reflection, which disclose precisely what they are meant to keep silent, *HA* VII:522).[10]

The incestuous act to which Mignon owes her existence is the "Other" of Natalie's analysis, which, by virtue of its sheer deductive reasoning, renews the enmity of oedipal structures toward incest. The tower is one such structure, and Wilhelm's admission to it constitutes entry into the law of the father. The fact that this initiation occurs under the shroud of mysterious ritual may point to an archaic psychical residue; for the formation of the superego repeats an ancient act of remorse for a crime motivated by incestuous desires. As Rainer Nägele points out, the tower not only facilitates the identification with the spirit of the departed father, but it also anchors the modern rationality that issues from it in an ambivalence aptly characterized as "twilight":

> The secret of the tower-society is the manifest secret of internalized authority. It is a common trait of literary fictions from the Enlightenment to Fontane's *Effi Briest* that the paternal authority enters the subject, if not literally as ghost, at least accompanied by mysterious, uncanny machineries and rituals. It is from this twilight of mystery and paternal machineries that a new genre is born: the detective novel and its hero, the immaculate rationality of the master detective.[11]

By means of this rationality the Society of the Tower resolves the doubt that underlies family romance. Wilhelm believes he may have fathered the illegitimate child of his former lover, who died in childbirth after Wilhelm, believing himself betrayed, had begun his travels. His hopes are confirmed now with a verbal gesture that brilliantly links happiness, proclaimed by the child's very name, with the autonomy that uncertain paternity invariably threatens: "Felix ist Ihr Sohn" (Felix is your son).[12] The society, which has also conjured the ghost of Wilhelm's father,[13] extends this patrilineage by enacting a kind of motherless birth, presenting Wilhelm with his son and urging him to pursue a happiness that, like the child, is of his own making: "Empfangen Sie das liebliche Kind aus unserer Hand . . . und wagen Sie es, glücklich zu sein!" (Receive the lovely child from our hand . . . and dare to be happy! *HA* VII:497).[14] The abbot's challenge intones a recuperative counterpoint to the bereaved Lessing, whose loss of wife *and* child following a difficult labor compelled him to acknowledge that happiness itself was always contingent on the fortune of birth, and was thus not happiness at all.[15] Freud's eventual formalization of this despair came in direct contradiction of Enlightenment teleology: "man möchte sagen, die Absicht, dass der Mensch 'glücklich' sei, ist im Plan der 'Schöpfung' nicht enthalten" (one might say that the intention that man be 'happy' is not contained in the plan of 'creation,' *SA* IX:208).

The tension between the Goethean and Freudian moments belies a common struggle with heterogeneity—one that associates Freud with a modern novel tradition that, following Lukács, mourns the loss of the immanence of meaning in life indigenous to epic.[16] Like Marxism, psychoanalysis is a theory of nonimmanent meaning, indeed, of its progressive nonimmanence, and the fabula/sjužet distinction has its cognates in the conceptual pairs infrastructure/superstructure and unconscious/consciousness. In Freud, the regression toward fabula is historical as well as formal—a return to the phylogenetic fables that reproduce themselves in the individual and represent the informing intelligence behind the seemingly unintelligible. In Novalis's *Ofterdingen,* this regression is a pilgrimage repeatedly described as a quest for the beginning rather than the end.[17] It is noteworthy, therefore, that the Provençal manuscript Heinrich discovers, unlike the parchment found by Wilhelm Meister, is not a coherent and closed master narrative—that is, not the fabula behind the dream it replaces—but a fragmented and incomplete text that duplicates the original enigma. Although Novalis seems on one level to have written Goethe's bourgeois romance back into an age in which the beneficent machinations of the *Turmgesellschaft* are commensurate with a belief in providence, he nonetheless refuses access to a stable origin. In fact, Hohenzollern's description of the manuscript preserves, via the word *mannichfach,* the heterogeneity invoked along with *Bildung* in the passage quoted earlier: "es [ist] ein Roman von den wunderbaren Schicksalen eines Dichters, worinn die Dichtkunst in ihren mannichfachen Verhältnissen dargestellt und gepriesen wird" (it is a romance about the wondrous fortunes of a poet, in which poesy is presented and praised in its manifold relations, 265; *PH* 91).

The premises behind the following discussion may be summarized as a three-part progression: (1) the structuralism that distinguishes fabula from sjužet and accords all privilege to the former extends a post-revolutionary morphology that sought to reestablish stability within change—the famous *Dauer im Wechsel* imputed by Goethe to plant metamorphosis; (2) *Bildung,* as a concept that incorporates change into a larger structure of continuity, is an earlier expression of the same formalism; and (3) *Heinrich von Ofterdingen,* as a narrative that subverts continuity by celebrating the gaps and dislocations of the dream, is a revolutionary novel, at least in the sense that it resists the hegemony of the "superindividual necessity" of fabula.[18] Because the concept of *Bildung* was borrowed from botany, flower imagery becomes the curious occasion for exploring its political implications. This analysis will move toward Philipp Otto Runge's engraving *Fall des Vaterlands* (1809), in which those implications become explicit. Generally, it may be said that the flower-imagery in Novalis and Runge formalizes, under the aegis of the Grotesque, the kind of unprecedented metamorphosis that the French Revolution had come to represent and that—in the writings of Kafka a century later—became virtually identical with modernism.

## METAMORPHOSIS AND THE BIRTH OF NARRATIVE

Heinrich's journey begins with a moment of infantlike speechlessness. An infant yet at the age of twenty, he awakens, groggy and dream-possessed, to the tender embrace of his mother, in whose arms he momentarily reclaims the oneness of self and world he knew in sleep. While she bids him eat and drink that he might awaken more fully, Heinrich's artisan-father chides him for rising late and complains that his mother's insistence on quiet has disrupted the morning work routine:

> Du Langschläfer, sagte der Vater, wie lange sitze ich schon hier, und feile. Ich habe deinetwegen nichts hämmern dürfen; die Mutter wollte den lieben Sohn schlafen lassen. Aufs Frühstück habe ich auch warten müssen. (197)

> You lazy bones, his father said, how long I've been sitting here filing. For your sake I was not allowed to hammer; your mother wanted to let her dear son sleep. I even had to wait for breakfast.

A struggle is hereby delineated, restrained to be sure, but a struggle none-theless—one that sets the introspective and essentially autoerotic youth against a world in which work, discipline, time, and productivity are the governing criteria. The same contest is displayed in rather more agonic terms in *Die Christenheit oder Europa* when a nascent Romanticism fighting to loosen the grip of the Enlightenment is likened to the infant Hercules standing his first trial:

> Aus dem Morgentraum der unbehülflichen Kindheit erwacht, übt ein Theil des Geschlechts seine ersten Kräfte an Schlangen, die seine Wiege umschlingen und den Gebrauch seiner Gliedmassen ihm benehmen wollen. (III:519)

> Awakened from the morning-dream of awkward childhood, one member of the species tests its first powers on snakes that entangle his cradle and seek to rob him of the use of his limbs.

In *Ofterdingen*, this is not simply a conflict between eros and civilization, for as the vessel of the novel's beginning intention and as the locus of what the narrator will eventually term *Bildung*, Heinrich embodies the aspirations of the novel *to be*—to assert itself in the face of a full-fledged reality that would impose on that new life its own notion of order and purpose in the form of plot. With Heinrich's awakening, the novel proclaims its infancy to not only the world but also, and especially, a modern narrative tradition that seems to have dispatched its agents throughout Novalis's text in a plot to assimilate the novel, along with its poet-hero, to the world's prosaic economy. Narrative itself emerges as epic protagonist.

The modernist implications of this conflict become markedly apparent in the works of Kafka which, by making plot itself the ever elusive object of quest, directly challenge a German novel tradition in which plot is an explicit function of a character's own natural development. Kafka writes of this struggle in a fragment examining how a story just begun, like a new and fragile life form, must fight to survive in a world already fully formed and closed:

> Anfang jeder Novelle zunächst lächerlich. Es scheint hoffnungslos, dass dieser neue, noch unfertige, überall empfindliche Organismus in der fertigen Organisation der Welt sich wird erhalten können, die wie jede fertige Organisation danach strebt, sich abzuschliessen.[19]

> The beginning of every story is ridiculous at first. There seems no hope that this newborn thing, still incomplete and tender in every joint, will be able to keep alive in the completed organization of the world, which, like every completed organization, strives to close itself off.[20]

These apprehensions are quickly countered with the remark that a story whose existence is justified will contain the seeds of its own completed organization, by virtue of which its survival is assured. This redemptive gesture acquires new shades of ambiguity, however, when Kafka draws an analogy to the anxieties of parents who fear for the life of a newborn child. Intuition suggests that Kafka, in a reversal of the analogy, identifies less with the parents than with their "pathetic" and "ridiculous" progeny. With an image that recalls Lessing's despair over the ultimate involuntariness of procreation, Kafka erodes the rationalistic premises of authorship by undermining the beginning intention that is the condition of any rational sequence: "ebenso müssten Eltern vor dem Säugling verzweifeln, denn dieses elende und besonders lächerliche Wesen hatten sie nicht auf die Welt bringen wollen" (in a like case parents should have to despair of their suckling infant, for they had no intention of bringing this pathetic and ridiculous being into the world).

Kafka's description of a new organism that is "tender in every joint" (überall empfindlich) evokes immediately the figure of Gregor Samsa, whose nightmarish awakening makes explicit the struggle that in

Novalis's work is generally subdued and surfaces only occasionally in supernatural form. Like Heinrich, but more so, Gregor incurs the displeasure of his father by sleeping late, awakening from dreams that grant him a new physical self-awareness and thus leave him inarticulate. "Dass ich auch nicht einmal von meinem wunderlichen Zustande reden kann!" (That I can't even speak of my curious condition! 195)—Heinrich's exclamation could well apply to Gregor, whose bodily transformation has rendered his speech unintelligible and made him strange unto himself. The opponent of this new and tender organism, that "completed organization of the world," is embodied by the corporate bureaucracy that watches over Gregor, an order that has a more monolithic counterpart in another of Kafka's works, namely *Das Schloss*.[21] The castle itself is the mysterious structure that, like the Freudian unconscious, would if penetrated yield up a hidden syntax connecting all particulars to form a comprehensive and meaningful whole. Yet as much as Gregor Samsa's metamorphosis indicates a deformation of *Bildung*, so does Kafka's novel, by refusing entry to the habitat of narrative rationale, represent a subversion of the *Bildungsroman*, that peculiar German invention in which the controlling consciousness that makes the story in effect "come together" enters the text as a character or group of characters, making plot a matter of conspiracy and displacing the responsibility for contrivance away from the author and onto an agency within the narrative frame.[22]

*Das Schloss* might also have been a fitting title for a Goethe's *Meister*, for it is in Lothario's castle that the completed organization of the world, to which the central character is assimilated, is revealed to be a secret order of men. Wilhelm's introduction to this society marks the point of retrospection at which all previous episodes, however discrete and coincidental they might once have appeared, are recognized as part of a masterplan that seems hopelessly arrogant in the self-assurance of its success. Even the most trivial detail of Wilhelm's adventure is now inscribed with the necessity of meaning, and the fact that this revelation takes the form of an obscure ritual suggests that one must indeed resort to magic to discover, in the words of Goethe's loquacious alchemist, "How all things as one are interwoven" (Wie alles sich zum Ganzen webt, *Faust, HA* III:22). Wilhelm's investiture represents a hybridization of novel and epic romance that betrays a nostalgia for a totality denied the modern novel; his introduction underscores as well Hegel's distinction between the two forms. In a lastingly paradigmatic passage that seems to allude to Goethe's text, and in which *meaning* and *ending* are shown to be coextensive, Hegel declares that the novel replaces the subjective trials of chivalry with a process of socialization through apprenticeship:

Diese Kämpfe nun aber sind in der modernen Welt nichts Weiteres als die Lehrjahre, die Erziehung des Individuums an der vorhandenen Wirklichkeit, und erhalten dadurch ihren wahren Sinn. Denn das Ende solcher Lehrjahre besteht darin, dass sich das Subjekt die Hörner abläuft, mit seinem Wünschen und Meinen sich in die bestehenden Verhältnisse und die Vernünftigkeit derselben hineinbildet.[23]

These battles are in the modern world nothing more than the apprenticeship, the education of the individual to the reality at hand, and so they attain their true meaning. For the end of such apprenticeship consists in the subject shedding his horns, growing with his desires and opinions into the existing state of affairs and its rationality.

The image of the subject "shedding his horns" implies a progressive sequence of transformations within which any radical change—be it puberty or revolution—is reduced to a "passing phase" and thus absorbed into a process that aims finally at the individual's incorporation into the aforementioned "completed organization of the world." This teleology is subverted by the regressive transformation undergone by Gregor Samsa and corrected after his death by his sister who, to the great satisfaction of their parents, has "blossomed into a beautiful and voluptuous girl" (zu einem schönen und üppigen Mädchen aufgeblüht). The metamorphosis she undergoes facilitates her integration into an order that includes marriage and excludes the kind of incestuous urges felt by Gregor. In these final lines of *Die Verwandlung*, the innocent freedom of a young woman reveling in her changing body is undercut by the insidious suggestion of surveillance and the impending appropriation of her development for the secret ambitions of others. The completion over time that *Bildung* implies seems to require the idiom of quest:

Stiller werdend und fast unbewusst durch ihre Blicke sich verständigend, dachten sie daran, dass es nun Zeit sein werde, auch einen braven Mann für sie zu suchen. Und es war ihnen wie eine Bestätigung ihrer neuen Träume und guten Absichten, als *am Ziele ihrer Fahrt* die Tochter als erste sich erhob und ihren jungen Körper dehnte.[24]

Falling silent and communicating almost unconsciously with their glances, they considered that the time had come to find her a good man. And it was as if their new dreams and good intentions were being confirmed when, *at the destination of their trip*, their daughter stood up first and stretched her young body.

That Gregor experiences his metamorphosis as fragmentation—he is aghast at the countless armorlike plates into which his new body is divided—underscores the lack of the wholeness that is the *telos* of proper formation. Mignon, who like Gregor is sacrificed to this ideal and whose formation is described as "irregular" ("Ihre Bildung war nicht regelmässig," *HA* VII:98), is a composite of individual features that, however charming in themselves, do not constitute an harmonious whole. Lack of harmony in this case means absence of order, for as a child of incest, Mignon marks the link between such misshapenness and an origin that does not conform to law. Her innately flawed composition forecasts a criticism of Romantic form, confirmed by Novalis when he defines the novel as an unfolding of the initial, unalterable, and unforeseen contingency of birth: "Das Individuum wird das Vollkommenste . . . seyn, das nur durch einen *einzigen absoluten Zufall* individualisirt ist—z.B. durch sein Geburt" (The individual shall . . . attain a perfection that is individualized only by means of a *single absolute coincidence,* e.g., through birth, II:579). The same fragment anticipates the modern notion of the "lyrical novel" by suggesting that a novelist creates an "end rhyme"[25]—a trajectory guided throughout by a sense of final destination:

> Ein Romanschreiber macht eine Art Bout rimes—der aus einer gegebenen Menge von Zufällen und Situationen—eine wohlgeordnete, gesetmässige Reihe macht—der ein Individuum zu einem Zweck durch alle diese Zufälle . . . zweckmässig hindurchführt. (II:580)

> A novelist creates a kind of Bout rime—which out of a given quantity of chance circumstances begets a well-ordered, regular sequence—which leads the individual through all of these coincidences purposively . . . to a single purpose.

This redundancy of calculated movement ("zu einem Zweck . . . zweckmässig") is echoed by the persistence with which, in *Ofterdingen,* Heinrich is urged to sidestep the whims of chance by learning "how everything . . . fits together according to laws of sequence" (wie alles . . . nach Gesetzen der Folge zusammenhängt, 281). It is a purposiveness reminiscent of the tower, and Novalis's novel is well populated with figures who seem to be expecting Heinrich, who gently nudge him and take secret pleasure in his development. One of these figures is the old miner, for whom the skilled navigation of the underground labyrinth is a metaphor for the discipline with which the individual conquers chance and distraction in the steadfast pursuit of a goal. The analogy is revealing in its juxtaposition of forward progress and the fragment: "Oft zerschlägt [der Gang] sich vor dem Bergmann in tausend Trümmern" (Often [the vein] crumbles into a thousand fragments right in front of the miner, 246; *PH* 71). The antithetical charge of the miner's teaching is illuminated by the fact that Heinrich's own two forays beneath the earth's surface produce fragmentary narratives, namely the dream and the Provençal manuscript. The latter also mirrors the scroll found by Wilhelm Meister during his initiation, but in contrast to that master-text, the very title of which proclaims a retrospection tantamount to "the end," the romance Heinrich discovers is incomplete: "der Schluss des Buches schien zu fehlen" (the end of the book appeared to be missing, 265). This subversion of the primacy of fabula conforms to Novalis's own nonteleological conception of the novel,[26] and *Ofterdingen*, itself unfinished, is one of a generation of German novels that resist completion by ironizing their existence between finite possibilities and infinite desires.[27] That Novalis died before he could finish his work simply reinforces the association, prevalent throughout, between the fragment and death. This link becomes palpable in the last pages when the sight of a ruin reawakens Heinrich's grief for his beloved. Here as elsewhere, the ruin functions as the allegory par excellence by both making visible the decay that defines allegory and serving as a reminder of the limits on representation imposed by death.[28] Such disintegration is what the *Bildungsroman*, with its claim to wholeness, works to transcend. The futility of this struggle is asserted by Novalis when, at this advanced stage of Heinrich's pilgrimage and with pointed intertextual reference, he places his protagonist beside "several crumbling towers" (einige verfallne Türme, 325).

### FRAGMENTARY TEXTS IN NOVALIS AND FREUD

In his historical overview of dream-theories (*SA* II:104), Freud quotes, with minimal commentary and vague appreciation, Heinrich von Ofterdingen's impassioned response to his father's contention that "dreams are froth" (Träume sind Schäume, 198)—that they are of ephemeral and intangible importance:

> Mich dünkt der Traum eine Schutzwehr gegen die Regelmässigkeit und Gewöhnlichkeit des Lebens, eine freye Erholung der gebundenen Fantasie, wo sie alle Bilder des Lebens durcheinanderwirft, und die beständige Ernsthaftigkeit des erwachsenen Menschen durch ein fröhliches Kinderspiel unterbricht. (199)

The dream strikes me as a defense against the monotonous regularity of life, a free recovery of the fettered imagination, in which all images of life are jumbled together, and the constant ernestness of adulthood is interrupted by the joyous play of children.

Freud admits to quoting this passage second-hand, and he seem to have lost sight of the censorial gesture implicit in the father's denial of the dream's significance; the illusion of meaninglessness is the strategic contrivance of preconsciousness. But the late-sleeping Heinrich has already offended his father's work ethic, and the youth's assessment of the dream, with its emphasis on play, confusion, and disruption—its "strange metamorphoses" (seltsame Verwandlungen, 198)—extends that conflict: the significance of the dream lies not in its translatability into a rational sequence, but, on the contrary, in its resistance to any such incorporation.

Arguing that the age of revelatory dreams is long past, Heinrich's father directs his son to "old histories and writings" (alte Geschichten und Schriften) in which the Holy Spirit is mediated by the "intellect of wise and beneficent men" (den Verstand kluger und wohlgesinnter Männer, 198). This patriarchal opposition of book and dream is subverted when Heinrich, in the company of the old miner, descends into an underground cavern closely resembling the earlier dream-scape and there discovers the illuminated Provençal manuscript that appears to tell his story:

> Es hatte keinen Titel, doch fand er noch beym Suchen einige Bilder. Sie dünkten ihm ganz wunderbar bekannt, und wie er recht zusah entdeckte er seine eigene Gestalt ziemlich kenntlich unter den Figuren. Er erschrack und glaubte zu träumen. (264)

> It had no title, yet in searching he found a number of pictures. They seemed strangely familiar to him, and as he peered carefully he discovered his own image quite distinct among the figures. He started and thought he was dreaming.

The illuminations show Heinrich in a variety of situations, past and future, familiar and exotic, yet the spacing of the pictures allows these situations simply to be listed, not interrelated. The book neither elucidates the dream nor renders it coherent; instead it duplicates its opaque discontinuities. Most important, it reproduces the desire that obscurity provokes and, if somewhat tentatively, places totality at the opposite end of that desire:

> Er sah sich am kayserlichen Hofe, zu Schiffe, in trauter Umarmung mit einem schlanken lieblichen Mädchen, in einem Kampfe mit

wildaussehenden Männern, und in freundlichen Gesprächen mit Sarazenen und Mohren. . . . Die letzten Bilder waren dunkel und unverständlich; doch überraschten ihn einige Gestalten seines Traumes mit dem innigsten Entzücken; der Schluss des Buches schien zu fehlen. Heinrich war sehr bekümmert, und wünschte nichts sehnlicher, als das Buch lesen zu können, und vollständig zu besitzen. (265)

He saw himself at the imperial court, on shipboard, in loving embrace with a slender and lovely maiden, in battle with savage-looking men, and in friendly conversations with Saracens and Moors. . . . The last images were dark and incomprehensible; yet several figures from his dream surprised him with the innermost delight; the ending of the book appeared to be missing. Heinrich was uneasy, and there was nothing he yearned for more than to be able to read the book, and to possess it totally.

Because the manuscript has no ending and because the yearning it induces in Heinrich is a function of its incompleteness, it seems reasonable to suggest that the book has no other end than desire itself. Fragmentary and open-ended, the mysterious romance prefigures a modernity in which psychoanalysis partakes and works to remedy; by mirroring the structure of the dream, the book poses the same explanatory challenge as dream-interpretation, which seeks to uncover the hidden logic that would transcribe those discontinuous elements onto an ascending scale of meaning.

Novalis's pairing of the dream and the cryptic find at the heart of Hohenzollern's cave recalls the similarity, so often suggested by Freud, between dream-interpretation and archaeology. And like the old miner, who specifies the fragment as the obstacle to his project, Freud develops his archaeological metaphors with respect to the status of the fragmentary in psychoanalysis. In the introduction to the case study of Dora, titled a "fragment" (Bruchstück),[29] Freud again likens himself to the explorer who endeavors "to bring to light, after long burial, the invaluable if but disfigured remains of antiquity" (die unschätzbaren wenn auch verstümmelten Reste des Altertums nach langer Begrabenheit an den Tag zu bringen, *SA* VI:92).

The archaeological metaphor becomes most interesting, however, when Freud addresses its particular inadequacy for representing the structure of the unconscious. Toward the beginning of *Civilization and its Discontents*, he asserts that even the most archaic strata of psychic life are indestructible and can, under the proper conditions, be recovered. These strata he compares to the deepest layers of the city of Rome, and he recounts in loving detail the supersession of one layer by the next—a process that results in the eventual disappearance of the earliest stages. Even the ruins that remain are not of the original structures, but of others that took their place:

> Was jetzt diese Stellen einnimmt, sind Ruinen, aber nicht ihrer selbst, sondern ihrer Erneuerungen aus späteren Zeiten. . . . Manches Alte ist gewiss noch im Boden der Stadt oder unter ihren modernen Bauwerken begraben. Das ist die Art der Erhaltung des Vergangenen, die uns an historischen Stätten wie Rom entgegentritt. (*SA* IX:202)

> Occupying these places now are ruins, not of themselves however, but of their replacements from later times. . . . Certainly there is still much of the old buried in the floor of the city or beneath its modern buildings. This is the kind of preservation of the past that we encounter at historical sites like Rome.

Freud argues that this process of historical sedimentation, in which more recent periods are palimpsested over earlier ones, differs from the psychical apparatus, in which even the earliest stages remain intact and exist alongside later ones. It is something that defies visual representation, for one would have to imagine a Rome in which everything that ever stood continues to stand, that is, in which monuments from separate ages occupy the same spot simultaneously. In a passage that seems to confront the age of Picasso with the proprieties set forth in Lessing's *Laokoon,* Freud insists that any pictorial representation inaccurately compresses the timelessness of the unconscious into a spatial simultaneity: "Wenn wir das historische Nacheinander räumlich darstellen wollen, kann es nur durch ein Nebeneinander in Raum geschehen; derselbe Raum verträgt nicht zweierlei Ausfüllung" (If we want to represent historical succession spatially, it can only be done by means of an adjacency in space; the same space cannot be filled in two different ways, 203).[30]

By way of contrast, it is helpful to remember that the fascination the Egyptian hieroglyphs held for Romanticism was predicated on the view that they were indecipherable; the presumed loss of an original key made it impossible to reconstruct their esoteric meaning. Freud immunizes the unconscious against such loss, for, unlike Rome, the unconscious contains no ruins. To adopt the terminology of Russian Formalism, the fragment with all the discontinuity it entails is, for Freud, the property of sjužet, the disjunctures of which are the result of the censoring mechanism of preconsciousness. The far-reaching regression that allows even the most archaic experiences to return and that the process of analysis recreates moves toward fabula.

Likewise the progressive semiotics of the Enlightenment, with its ideal of sheer transparency, aims toward the restoration of a clarity and coherence that would confirm the influence of reason in the historical process. Applied to the metahistory of rationalism, sjužet describes a temporary confusion of fabula and as such forms the object of a certain gnostic divination.[31] Freud uses the word "aufklären" to denote the revelation of a meaningfulness, the agency of which is located in a forgotten past. Freud voices this ideal when he contends that the analysis of Dora, had the patient allowed it to continue, would have irradiated every unexplained detail with the light of a totalizing rationality (*SA* VI:91). The narratological framework discussed above gains in relevance if one accepts, following Toril Moi, that Freud "imposed a fictional coherence on Dora's story, in order to render the narrative readable."[32] Moi speculates that Freud's obsessive preoccupation with the incompleteness of this case history is motivated by "his fear of epistemological castration," which "manifests itself . . . in his oddly intense discussion of the fragmentary status of the *Dora* text."[33]

The local thrust of Moi's interpretation exposes Freud's own phallocentrism and folds his analysis into the anxieties he attributes to others. The more global import of this conclusion is that psychoanalytic theory is itself a product of a general anxiety vis-à-vis modern dispersal. The metaphorical broadening of castration lends a new urgency to the desire for readability, and the narratological model of "reading out"—that is, of extracting fabula from sjužet—emerges as a creature of the same anxiety. *Bildung,* an anthropomorphism for establishing the narratability of natural transformations and thus for identifying the continuity that underlies change, is an earlier scientific articulation of the same distinction. If the *Bildungsroman* indeed represents a disavowal of the French Revolution, or at least a denial of the irreversibility of its effects,[34] this is undoubtedly linked to the fact that its governing morphological concept was devised to exclude changes so abrupt and unexpected as to resist narration.

## THE BLUE FLOWER AND REVOLUTIONARY FORM

At one point in the *Lehrjahre,* Wilhelm defends Shakespeare's *Hamlet* against the criticism that it was an admixture of the essential and the incidental—of wheat and chaff—and would thus require editing before being presented on the German stage. Taking recourse to a botanical analogy that imprints every detail with the necessity of final purpose, he describes the play as the progressive realization of formal perfection: " 'es ist ein Stamm, Äste, Zweige, Blätter, Knospen, Blüten und Früchte' " ("it is a trunk, limbs, branches, leaves, buds, blossoms and fruit," *HA* VII:294). Defensible or not, Wilhelm's comparison echoes what Goethe, in his study of plant morphology, called a "progressive" (*fortschreitend*) metamorphosis, "which can be observed, working step by step, from the first seed sprouts to the final formation of the fruit" (welche sich von den ersten Samenblättern bis zur letzten Ausbildung der Frucht immer stufenweise wirksam bemerken lässt, *HA* XIII:64–65).

This progressive development, in which every subsequent stage represents a refinement of the previous one, parallels the Enlightenment's conception of history as the gradual and peaceful advance toward perfection. The fact that this teleology had become less tenable in light of the French Revolution seems reflected in the fact that Goethe declares himself more interested in metamorphoses in which the continuity is less apparent, but which, once found, is all the more convincing. In these transformations, which he calls "irregular" (*unregelmässig*) or "regressive" (*rückschreitend*), the order of growth seems temporarily reversed. Goethe the botanist describes himself as being engaged in a process of detection, the object of which is a "secret affinity" (geheime Verwandtschaft)—an underlying *fabula* the very clues to which are provided by those sequential disruptions on the surface:

> Durch die Erfahrungen, welche wir an dieser [unregelmässigen] Metamorphose zu machen Gelegenheit haben, werden wir dasjenige enthüllen können, was uns die regelmässige verheimlicht, deutlich sehen, was wir dort nur schliessen dürfen (*HA* XIII:65).

> By means of the opportune experiences furnished us by this irregular metamorphosis, we shall be able to uncover what the regular one keeps secret from us, to see distinctly what in that case we can only suppose.

In addition to these regular and irregular metamorphoses, Goethe also mentions those that occur "randomly" (*zufällig*), influenced from without (especially by insects), the products of which he characterizes as "monstrous deformities" ("monströse Auswüchse," *HA* XIII:65). It is an apt description of Kafka's aforementioned story, not only because of the monstrous transformation Gregor undergoes nor because he, like other protagonists in Kafka, seeks desperately to orient himself within an inexorably random sequence of events, but because it also links Kafka's work to an ongoing quest for sustained narratability in the face of daunting odds. This argument in no way presupposes that Kafka had read Goethe's *Botanik;* instead, Goethe's studies in plant morphology already represent an attempt to exclude randomness and chance, to find order in what was seemingly chaotic, and thus to rescue the teleology of Enlightenment in the wake of the French Revolution, which had been received as an absolute rupture.

This disruption is registered by the "monstrous deformities" that characterize much of the flower imagery of Romanticism. The painter and graphic artist Philipp Otto Runge, whose death in 1810 at age thirty-three was read by Goethe as an apocryphal symptom of Romantic imbalance,[35] is known for the voluptuous plant forms that both fill and contain his works. His compositions are typically encircled by decorative borders of floral vines in which human or animal shapes metamorphose out of the cups of exotic blossoms. This kind of metamorphosis suggests a revolutionary *style,* the appropriate term for which is "grotesque." Writing on foreign perceptions of the French Revolution, Ronald Paulson discusses how observers abroad, who found in the Revolution neither historical precedent nor natural rationale, resorted to nonmimetic aesthetic categories, specifically the Sublime and the Grotesque. These categories, writes Paulson, "resolved themselves into various types of progression, and the French Revolution was above all else . . . a questionable sequence of events."[36] This implausibility of sequence led eighteenth-century aestheticians to reject the Grotesque as unnatural. The following criticism, while dating from the age of Augustus, was an authority frequently invoked during the Age of Reason: "The little stems . . . support half-figures crowned by human or animal heads. Such things, however, never existed, do not now exist, and shall never come into being. For how can the stem of a flower support a roof, . . . how can a tender shoot carry a human figure, and how can bastard forms composed of flowers and human bodies grow out of roots and tendrils?"[37]

The reference to "bastard forms" indicates the particular capacity of the Grotesque for representing improper alliances. Like the Gothic, the Grotesque had become for the eighteenth century a generic concept for the violation of classical harmonies—a mingling of what simply did not belong together. The political implications of this offense are immanent in the criticism leveled at Shakespeare by none other than Frederick the Great, who perceived in *Hamlet* (the integrity of which Wilhelm Meister defends) a "mélange bizarre" of the common and the noble.[38] As the formalization of such bizarre mixtures, the Grotesque acquires an antioedipal force and makes incest itself a representation of revolution. The resistance of the Oedipus complex to revolution, which since 1793 had come to be equated with patricide, is simultaneously a shield against incest, the condition of which is the removal of the father; it ensures adequate respect for proper boundaries and thereby protects against the over-sameness that incest and narcissism represent.[39]

By depicting incest and revolution in a single gesture, the Grotesque enlists political upheaval into a repertoire of unnatural acts. But within the framework of a theory that accounts for unanticipated transformations in terms of an underlying continuity, the Grotesque also represents the potential for "naturalizing" what had been deemed unnatural. The potential for ambiguity, which such imagery holds, is demonstrated in the *Lehrjahre* by Augustin, Mignon's father, who employs a botanical analogy to identify in nature a precedent for the incest of which he is guilty: "Seht die Lilien an: entspringt nicht Gatte und Gattin auf einem Stengel?" (Consider lilies: do not husband and wife emerge on a single stalk? *HA* VII:584).[40] In *Ofterdingen,* Augustin's metaphor is given stunning literal fullness by the poet Klingsohr, and the union he describes, replete with a fluid undifferentiation reminiscent of Heinrich's original immersion, comes as the crowning event in a tumultuous sequence characterized as a total upheaval of heaven and earth:

> Eine wunderschöne Blume schwamm glänzend auf den sanften Wogen. Ein glänzender Bogen schloss sich über die Flut auf welchem göttliche Gestalten auf prächtigen Thronen, nach beyden Seiten herunter, sassen. Sophie sass zu oberst, die Schaale in der Hand, neben einem herrlichen Manne, mit einem Eichenkranze um die Locken, und einer Friedenspalme statt des Szeptors in der Rechten. Ein Lilienblatt bog sich über den Kelch der schwimmenden Blume. . . . In dem Kelche lag Eros selbst, über ein schönes schlummerndes Mädchen hergebeugt, die ihn fest umschlungen hielt. Eine kleinere Blüthe schloss sich um beyde her, so dass sie von den Hüften an in Eine Blume verwandelt zu seyn schienen. (300)

> A flower of wondrous beauty swam glistening upon the gentle swells. A brilliant arch joined above the current down either side of which divine forms sat on splendid thrones. Sophie sat uppermost, the bowl in her hand, beside a splendid man with an oak wreath about his locks and a palm of peace instead of the scepter in his right hand. A lily pad curved over the calyx of the floating flower. . . . In the calyx lay Eros himself, bent over a beautiful, slumbering maiden who held him in fervent embrace. A smaller blossom enclosed both of them, so that from the hips down they appeared to be transformed into a single flower. (*PH* 131)

This epiphanic tableau bears comparison to any number of compositions by Runge in which divine ascension mimics the upward reach of a stem that spreads outward to form a Gothic vault upon which angelic figures are perched. This vision comes not long after the earlier prohibition against incest is explicitly violated, and Eros's journey, like Heinrich's, traces the route of desire through narcissim and incest—moments from which desire will never fully separate itself.[41] The blue flower, as the carrier of a strange metamorphosis that leads immediately to the mother, places the child's attachment to her between the autoeroticism of the dream and the object-relations of maturity; yet it also reveals every subsequent experience as a return to a prior position.[42]

If the permutations undergone by the blue flower are by themselves insufficient to qualify it as grotesque, one need only consider the literalness with which Novalis traces its genesis from out of a subterranean cavern exhibiting the features of the Roman grottoes whence the term is derived. This may be the shrewdest of all links between the dream and the archeological site; the *grotte* were discovered beneath the baths of the emperor Titus.[43] Novalis's narrative, which eventually dissipates into fragmentary paralipomena that chart metamorphoses worthy of Ovid,[44] is from the outset a fragment, and the blue flower, which all but invites interpretations that invest it with a univocal wholeness, is born of the ruin that is allegory itself. This aetiology of the flower is explicitized in Part Two when Heinrich finds himself in Sylvester's garden, which lies in full flower beside a mouldering ruin picturesquely overgrown with lush vegetation. Heinrich, now in mourning for Mathilde (and perhaps his own mother), describes the blooms not only as children of the ruins, but as signs of life predicated on death:

> Ruinen sind die Mütter dieser blühenden Kinder. Die bunte, lebendige Schöpfung zieht ihre Nahrung aus den Trümmern vergangener Zeiten. Aber musste die Mutter sterben, dass die Kinder gedeihen können, und bleibt der Vater zu ewigen Thränen allein an ihrem Grabe sitzen? (327)

> Ruins are the mothers of these blossoming children. The colorful, vital creation draws its nourishment from the fragments of past ages. But did the mother have to die in order for the children to prosper, and shall the father remain sitting alone at her grave in eternal tears?

When Sylvester consoles the grieving Heinrich with a "forget-me-not" grafted onto a cypress twig, the gift, itself a grotesque hybrid, marks the flower with discontinuity and loss.

The above juncture in Heinrich's pilgrimage seems to support Thomas McFarland's suggestion that the Romantic theory of organicism, like that of the symbol, constitutes an attempt to come to terms with fragmentation by supposing a wholeness where none is apparent. (In essence we are back to Walter Benjamin's *Sammler,* whose collection is an aggregate of parts that replaces the lost unity it allegorizes.) Goethe, an avid collector of botanical specimens, saw the diverse multiplicity of forms as evidence of a "primal plant" (*Urpflanze*), a Platonic idea not manifest in any one particular phenomenon but expressed precisely as a formal diaspora.[45] This logic, which accepts the very lack of visible unity as proof of that unity, is reminiscent of Freud, for whom meaningfulness is confirmed by the apparent absence of sense. Like Freud's "primal scene" (*Urszene*), Goethe's primal plant exists entirely as inference; and like the narratologist's fabula, also a construction inferred from a disturbed chronology, it is superindividual. Fabulations about the meaning of the blue flower, which presuppose an integral, unified consciousness as the originary locus of that meaning, partake of Heinrich's desire for an "undivided existence" (ungetheiltes Daseyn), which he ascribes to Mathilde, the human metamorphosis of the blue flower (277). Yet her death by drowning leaves Heinrich with only a disembodied forget-me-not, a blue flower that flourishes amidst the decay of the ruin surrounding Sylvester's garden. It is the product of a "revolutionary" development contingent on a shattered past—an allegory whose disguise as symbol is unsustainable.[46] It is worth remembering here that Hohenzollern's subterranean home, the topographical counterpart to Heinrich's dream-cave, contains not only the Provençal manuscript but also the more literally cryptic tomb of the hermit's wife. Like the Grotesque, the blue flower alludes to a vaporous, underground source of poetic inspiration,[47] but it exposes that underground as a ruin, pointing moreover to the body that lies buried there.

## THE FALL OF THE FATHERLAND

The syntactic regression from sjužet to fabula is commensurate with an impulse behind Goethe's twin formalisms—his theory of plants and his classicism. At the heart of the latter is an aesthetics that requires of visual works of art an immanence of plot that renders any secondary fabulation superfluous. This insistence on autonomy and closure stands in distinct opposition to Diderot's philosophy of art criticism, which gained considerable currency among the German Romantics, according to which the absorption in the painting or sculpture incites the beholder to forget the work itself and weave a narrative about events not depicted. Goethe, whose organicism dictates a self-containment that precludes such forays beyond the work, deploys the famous *Laocoön* statue to exemplify an internal dynamics that makes any reference to the mythological context (the punishment of the priest who violated the secret of the Trojan Horse) extraneous. The sculpture displays a "pictorial syntax" in which every gesture, movement, and expression is intuitively recognized as the effect of a primary contingency, in this case the initial sting of the snakebite on the central figure's flank. In keeping with the requisites of fabula, spatial adjacency does not impede the visibility of causal sequence. In the words of Neil Flax, "The statue is a conditional sentence in stone, an occasion to think a grammatical relation and to see it at the same time."[48]

That Goethe's resistance to the allegorical predates his classicism is made evident in his *Von deutscher Baukunst* (On German Architecture, 1772), an essay that claims the Gothic cathedral at Strasbourg for a native German tradition, and in which a structure as yet unfinished represents not fragmentation, but a totality in the process of being realized. Indeed, this teleology had suffused each particular component to such an extent that the actual completion of the building would have been redundant. In a manner consistent with the later postulate of the primal plant, Goethe denies—in the Gothic as well as in nature—the existence of parts in the absence of a whole: "wie in Werken der ewigen Natur . . . alles zweckend zum Ganzen" (as in products of eternal nature . . . everything striving to complete the whole, *HA* XII:12). The narrative begins with Goethe recalling his vain attempt to locate the stone marking the grave of the master builder, Erwin von Steinbach; Goethe then concludes that the great structure alone was sufficient—that is, self-sufficient—as a monument to the genius that formed a "vital whole" (lebendiges Ganze) out of "dispersed elements" (zerstreute Elemente, 12). The modern collector can only dream of such wholeness; Goethe's own modest tribute to Erwin is a collection, an assortment of plants he has gathered and placed on a handkerchief tied to a sapling. With reference to a more venerable allegory, he intimates that this meager and transitory offering is an adequate monument only to the process of decay, but not to that which survives decay:

> Nicht ungleich jenem Tuche, das dem heiligen Apostel aus den Wolken herabgelassen ward, voll . . . Blumen, Blüten, Blätter, auch wohl dürres Gras und Moos und über Nacht geschossne Schwämme, das alles ich . . . dir nun zu Ehren der Verwesung weihe. (8)

Not unlike that cloth, which was lowered down from the clouds to the holy apostle . . . full of flowers, blossoms, leaves, as well as dry grass and moss and mushrooms that shot up overnight, all of which . . . I now consecrate, in your honor, to decay.

New Criticism before the fact, Goethe's outdoor sacrifice, destined to repeat the decomposition of the architect's remains, celebrates a formal integrity so perfect as to erase the memory of its author, whose anonymity is assured by the absence of a gravestone. Or perhaps less naively, Goethe's account shows the achievement of the autonomy and wholeness he knew as "symbolic" (and not "allegorical") to be tantamount to the concealment of a body.

Even a cursory examination of *Fall des Vaterlandes* (fig. A), Runge's allegory of German national resurrection, reveals a linkage between the buried corpse and the architecture of transcendence, which appears here as a skeletal structure entwined with floral vines fed by natural decay. "What leaf-fring'd legend haunts about thy shape[?]" John Keats's immortal though vain interrogation of a Grecian urn begets a Goethean identity of beauty and truth, but that unity is eroded by the incipient awareness of the urn as memento mori—a funerary vessel whose aesthetic self-containment alludes to a transcendence denied: "That is all / Ye know on earth."[49] The "flowery tale" that both issues from and envelops the central scene in Runge's drawing constitutes a narrative of transcendence that incorporates death and decay into a cycle of regeneration. Yet the transformation depicted is revolutionary in nature, one to which the term "development" seems inappropriate. Intended as the frontispiece to the *Vaterländisches Museum* (1809) but deemed too incendiary, *Fall des Vaterlandes* registers the artist's dual disappointment with Napoleon's defeat of Prussia and the dull militarism of Prussia itself. The rejuvenation of the latter could come only as the consequence of catastrophic upheaval—of total war. Runge's highly unliberal conception of change is made visible by the grotesque metamorphoses that fill his works, which are equal to what he lauded as "a vital striving by the human spirit to overcome all the old forms that imprison and suppress it" (ein lebendiges Bestreben des Menschengeistes, alle alten Formen zu überwältigen, die ihn gefangen halten und unterdrücken).[50]

Yet the claims made on Runge's work by rupture and discontinuity have not deterred commentators from seeking an indivisible vantage point from which it might be read. While his republican sympathies have been acknowledged, these have been subordinated to religious concerns, specifically his conviction that Prussian rebirth was possible only as a spiritual awakening: "Man darf Runges politische Stellungnahme nicht von seiner religiösen trennen und für sich betrachten" (One may not separate Runge's political stance from his religious one and consider it by itself).[51] This almost holistic insistence on the inseparability of discourses is replicated by the tendency to reduce Runge's work to a system of symbolic equations:

> solange sich die Deutschen opfern für ihr Land, wird dieses Land fruchtbar sein—darauf deuten der Pflug, das Kind, die Frau, die den Pflug nur mit einer Hand lenkt, weil die Liebe ihn zieht, die Liebe zum Vaterland.[52]

> as long as Germans sacrifice themselves for their country, this land will be fertile—this is signified by the plow, the child, the woman who is guiding the plow with a single hand because love is pulling it, love of the fatherland.

The ease with which this interpretation translates Runge's uniquely unsettling image into a "conditional sentence" with a promise of continuity overlooks something as hard to ignore as the rock pressing into the back of the fallen patriot. A redemptive reading of this kind is not surprising, though, given a work that so completely confirms, if by sheer negation, the classicism of Lessing's *Wie die Alten den Tod gebildet* (How the Ancients Portrayed Death) and Schiller's "Die Götter Griechenlands" (The Gods of Greece), in which the integrity of form coincides with the absence of religion. Runge's *Fall des Vaterlandes* derives the very origins of religion from decomposition; as a recognizably arbitrary sign of Christian resurrection, the emerging passion flower underscores the mechanics of allegory, binding together a structure composed explicitly of *parts*—empty helmets and disconnected heads.

I must likewise mention the oedipal implications of a father being buried by mother and infant with the assistance of love; the father, his hands and ankles bound by the very vines that promise renewal, seems arched in agony as the plough-blade cuts directly above his genital region. Without exploiting this theory for yet another transcendental fabulation about Runge's work, one should add only that Freud described the death of his own father in terms of *Vaterlandslosigkeit* ("lack of a fatherland") and conveyed his grief in words that suggest the more specific oedipal anxiety that, as was seen earlier, may manifest itself broadly as a fear of incompleteness: "Ich habe nun ein recht entwurzeltes Gefühl" (I feel torn up at the roots).[53]

Courtesy of Hamburger Kunsthalle.

A more radical application of Runge's special treatment of swords and ploughshares is indicated by the crisis that underlies family romance, namely the threat to paternal identity posed by the inexorable fertility of the maternal body. The mother in this drawing represents the kindred fecundities of womb and soil and thus realizes the mythological link between the certainty of maternal identity and the matriarchal origins of agriculture. This myth placed fertility rites in the hands of women—rites that a more patriarchal age came to associate with witchcraft. The Grimm brothers' insertion of a stepmother into the story of "Hänsel und Gretel," while an attempt to cover the tracks that lead from the natural mother to the witch's cottage, only explicitizes the question of certain maternity as the crucial factor in the invention of the witch. In Coleridge's poem "Kubla Khan," the creation of a paradise by patriarchal decree represents a distinctly motherless birth that is quickly undermined by upheaval within the dark and enchanted depths of mother-earth. A "deep romantic chasm" out of which "Huge fragments" erupt, the site of the witch's illicit couplings seems also to be the birthplace of Romanticism itself.

# 6

# "Kubla Khan" and The Oriental Hallucination

## THE OMNIPOTENCE OF THOUGHTS

"O! In the virgin womb of the imagination the word was made flesh."
This exclamation, from James Joyce's *A Portrait of the Artist as a Young
Man,* places divine creation opposite sexual birth and echoes the enmity
toward sexuality that attended the very inception of *Einbildungskraft:* the
imagination, like genius before it, was the instrument of bourgeois self-
production. One of my general contentions has been that while the Enlightenment simply averted its eyes from the maternal body, Romanticism
appropriated it, though to similar ends; the aim was still that of circumventing the sheer irrationality of sexual origins. The virgin birth of Christ
is a mythical family romance, a compensatory response to the inevitable
doubt surrounding the identity of the biological father. It represents a com-
plicity between the mind of God and the body of woman, establishing a
sequence in which an intention—a vision—is resolutely anterior to the
procreative act.

Jakob Böhme, the seventeenth-century mystic whose importance for
both Novalis and Coleridge has been charted, implicates the conception of
Christ as a repetition of original creation, which for him was the result of
God's desire to see himself reproduced in the physical universe. To this
end God created the virgin Sophia, figure of eternal wisdom, as a mirror
in which to behold his own reflection. Genesis too is a virgin birth in
which the imagination is a prolific counterpart to a devitalized woman:

> So imaginiret er aus dem Ungrunde in sich selber, und machet ihm
> in der Imagination einen Grund in sich selber, und schwängert sich

mit der Imagination aus der Weisheit, als aus dem jungfräulichen Spiegel, der da ist eine Mutter ohne Gebären, ohne Willen.[1]

Thus he imagines out of the abyss within himself, and creates in the imagination a ground within himself, and impregnates himself with imagination out from wisdom, as from the virgin mirror, which is there, a barren mother without a will.

The autoeroticism of this process, in which the female image is but a stimulus to male self-realization, suggests the Romantic narcissism represented by Fichte's self-positing *Ich*. The feminist ramifications of a woman without will (*ohne Willen*) serving as an instrument of stimulation are far-reaching and extend to the more elemental movement from abyss (*Ungrund*) to ground (*Grund*)—an impulse away from fluid shapelessness and towards clear divisions and distinct forms.

Böhme's is an aetiology that exposes what the act of creation conceals. The abyss, the primordial waters (*Urgewässer*) out of which the world is formed,[2] is a void that creation both fills and erases. (Goethe's Faust, who builds dikes and turns sea into land, is a monument to the secular application of this process and demonstrates the link between the creative imagination and the more worldly projects of the social class that championed it.) In the topography of Coleridge's "Kubla Khan," a "sunless sea" lurks beneath an earthly paradise; the "deep romantic chasm" that cleaves the sunlit surface and leads down to the waters below threatens the phallic order signified by the Khan's erection of a "pleasure-dome."[3] The parallel between divine cosmogony, as suggested by Kubla's creation by decree, and poetic invention defines the latter as an intellectual birth that stands in opposition to the procreative act, which here is instinctual, female, dark, demonic, and destructive. The abyss is an opening that inspires impotence—in this case the inability to recall a poem composed in sleep—and the poet's wish to "build that dome in air" resembles the "omnipotence of thoughts" (*Allmacht der Gedanken*) ascribed by Freud to the narcissism common to young children and primitive peoples (*SA* IX:374–86).

The narcissistic magic by which thoughts become instantly manifest and wishes are tantamount to deeds is evident during Heinrich's dream when the contents of his imagination acquire a physical existence in the space about him: "neue, niegesehene Bilder entstanden, die auch in einander flossen und zu sichtbaren Wesen um ihn wurden" (images such as he had never seen appeared, flowing into each other and turning into visible presences around him, 196–97). It is an experience repeated by Stephen Dedalus, the young artist in Joyce's novel, who passes from a dream into a reverie resembling that of Novalis's poet-hero. Stephen too awakens amid a cool and liquid radiance, and his lingering dream-imagery, rather like Heinrich's, evokes a combination of nocturnal emission and seraphic visitation: "Towards dawn he awoke. O what sweet music! His soul was all dewy wet. Over his limbs in sleep pale cool waves of light had passed. He lay still, as if his soul lay amid cool waters, conscious of faint sweet music. His mind was waking slowly to a tremulous morning knowledge, a morning inspiration. A spirit filled him, pure as purest water, sweet as dew, moving as music."[4] As the reverie threatens to fade, Stephen strains to adapt his near delirium to the formal intricacies of a villanelle. This struggle for form aims not simply to recollect the dream but also to endow it with a permanence and structure alien to that pre-oedipal ecstasy. The poem begins to take shape; the product of a recombinant imagination ultimately distills a symbolic order of language out of these watery surroundings: "Her nakedness . . . enfolded him like water with a liquid life: and like a cloud of vapour or like waters circumfluent in space the liquid letters of speech, symbols of the element of mystery, flowed forth over his brain."[5]

It is a dense solution of Romantic image and analogy which Joyce, with no small measure of irony, conjures in the name of the epic revision of lyrical subjectivity that his own narrative represents. When Stephen Dedalus, "fearing to lose all," scribbles his poem on a hastily emptied cigarette carton,[6] he commemorates vividly Coleridge's "Author," whose attempt to recover lines composed during an opium-induced sleep met with only fragmentary success. The cigarette wrapper, impinging prosaically on the sovereignty of the lyrical subject, is but one of several mundane objects—a table, a soup plate, a candlestick, a coat, a window ledge—whose emergence out of the early morning gloom marks the advent of epic, in which the subject stands vis-à-vis a substantial world of things. If Novalis's *Ofterdingen* and Joyce's *Portrait* constitute struggles with the latter idiom, then the "lyrical novel" is more than a matter of narrative structure: it represents a narcissistic retreat from an outside reality not of the self—an insulary gesture against the prose of the world.[7]

This discussion is heir to a later eighteenth-century German habit of understanding the history of human consciousness as the history of literary genres where lyric, epic, and drama represent progressive stages in the development of the subject in relation to the world. Heinrich's admission that he had never actually seen any poems, only "heard tell" of them ("Von Gedichten ist oft *erzählt* worden," 208),[8] signals a belatedness that is also the condition of an epic quest the destination of which is a self outside the self. "Kubla Khan" too is wrapped in a prosaic preface complete with footnotes, which (like *Ofterdingen*) juxtaposes the two senses of "source" and tells of not only the poem's origin but also the interruption that deprived it of closure. A kind of ruin, "Kubla Khan" is itself a contracted romance, a remnant of Coleridge's plan for an epic poem he meant to call *The Fall of Jerusalem*.[9] Poised between departure and return and thus between two moments of purported immediacy, epic is commensurate with a Romantic aesthetics grounded in difference and deferral. All three of these texts predicate epic on the loss of the dream and its lyric spontaneity, and Joyce, whose novel includes a discussion of German poetics, echoes Hegel in making drama, wherein the subjectivity of lyric is wholly objectified, the end of epic. In other words, drama embodies the identity toward which epic strives; as the complete externalization of self, it is an act of creation to which the divine analogy is appropriate. Says Stephen: "The artist, like the God of the creation, remains . . . invisible, refined out of existence, indifferent, paring his fingernails."[10]

Such godlike indifference, insofar as it accompanies an identity fully realized in the work of art itself, is reminiscent of the *Indifferenz*—that is, undifferentiation, of subject and object that Schelling described as the unique accomplishment of aesthetic intuition (*SW* III:625). Schelling had defined aesthetic intuition as the objectification of intellectual intuition, which he in turn understood as "a producing that becomes its own object" ("ein sich selbst zum Objekt werdendes Produciren," (*SW* III:370). A self-positing ego was the concept by means of which Schelling, along with Fichte, roughly circumnavigated Kant's insistence that to have extrasensory knowledge of something was to bring it forth and that only God creates what he thinks simply by thinking it.[11] The "omnipotence of thoughts" that Freud relates to narcissism—the belief in the voodoo-like power of thoughts and words to generate a correspondent phenomenon outside the mind—retains a sense of the hubris of which the Romantic imagination has often been accused and more generally reinforces the suggestion that the philosophy of German idealism was in some way narcissistic. I argued in Chapter 3 that this philosophy constituted a kind of unconscious in which initially or explicitly social wishes, in particular the desire for self-creation through reason, were displaced by their metaphors, which brought these desires into association with an ostensibly more universal, psychological drama. Literary Romanticism, because of its concentrated engagement of this imagery, already represents an analytical moment through which both the psychological and political implications of that philosophy find articulation.

Thus in "Kubla Khan" the creative imagination, a concept that accompanies the desire for social emancipation, appears as an "omnipotence of thoughts'' in which sheer sexual potency and outright political power are conjoined through the decree of the Eastern potentate:

> In Xanadu did Kubla Khan
> A stately pleasure-dome decree:
> Where Alph, the sacred river, ran
> Through caverns measureless to man
>   Down to a sunless sea.

Coleridge, for whom the imagination was a faculty of self-origination,[12] prefaced his Oriental poem with an account of how he, under the influence of medicinal opium, fell into a dream in which his mental images appeared before him as external objects. His description emphasizes the extrasensory nature of the experience: "The Author continued for about three hours in a profound sleep, at least of the external senses, during which time he has the most vivid confidence, that he could not have composed less than two or three hundred lines; if indeed that can be called composition in which all the images rose up before him as *things*."[13] Coleridge recounts how his subsequent attempt to commit these lines and figures to paper was thwarted by the arrival of a visitor "on business," after which interruption he found that, in Joyce's words, "the heart's cry was broken":[14]

> On awaking he appeared to himself to have a distinct recollection of the whole, and taking pen, ink, and paper, instantly and eagerly wrote down the lines that are here preserved. At this moment he was unfortunately called out by a person on business from Porlock, and detained by him above an hour, and on his return to his room, found . . . that . . . with the exception of some eight or ten scattered lines and images, all the rest had passed away like the images on the surface of a stream into which a stone has been cast, but, alas! without the after restoration of the latter!

It is not so much the mundane affairs of the visitor that matter, for the corresponding rupture in "Kubla Khan" is the chasm, deep and romantic, which divides and undercuts an idyllic landscape devoid of lack. The inability to recover the lines composed in sleep corresponds, following the preface, to the loss of a state of reflection, which in the poem is more overtly rendered as the kind of erotic self-contemplation Freud termed "narcissistic." The ensuing wish to drink "the milk of paradise" indicates that the revival of the dream-imagery requires the restoration of the unity of self and world specific to infancy—a unity that conditions the identity of wishes and their gratifications. The chasm and the person from Porlock have in common that they both announce the existence of a world apart from the self.

### DREAMTIME

Like psychoanalysis, the Romanticism of "Kubla Khan" may represent a moment at which social and political desires threaten to disappear behind individual sexuality, but only by means of a condensation that leaves the latter forever indissociable from the former.[15] Even when the wish for autonomy was still framed by overtly political events, the aesthetic theory of the Sublime, claiming the superiority of the inner self over the world without, eluded fear by treating awesome natural phenomena as ciphers of moral strength. This theory is part of a general intellectual absorption of external forces, something that Horkheimer and Adorno, in their criticism of the Enlightenment, regarded as a modern extension of the primitive impulse to incorporate everything foreign. All that is missing from their description is the word "narcissism": "Es darf überhaupt nichts mehr draussen sein, weil die blosse Vorstellung des Draussen die eigentliche Quelle der Angst ist" (Nothing at all is allowed outside any more because the mere idea of the outside is the true source of fear).[16]

The above remark is cited by someone who discerns among the "primitives" a greater tolerance for the outside. In his *Traumzeit: Über die Grenze zwischen Wildnis und Zivilisation* (Dreamtime: On the Boundary between Wilderness and Civilization, 1978), Hans Peter Duerr seeks to implicate both Marxism and Freudian theory in a process of modernization that obliterates the insights contained in premodern practices, especially those concerning witchcraft. Duerr takes issue with theories that explain such phenomena as projections of "inner demons," and his accusation that the Enlightenment "banished fairies and elves to the subconscious" (die Feen und Elfen ins Unterbewusstsein vertrieb) suggests a Romantic caricature.[17] This may be more the consequence of provocative intent than actual naiveté, but in any case, *Traumzeit* has the effect of a Romantic eruption. And what Duerr calls the "crisis of civilization" seems to be nothing other than the unresolved family romance of the Enlightenment. It provides an apt and suggestive description of the crisis of "Kubla Khan"—one that commences with a discussion of drug-induced visions.

147

Duerr begins by citing numerous documents indicating that hallucinogenic substances played a role in the supernatural experiences reported by women and men accused of witchcraft in Early Modern Europe. He contends that the Church, having a considerable stake in the objective reality of Satan, suppressed evidence that would have exposed him as the product of narcotic hallucinations. Duerr's criticism is less of the Church than of those theories of projection in which the very concept of hallucination is sufficient to deprive the outside of a reality independent of a psychic interior. He deploys a variety of ethnological sources to locate the so-called *Hexenflug* ("flight of the witch") within a ritual tradition whose destination is an aboriginal dreamtime wherein the divisions upon which civilization is built are revoked. He does not regard this as a threat to civilized order, but as a rite of initiation by which a commitment to society is renewed through exposure to the wilderness. Duerr proposes that a Church that grew increasingly patriarchal could less and less tolerate the sight of what amounted to ecstatic, nocturnal gatherings of women at places in the landscape which resemble the reproductive openings of the woman's body. These celebrations of the matriarchal origins of agriculture exhibited residues of a time when it was thought that women received the "soul" of the child not from the seed of a male partner, but directly from the womb of the earth.[18] The cave in the following passage exemplifies this "womb," and Duerr's description echoes even the details of similar topographies in Novalis's novel:

> Ein derartiger Schoss wird etwa die Höhle der Eileithyia bei Amnisos an der kretischen Nordküste gewesen sein, in deren Öffnung ein Feigenbaum wächst und in welcher . . . ein runder Stalagmit, ein *omphalos,* ahnen lässt, dass man sich hier am Nabel der Welt befindet. . . . Im Hintergrund der Höhle—von deren Decke beständig ein leicht mineralhaltiges Wasser tropft—öffnet sich im Boden fast senkrecht ein schmaler Schlund. Lässt man sich . . . in diese Öffnung hineingleiten . . . , gelangt man nacheinander in drei kleine Grotten, wohl einstmals der Uterus der Erde, wenn die Höhle selber die Vagina war.[19]

> A womb of this kind might well have been the cave of Eileithyia at Amnisos on the northern coast of Crete, in the opening of which a fig tree grows and in which . . . a round stalagmite, an *omphalos,* gives one the sense of being at the navel of the world. . . . At the far back of the cave—from whose ceiling water of slight mineral content drips constantly—an almost vertical chasm opens up. If one slides down into this opening . . . , one comes in succession to three

small grottoes, certainly once the uterus of the earth, if the cave itself was the vagina.

Duerr argues further that the devil seldom played a role in the original
confessions of the accused witches, but rather was interposed, often
through torture, by inquisitors seeking to correct the anathematic image of
the so-called "unbemannte Frau" (unmanned woman)—an image as
threatening to the patriarchal order as the gaping vagina of the earth
itself.[20] The insertion of Satan into these "witches' sabbaths" effectively
organizes chaos under a single despotic sign, which becomes the object of
female desire: the witch enters the wilderness to copulate with the devil.
One is familiar with recent accusations that Freud, especially in his treatment of "Dora," performed a similar colonization of female desire.[21] It is
also interesting to consider his *Eine Teufelsneurose im siebzehnten Jahrhundert* (A Demonic Neurosis in the Seventeenth Century, 1923), an analysis of documents pertaining to an exorcism, in which the devil emerges as
a projection of a critical ambivalence stirred by the death of the subject's
father. These documents included testimonial paintings depicting Satan
with multiple pairs of female breasts, an image revealing in its conflation
of paternal authority and the desire it rises to oppose (*SA* VII:287–319).

An individual father's death activates the forces that counter the threat
to patrilineage of which his death is a reminder. On the occasion of his
own father's death, Freud informed his friend Fliess that feelings toward
his father—feelings that in recent years had lost their urgency as the elder
Freud's own vigor had declined ("ausgelebt")—were suddenly being revived within him: "Im Innern ist wohl alles Frühere . . . aufgewacht"
(Everything from before has been . . . awakened within me).[22] The words
"ausgelebt" and "aufgewacht" define a trajectory along which the
mourning labor of analysis would be performed. The object of that labor
was to be a dreamtime in which ontogeny does not replicate phylogeny, but
is overtaken by it. It is, to quote Duerr, "an age between the ages" (eine
Zeit zwischen den Zeiten),[23] a place outside the continuum of time where
distinctions between oneself and one's ancestry are dissolved. There is a
sense in which the oedipal theory, by describing the mechanism by which
the son, like Hamlet, becomes the agent of his father's ghost, avows the
same dissolution and renders the boundary between father and son an internal one. In the same letter, Freud tells of a dream in which a placard
appears bearing the words: "es wird gebeten, die Augen zuzudrücken" (it
is requested that the eyes be closed). This enjoinder, which Freud associated with feelings of guilt toward his father, betokens a self-identification
with Oedipus, whose own sense of guilt led him to take the injunction

against seeing to a notorious extreme. The expulsion of Oedipus from Thebes appears as an attempt to make out of that inner division an outer one and thus to restore the savage to the wilderness whence it came. The final act of banishment reasserts the division of *inside* and *outside* and moves contrary to the modern process whereby, according to Duerr, "the 'outside' slips inward" (das "Draussen" rutscht nach innen).[24]

In "Kubla Khan," a poem that represents the establishment of civilization in terms of the boundary between inside and out, the closing of the eyes becomes an act of piety in the face of evil discovered within. Having cast his own desired act of spontaneous poetic creation as a kind of witchery, the speaker becomes himself a ritual outcast, a foreign agent to be expurgated from the body within which it has been isolated:

> And all shall cry, Beware! Beware!
> His flashing eyes, his floating hair!
> Weave a circle round him thrice,
> And close your eyes with holy dread

This gesture of encirclement repeats a similar moment earlier in the poem when, in fulfillment of Kubla's decree that a palace of pleasure be built, the territory of a civilization is claimed, indeed secured, by means of fortified enclosure:

> So twice five miles of fertile ground
> With walls and towers were girdled round.

The interval of these two passages does more than point to the familiar insight that every act of inclusion is simultaneously one of exclusion. It emphasizes that the latter is necessary to represent the former; a society represents itself by both what it shuts out and whom it banishes. The role of the classical *pharmakos* is to illuminate the boundary of inside and out by crossing it. Such, according to Duerr, is the function served in traditional societies by shamans, witches, even werewolves; that is, to be on both sides of the fence at once and thus remind those on the inside of their own potential for chaos. When communities began burning witches, they exposed themselves completely to the outside, for the witch only became a threat when she ceased to sound a warning, and that she could only do from a position of proximity. Deprived now of an external existence, the witch, like Freud's dead father, reappeared within: "Jetzt drohte die Hexe nicht mehr von aussen, sie erwachte im Innern" (Now the witch no longer threatened from without, she awakened within).[25]

Coleridge alludes unmistakably to witchcraft, and he does so at the very point where his poem describes what lies beyond the walls of Kubla's Eden. The witch is associated with the line that separates civilization from the wilderness, for that is the frontier she violates when she enters into the night to consummate her passion for the Beast. This is the realm of the maternal-feminine; the site of said consummation is a natural topography that evokes the female cavity:

> But oh! that deep romantic chasm which slanted
> Down the green hill athwart a cedarn cover!
> A savage place! as holy and enchanted
> As e'er beneath a waning moon was haunted
> By woman wailing for her demon-lover!

Clearly and abruptly, the opposition to the civilized world is articulated: "A savage place!"[26] Yet to specify the function of the witch entails identifying the boundary she demarcates, and it becomes necessary to ask what specifically is nonsavage about Kubla's domain. Those walls and towers, by encircling ten miles of "fertile ground," locate *fertility* at the center of civilization. The poem redefines the opposition of inside and out in terms of fertility and something else, not *in*fertility, but rather that which is savage about the process that brings fertility about. Following the lines just quoted is a sustained and erotically explicit rendering of the act of fecundation: a "sacred river" erupts forcefully from beneath Kubla's sunny paradise before returning to its subterranean source. The climax itself is represented by two similes that, given the out-of-placeness of their figures, interrupt a stream of images linking the earth to the body of woman:

> And from this chasm with ceaseless turmoil seething,
> As if this earth in fast thick pants were breathing,
> A mighty fountain momently was forced:
> Amid whose swift half-intermitted burst
> Huge fragments vaulted like rebounding hail,
> Or chaffy grain beneath the thresher's flail.

The act of threshing or flailing, which signifies harvest, and hail, which represents a threat to it, are reminders that the fruits of the earth are not freely given, but are the stakes of an often fierce contest between society and nature. The apposition of harvest and human procreation reminds one further of the immediate consequence of the biblical expulsion from Eden:

namely, cultivating the earth and bearing children were to become two kindred exercises in pain. To a patriarchal conception of agriculture is juxtaposed an image of virgin birth, what the poem later calls "a miracle of rare device," and it is worth observing that the mighty fountain does not issue from the phallic "pleasure-dome" of Kubla's making, but from the "deep romantic chasm." Interrupting the experience of pleasure is a threat that resonates of patrilineage, yet its source is no longer a voice from within:

> And 'mid this tumult Kubla heard from far
> Ancestral voices prophesying war!

The obstetric treatment of the earth reminds us of Kleist's *Das Erdbeben in Chili* (The Earthquake in Chile), in which the immediate result of a cataclysm that destroys all social divisions is the unprecedented sight of women throughout the city giving birth *for all men to see* ("vor den Augen aller Männer").[27] This event mirrors the moment where the heroine, Donna Josephe, goes into labor on the cathedral steps during the procession of *corpus Cristi,* a coincidence that establishes a sharp opposition between the fertile body of woman and the chaste body of Christ. Perhaps for this unwelcome reminder the illicit lovers are confined to those two places of internal exile, the prison and the convent, institutions that render the outside innocuous by burying it within. Implicit here is a definition of civilization as a repeated closing of the eyes to the procreative role of woman, the simple knowledge of which seriously threatens patriarchal order. This threat was clarified by Freud in the now familiar discussion of family romance, which describes how children, once they acquire a rudimentary awareness of where they come from, know for certain who their mothers are, but may readily doubt the identity of their fathers. The problem of uncertain paternity is a key factor in Kleist's tale, in which social turmoil is resolved through the constitution of an adopted family, and in which the outbreak of savage violence coincides with the question: "Wer ist der Vater zu diesem Kinde?" (Who is father to this child?).[28] Having discovered the intruders in their midst, the people issue cries that echo the "Beware! Beware!" of "Kubla Khan": "Weichet fern hinweg, ihr Bürger . . . !" (Give a wide berth, you citizens . . . !).[29] And much as Coleridge's visionary becomes the object of ritual encirclement, so do Kleist's protagonists find themselves at the vortex of a circle the dynamic principle of which is the centrifugal force of revulsion: ("indessen sich ein weiter Kreis des Entsetzens um sie bildete"[as a broad circle of horror formed around them]).[30]

How peaceful, by contrast, is the resolution of a similar conflict in the tale of Atlantis, the second of two stories told by the traveling merchants in Novalis's novel! Here the survival of a kingdom is assured through the conception of an heir, yet the conception itself must occur in the wilderness, as it violates social divisions stubbornly guarded by the King. Like Dido and Aeneas, the princess and her lover realize their union in a cave where they have taken refuge from a storm. The cave emulates the womb, and the natural shelter mimics the act of love it both contains and inspires: "Ein wilder Mandelstrauch hing mit Früchten beladen in die Höhle hinein" (A wild almond branch laden with fruit hung into the cave, 221). When the princess returns to her father one year later, she brings a baby and thus presents the court with an exemplary image of motherhood. The youth who has fathered the child sings a song proclaiming the melting of a rigid patriarchy, the King himself entering the equivalent of the "deep romantic chasm": "Da tritt, gelockt von den Gesängen, / Der König in die Kluft hinein" (And to the lure of song succumbing, / The King steps down into the gorge, 228). The warm acceptance of the child, who is not only illegitimate but also the product of a social *mésalliance,* suggests a counterpoint to the bloody reception in Kleist's narrative, but the legendary fate of Atlantis places both stories in a tradition bent on concealing erotic origins. Indeed, what one natural catastrophe has exposed for all to see, another covers over, the mythical city of Atlantis having been "removed from view by mighty flood waters" (von mächtigen Fluten den Augen entzogen, 229). Heinrich has access to this fluid, maternal world by way of his dreams. His Oriental quest, which also anticipates a journey planned but not taken by Kleist's ill-fated lovers—a journey home by way of a port named La Conception—is an expression of that "will to knowledge regarding sex" which, according to Foucault, defines the modern Occident.[31]

## MALE FANTASIES AND THE ROMANTIC MOTHER

Edward Said, for whom the will to knowledge regarding the Orient is constitutive of the Occident—a project by means of which the latter gained a fortified self-definition—has remarked on the significance of the fact that Goethe's *West-östlicher Divan* was based on a journey to the Rhineland.[32] This irony underscores the irreality of the Orient for the Germanies, which did not have the same political investment in the Middle East as the French and British empires. "Kubla Khan" makes clear that the Orient was first and foremost a site in the imagination; but it never became otherwise for Germans, much of whose philological fascination for those exotic cultures was soon displaced onto forgotten German and Germanic languages, that is, onto the exotic within.[33] It is a reorientation in the fullest sense of the word—one that a completed *Ofterdingen* would presumably have realized, Heinrich returning to a homeland made unfamiliar by his experience of those strange and distant places.

As it stands, the only Oriental encounter presented by the unfinished *Ofterdingen* occurs on German soil, and the concreteness ascribed to this experience seems to mark the Orient as the product of a colonizing imagination. The ostensibly disinterested and unpolitical nature of German Orientalism is complicated by the fact that Novalis's novel is set during the crusades, when the Middle East was also an object of conquest for Germans. German crusaders appear in Chapter Four when Heinrich, his mother, and their companions find lodging in the castle of a warrior who has already been to the Holy Land and is now eagerly awaiting the next call to arms. During a feast, he and his fellow knights seek to enlist Heinrich in their cause by firing his enthusiasm with a sword taken from a slain Saracen. The unavoidable phallic significance of the weapon is heightened by an erotic gesture that suggests homage to the object that also threatens castration, and the scene amounts to an initiation into an order replete with symbols (the cross, coats of arms) and the language of patrilineage:

> Alle besahen das prächtige Schwerdt, auch Heinrich nahm es in seine Hand, und fühlte sich von einer kriegerischen Begeisterung ergriffen. Er küsste es mit inbrünstiger Andacht. Die Ritter freuten sich über seinen Antheil. Der Alte umarmte ihn, und munterte ihn auf, auch seine Hand auf ewig der Befreyung des heiligen Grabes zu widmen, und das wunderthätige Kreuz auf seine Schultern befestigen zu lassen. Er war überrascht, und seine Hand schien sich nicht von dem Schwerdte losmachen zu können. Besinne dich, mein Sohn, rief der alte Ritter. (231)

> Everyone examined the splendid sword, and Heinrich also took hold of it and felt seized by a warlike enthusiasm. He kissed it with passionate devotion. The knights were pleased at his interest. The old one embraced him and encouraged him to dedicate his hand eternally to the liberation of the Holy Sepulchre and to allow the miraculous cross to be fastened to his shoulders. He was surprised, and his hand seemed unable to release the sword. Think it over, my son, the old knight implored.

This attempted induction into a male order spells a temporary end to Heinrich's androgyny and results in the expurgation of the feminine as Other, as Orient. A decisive affirmation of sexual difference, the sword has its opposite, namely the beautiful captives promised to Heinrich in return for his bravery. Woman is now, to borrow Freud's characterization of the repressed, "internal foreign territory" (inneres Ausland, *SA* I:496); driven from within, she must be located in the landscape.

This happens after Heinrich abandons the drunken soldiers, wanders into the night, and there meets Zulima, a young Saracen mother whom Heinrich's host had widowed and captured. When the sound of her voice and lute is heard from deep within a wooded valley, indeed from a mighty depth ("aus der gewaltigen Tiefe," 234), it comes in response to a longing cast explicitly as lack: "Er fühlte, dass ihm eine Laute mangelte" (He felt that he was missing a lute).[34] The lute, which Heinrich will relinquish voluntarily before the chapter is over, replaces the sword, and Heinrich's newly recovered lack seems to mark a dissolution of sexual difference completed by his descent into the deep recess where Zulima is singing woefully of a "Distant, maternal country" (Fernes, mütterliches Land, 235). His contact with the landscape is characterized by a direct physicality reminiscent of his approach to the womblike cave of his dream: "Er schweifte durch das wilde Gebüsch und kletterte über bemooste Felsenstücke" (He rambled through the wild bush and clambered over moss-covered boulders, 234; *PH* 58). The song he hears from below, like "Kubla Khan" with its "cedarn cover," describes an Oriental landscape that evokes the body:

> Könnte ich dir die Myrthen zeigen
> Und der Zeder dunkles Haar!
> Führen dich zum frohen Reigen
> Der geschwisterlichen Schaar!
> Sähst du im gestickten Kleide,
> Stolz im köstlichen Geschmeide
> Deine Freundinn, wie sie war. (234)

> If I could you the myrtles show
> And the cedars' shady locks!
> In happy dance with me you'd go
> Amid the joyous sister-flock!
> In embroidered dress you'd see,
> Proud adorned in precious gems
> Your friend just as she used to be.

This strophe is even more reminiscent of Goethe's "Erlkönig," in which the child is tempted by a similar pre-oedipal phantasy—a world of play, plenitude, sibling affection, and a mother adorned in gold ("Meine Mutter hat manch' gülden Gewand,"*HA* I:155). Indeed, Heinrich's discovery of Zulima follows a temptation also associated with gold: "Heinrich, der . . . von der goldenen Ferne gelockt wurde . . . , eilte ins Freye" (Heinrich, tempted by the golden distance . . . , hurried out of doors, 233–34). The usual opposition of blue (distance) and gold (proximity) is suspended, and the landscape, otherwise a formal scaffolding for that opposition, now manifests the distance-in-proximity that defines the aura of the fetish.[35] Gold is the vehicle of contiguity that leads back to the mother and identifies other love-objects as receptacles of a passion first awakened by her. When Heinrich and Zulima part company, she gives him a golden band from her hair and accepts in exchange a veil that belongs to his mother (238–39). This exchange prefigures the moment in Klingsohr's tale where Eros's mother and Ginnistan, the wet-nurse whose name resonates of the East, exchange physical form, so that when Eros and Ginnistan succumb to their mutual passion, the distinction between mother and lover is rendered invisible.

The similarity between the above strophe of Zulima's song and the seductive tableau conjured by the Erl-king underscores a crucial difference, for Heinrich seems immune to the fear experienced by the child in Goethe's poem. The source of that fear is not the vision itself, but the father, whose repeated "mein Sohn" is a constant reminder of an order in which that fantasy is taboo. In *Ofterdingen*, the elder crusader's "Besinne dich, mein Sohn" (Think it over, my son) echoes the same order, but it is one Heinrich renounces with the ease of leaving a room. This renunciation includes the sword, which is replaced first by the lute and then by a hairband decorated with "unknown letters" (unbekannten Buchstaben, 238). Heinrich's return to his mother and to the eroticized landscape of his dream is a recovery of a realm of music and not-yet-comprehended speech—a stage of childhood prior to entry into language, the law of the father, and the prohibition against incest. As already noted, the exchange of garments between Zulima and Heinrich's mother presages the love scene between Eros and Ginnistan, the latter having assumed the appearance of the child's mother. This contiguous chain of associations implicates the following image, in which intercourse and nursing are indistinct, as the anathema against which the crusaders are struggling:

> [Ginnistan führte Eros] zu einem abgelegenen Bade, zog ihm die Rüstung aus, und zog selbst ein Nachtkleid an, in welchem sie

fremd und verführerisch aussah. Eros tauchte sich in die gefährlichen Wellen, und stieg berauscht wieder heraus. Ginnistan trock-
nete ihn, und rieb seine starken, von Jugendkraft gespannten
Glieder. Er gedachte mit glühender Sehnsucht seiner Geliebten, und
umfasste in süssem Wahne die reitzende Ginnistan. Unbesorgt über-
liess er sich seiner ungestümen Zärtlichkeit, und schlummerte endlich nach den wollüstigsten Genüssen an dem reitzenden Busen
seiner Begleiterin ein.(300)

[Ginnistan led Eros] to a secluded pool, removed his armor, herself
donned a nightgown that made her look strange and seductive. Eros
slipped under the dangerous waves and reemerged intoxicated. Ginnistan dried him and rubbed his strong members, which were tensed
with the vitality of youth. With ardent longing he thought of his beloved and embraced the enticing Ginnistan with sweet madness.
Without a thought he surrendered to his violent affection, and finally fell into a slumber after the most voluptuous pleasures at the
tempting breasts of his companion.

But why should such eroticism provoke the dread that powers fantasies of
military conquest? That the foregoing sequence begins with the shedding
of armor may be a clue to the actual function of armor: to reinforce the
boundaries of the self against the "dangerous waves" of seduction, and,
in the guise of a male chastity-belt, to restrict the outlets of bodily energy
to those appropriate to the battlefield. Ginnistan, who shoulders the blame
for transforming Eros into a master of destruction ("Sein Bogen richtet
überall Verwüstungen an" [His bow reaps destruction everywhere], 306),
describes their union as a dissolution of self, an act of degradation after
which she is no longer a narcissistic object in which he glimpses his idealized image. A victim of a veritable rape, she becomes a casualty of his
own fear of self-annihilation. And so she is annihilated:

Ich glaubte unter seinen feurigen Liebkosungen zu zerschmelzen.
Wie ein himmlischer Räuber schien er mich grausam vernichten und
stolz über sein bebendes Opfer triumphiren zu wollen. . . . Ich sah
meine Gestalt verändert. . . . Ich hätte mich mit Eros vor allen Augen verbergen mögen. Ich hatte nicht das Herz in seine beleidi-
genden Augen zu sehn, und fühlte mich entsetzlich beschämt und
erniedrigt. (305–306)

I thought I would melt away beneath his fiery caresses. Like a heavenly marauder he seemed to want to annihilate me cruelly and triumph proudly over his trembling victim. . . . I saw my form
altered. . . . I would have wished to hide myself with Eros before all

eyes. I had not the heart to look into his insulting eyes, and I felt a revolting shame and humiliation.

By revealing the brutality of war as a regressive deformation of eros, Klingsohr's tale allegorizes what Chapter Four of *Ofterdingen* makes clear and what Zulima herself explains; that is, there is something instinctual about military aggression.[36] The particular fact that, in Klingsohr's tale, the taboo against incest is spoken by the very object of incest (the mother)[37] brings this allegory into loose consonance with Klaus Theweleit's study of the *Freikorps,* an elite group of soldiers who after World War I became Germany's crusaders against the proletariat and eventually supplied the SA and the SS with their most practiced executioners. Theweleit is interested in the "male-fantasies" that appear in the writings of these men—fantasies in which, as a rule, the threat of sexual arousal is answered with the desire to eliminate violently the source of that arousal. These fantasies of brutality are interpreted as expressions of an outright fear of object-relations, which would suggest the lack of a fully developed ego (the ego being for Freud the mediator between the inner and outer worlds). The material Theweleit reproduces—novels, diaries, letters, autobiographies—exhibits a prevalence of anxieties surrounding incest and castration, and he notes with some emphasis that these anxieties tend not to be disguised. (Theweleit interprets this apparent absence of disguise as further evidence of an underdeveloped ego, because a fully formed ego would strive to repress these anxieties and allow them to surface only in distorted form.)

The absence of such distortion and disguise leads Theweleit to explain these fantasies in terms of crises that must have occurred prior to the formation of the Oedipus complex, the theory of which he thus deems inadequate to explain the phenomenon of fascism. Incest is feared not because of the potentially violent interdiction of the father, but because the very act of incest produces an undifferentiation that profoundly threatens the boundaries of the self. To experience sexual climax is to be lost, annihilated, inundated, dissolved. The "fear of orgasm" is a fear of one's own sexuality—the fear that a life without would arouse a vitality within. Out of these fears arises the need not simply to kill, but to kill massively—to eliminate all surrounding life and to create, on the inside, a correspondingly massive lifelessness:

Der Monumentalismus des Faschismus scheint sich als ein Sicherheitsmechanismus gegen die Vielfalt des Lebendigen verstehen zu lassen. Je lebloser, geordneter, monumentaler die Realität erscheint,

desto sicherer fühlen sich diese Männer. Die Gefahr ist die Leben-
digkeit selbst.[38]

It seems that the monumentalism of fascism can be understood as a
safety mechanism against the complexity of the living. The more
lifeless, ordered and monumental reality appears, the safer these
men feel. The danger is vitality itself.

This violent aversion to object-relations results in a split in the image of
woman. On the one hand, there is the eroticized female—the prostitute,
the proletarian woman, and especially the nurse, whose designation as
*Krankenschwester* ("sister to the sick") articulates the potential for incest. These women become the objects of the violence that their immediate and irresistible physicality threatens. At the opposite pole is the
devitalized or "white" woman, whose characteristic deathly paleness represents a purity tantamount to an absence of life. Theweleit discusses how
mothers are at once beatified and drained of life, left cold and distant
(even as they intercede to mitigate some paternal harshness), as if their
sons feared nothing other than their warmth and closeness. It is a twofold
devitalization, for these mothers are dispossessed of both their maternal
love and their men, "as if the fathers were never supposed to have touched
the mothers" (als ob die Väter die Mütter nie hätten berühren dürfen). The
consequence of this prohibition, namely that the sons would not have been
conceived, leads Theweleit to a set of questions that recall the crisis of
family romance:

> Daraus ergeben sich wichtige Fragen:—soll die Tatsache dieser Zeu-
> gung ausgelöscht werden? Wollen diese Söhne andere Väter haben/
> gehabt haben, oder wollen sie gar *keine* gehabt haben? wollen sie
> von der Jungfrau geboren sein? Oder die sein, die sich selber
> zeugten?[39]

> Some important questions arise:—is the fact of this conception to be
> eradicated? Do these sons want to have, or to have had, other fa-
> thers, or do they want to have had *none* whatsoever? Do they want
> to have been born by a virgin? Or is it that they wish to have con-
> ceived themselves?

To conceive oneself: this would appear to be the "miracle of rare
device" in "Kubla Khan"—the capacity for self-origination Coleridge
ascribes to the imagination, Schelling to intellectual intuition. In
Theweleit's analysis, this appropriation of the object-world can assume
more desperate forms when the "anxiety of influence" degenerates into

profound existential fear. Although less extreme, Kubla's erection of a stately dome is comparable to the aforementioned "monumentalism": if not a defensive shield against an encroaching vitality from without, at least a way of relocating and containing it on the inside ("Could I revive within me"). In any case, the kind of bifurcation of woman Theweleit describes becomes evident here when the "woman wailing for her demon-lover" is displaced by a maiden elevated and forever distant in her spiritualized noncorporeality:

> A damsel with a dulcimer
> In a vision once I saw:
> It was an Abyssinian maid,
> And on her dulcimer she played,
> Singing of Mount Abora.

Like Böhme's Sophia, barren and devoid of will, the Abyssinian maid evokes a contrast to the fecund force that erupts from the "deep romantic chasm" and undermines the power of the Khan. This rupture, like Kleist's earthquake, and like the French Revolution, disturbs a rational sequence ("rational," because it issues from the mind, not the body). This order of events is restored by the recasting of the female as something internal to the male imagination ("In a vision once I saw"). The poet dreams of becoming the birth-giving origin of the sequence by usurping the fertility that threatens order in the first place. The taboo this witchery violates provokes the reaffirmation of the boundary between inside and outside and makes the poet the object of "holy dread." Writing on Wordsworth's *Prelude,* Gayatri Spivak identifies a similar appropriation of the maternal via the poetic imagination, which she defines as "the androgyny of Nature and Man—Woman shut out."[40] So too in "Kubla Khan." The certain sterility of the Abyssinian maid is a condition of the dream to "build that dome in air." The parallel expulsion or introjection of the female exposes the defensive thrust of this uniquely Romantic triumph of the will.

# Epilogue

## THE ROMANTIC MOTHER AND THE FATHERLESS SOCIETY

The foregoing reference to Theweleit's analysis of the German *Freikorps* does not suppose a lineage between Romanticism and National Socialism—a line that has been drawn and overdrawn—but between Romanticism and aspects of Theweleit's analytical framework. In this study I sought to demonstrate that psychoanalysis and Critical Theory represent formal articulations of Romantic commonplaces. Romanticism is a kind of mythology, the *bricolage* of imagery theorized by Lévi-Strauss in which concepts are fully embedded in images—images that in turn provide models for understanding experience.[1] Narcissism is an example of the tenacious adherence of an image to the wisdom it contains, even while that wisdom undergoes successive reincarnations as knowledge and as theory. To the extent that Freud depended on the imagery of the tradition he interpreted, he was a *bricoleur,* limited to materials that had been left over from other projects and were thus "ready at hand."[2] Erik Erikson's analysis of Luther's contest with Satan, by salvaging the wisdom inherent in the superstition, makes psychoanalysis complicit in the myth it clarifies: "The fact that he called defeat the devil only meant he was using a diagnostic label that was handy."[3]

Although Freud was able to relinquish the devil as an image of neurosis, he could not give up the father as *the* image of authority. It has been noted that Freud neutralized politics by treating political conflicts as epiphenomena of crises undergone in early childhood.[4] Frustrations experienced by the adult within the public sphere derive their emotional "capital" from the family crises they revive. Freud's own myriad frustrations with Austrian politics, the nobility, the academic and medical bureaucracy, and anti-Semitism were important, from his standpoint, only insofar as they exhumed unresolved conflicts with his father. This effacement of the political and public in favor of the private betrays a nostalgia for the father in an age when the family had ceased to be the locus of cultural reproduction. Psychoanalytical theory itself appears to be a rearguard action against the irresistible rise of the "fatherless society." Freud's own lament at being without a fatherland (*vaterlandslos*) acquires a particular resonance in this context.[5]

The concept of the fatherless society, implicit in much of the work of the Frankfurt School, was elaborated by Alexander Mitscherlich in reference to a process of modernization that deprived the father's authority of its substance. This substance, once grounded in the immanent visibility of social relations within the domestic sphere, dissipated as the authority of the father was usurped by the ubiquitous and anonymous public agencies of power and administration. Industrialization ended the peasant existence in which every facet of parents' lives was played out before the eyes of their children. With the division of labor came a partitioning of space that separated the world of work from the home, removing from view the means by which the father earned a living. As the father ceased to pass on acquired skills to his children, teaching became the task of "professional parents" outside the family. A father left with nothing to bring home from work but his frustrations, says Mitscherlich, may appear to his children "only as a terror-striking figure, a bogy man."[6] One such figure is found in Goethe's "Erlkönig," in which the ogre in the trees deflects attention from a father powerless to help his son. If *Heinrich von Ofterdingen* constitutes a flight from this kind of primal scene, the refuge it presents seems to be the room of the parents—the "elterliche Stube" in which Heinrich awakens, an integral space that serves parents and son alike as bedroom and workroom and in which the full range of parental activities is visible to the son.

This literature might be read as a fantasy of sheer regression were it not for the consistency with which it links the so-called "fatherless society" to the specific transformations that brought it about. Like the theory set forth by Horkheimer, Mitscherlich, and others, post-Enlightenment texts trace the disappearance of a substantive father to an economy of pure exchange that leaves the father faceless and interchangeable. This development was seen earlier in Lessing's "Parable of the Ring," in which a loving and fallible father is displaced by a judge, in which teaching by demonstration gives way to opaque authority, and in which tradition-bound truth is supplanted by the plain coin (*bare Münze*) of reproducible abstraction. A similar transformation is apparent in Kleist's *Der zerbrochene Krug* (The Broken Jug) when a village judge, forced to don the mantle of impartial and impersonal authority, asks the plaintiff, a woman he has known for years, to identify herself. When she protests the ridiculous formality, he responds in a way that captures brilliantly the process of abstraction that empties social relations of their human content: "Ich sitz im Namen der Justiz. . . . , / Und die Justiz muss wissen, wer Ihr seid" (I sit in the name of Justice . . . , / And Justice needs to know who you are).[7] And in a text that makes "faith" and "love" the watchwords of the ideal state, Novalis criticizes the advent of a "mechanistic administration" while mourning the death of a king reputed for his paternalism: "Kein Staat ist mehr als Fabrik verwaltet worden, als Preussen, seit Friedrich Wilhelm des Ersten Tode" (No state was ever managed more like a factory than Prussia since the death of Frederick William the First, II:494).

Both Novalis's king and Kleist's judge reappear, via the ponderous ventriloquy of Emil Jannings, in two films made under the auspices of Joseph Goebbels (*Der alte und der junge König* [The Old and the Young King, 1935] and *Der zerbrochene Krug* [The Broken Jug, 1937]). The earlier of these works, which depicts the conflict between Frederick William and his son (Frederick the Great), adheres to the oedipal scheme by making revolt against the father the prerequisite for identifying with him. Janning's portrayal (in both cases) is successful in doing what a more overtly propagandistic film, Leni Riefenstahl's *Triumph des Willens* (1935), could not hope to achieve, namely, lending a convincingly human face to an authority as cold and remote as it was absolute.

According to Theweleit, whose analysis is underwritten by the theory of the fatherless society, but who is less attentive to the social conditions described earlier, fascism robs the family of anything positive it could provide—warmth, solidarity, protection—yet holds it aloft as a model of absolute obedience. The family thus becomes the site of domination by an authority without substance; as such it is something the child cannot but fear and hate.[8] The result is a nostalgia not for a preindustrial family, but for a "direct filiation" that bypasses the family altogether and makes the child a product of the earth, that is, a child whose ego is as boundless as nature itself.[9] The "inflationary 'we' feeling" that is hereby created represents an internal massiveness that combats the masses without, and the ambivalence Mitscherlich describes explains the mass behavior of fascism as an attempt to straddle the divide between the wish for an all-encompassing unity and the desire for an intact and autonomous ego: "At one end of the scale the individual has the exultant feeling of merging with the ocean in all its moods, and at the other he feels a solitary dwarf threatened by an incalculable giant."[10] These words echo those spoken by Faust when he remembers how the sight of the earth-spirit made him recoil in terror: "die Erscheinung war so riesengross, / Dass ich mich recht als Zwerg empfinden sollte" (the apparition was so gigantic, / That I truly felt myself a dwarf, *HA* III:27). The spirit identifies itself as the being at whose "sphere" Faust had often sucked ("An meiner Sphäre lang gesogen," 23)—an allusion, perhaps, to the breast imagery of Goethe's early poetry and one that vividly charts the conversion of an object of oral desire into a source of abject fear.

Oral desire is the point of departure in *Heinrich von Ofterdingen,* the prefatory poem of which acknowledges the primacy of maternal nurture: "An ihrem vollen Busen trank ich Leben" (At her full bosom I drank of life, 193). Heinrich's subsequent dream suggests a "direct filiation," as he is born out of the earth and into a home that, on the one hand, represents the immanence of preindustrial social relations and, on the other, displays a father already weakened, prevented from hammering while his son dreams a dream inherently threatening to paternal identity. In the novel's fragmentary continuation, Heinrich and Sylvester remember the elder Ofterdingen, whose failure to realize youthful ambitions had left him world-weary and alienated from his own labor. Heinrich recalls how his father, an accomplished artisan, worked "out of habit and not out of inner desire" (aus Gewohnheit und nicht aus innrer Lust) and was predisposed to treat all relations "like a piece of metal and a product of artifice" (wie ein Stück Metall und eine künstliche Arbeit, 326–27).

Mitscherlich argues that the self-sustaining super-state, the most extreme manifestation of the fatherless society, is a regressive fantasy that replaces the father not with a father-figure, but with a "mother-goddess lavish with her milk."[11] This sheds a different light on "The Mother" of Klingsohr's tale, who is burned at the stake and whose ashes are drunk as an elixir by all who remain. The result, a "new world" devoid of strife and lack, is an image virtually totalitarian in the unity of state and nature it produces (312–13).[12] This "neue Welt" is the polar counterpart to the "alte Welt" Heinrich left behind—the world of a father with whom he failed to identify and in whose footsteps he chose not to follow. There is something here of the nostalgia that informed psychoanalysis and, in Freud's tongue especially, made "fatherland" the geographical extension of the departed father. It is a nostalgia of which the theorists of the fatherless society are not innocent, and this is part of the unacknowledged legacy of Romanticism.[13] Novalis, whose ironies are lodged firmly between the Naïve and the Sentimental, represents this nostalgia as just that by placing the father at the far end of the landscape and endowing him with the distance (*Ferne*) that drew Heinrich away from home. The father is the metonymy of a destination that occurs to Heinrich even as he is leaving, for he feels "as if he were actually voyaging toward his fatherland" (als reise er [seinem Vaterland] eigentlich zu, 205).

# Notes

## INTRODUCTION

1. Sigmund Freud, *Briefe an Wilhelm Fliess,* ed. Jeffrey M. Masson (Frankfurt: S. Fischer, 1986), p. 345. See also Freud's essay on mourning and melancholia ("Trauer und Melancholie"), in which "fatherland" is identified as an abstraction that frequently substitutes for a loved one as object of mourning. *SA* III:197.

2. Raymond Immerwahr, *"Romantisch": Genese und Tradition einer Denkform* (Frankfurt: Athenäum, 1971).

3. Harold Bloom, "The Internalization of Quest-Romance," in *Romanticism and Consciousness: Essays in Criticism,* ed. Harold Bloom (New York: Norton, 1970), pp. 3–24.

4. "Die Blätter wurden glänzender und schmiegten sich an den wachsenden Stengel" (the leaves grew shinier and rubbed up against the growing stem, *Schriften* I:197). All subsequent references to Novalis, *Heinrich von Ofterdingen* are by page number only; references to other of Novalis's works are by volume number as well.

5. The dream of Heinrich's father (chap. 1) concludes with the appearance of an infant, presumably Heinrich, who acquires messianic stature; the "Tale of Atlantis" (chap. 3) includes the conception and birth of an heir to the throne; Klingsohr's "Weinlied" depicts the underground fermentation of wine in images suggestive of birth; the voice of the poem "Astralis" is that of a child born of a kiss.

6. Peter Brooks, *Reading for the Plot: Design and Intention in Narrative* (New York: Vintage, 1984), p. 24.

7. Michel Foucault, *The History of Sexuality: Volume One* (New York: Vintage, 1980), p. 65.

8. Acknowledging his own inability to "grasp" things due to an inadequate command of "words," Heinrich lapses into his dream; its imagery suggests the fluid diffuseness and inarticulate heterogeneity that Julia Kristeva in *La Révolution du langage poétique* (Paris, 1974) ascribes to the pre-oedipal stage, which is intimately connected with the moth-

er's body and exists prior to the Symbolic Order of fixed meanings and clear distinctions: "Es dünkte ihn, als umflösse ihn eine Wolke des Abendroths; eine himmlische Empfindung überströmte sein Inneres; mit inniger Wollust strebten unzählbare Gedanken in ihm sich zu vermischen; neue, niegesehene Bilder enstanden, die auch in einander flossen und zu sichtbaren Wesen um ihn wurden, und jede Welle des lieblichen Elements schmiegte sich wie ein zarter Busen an ihn. Die Flut schien eine Auflösung reizender Mädchen, die an dem Jünglinge sich augenblicklich verkörperten" (He felt as if immersed in a cloud reddened by the sunset; a heavenly sensation poured over his inner being; countless thoughts strove lustfully to intermix within him; images such as he had never seen appeared, flowing into each other and turning into visible presences around him, and each wave of the delightful element caressed him like a soft breast. The fluid was like a solution of voluptuous maidens who momentarily incarnated themselves at the youth's touch, 196–97). See Terry Eagleton, "Literary Theory: An Introduction," in *Feminist Literary Theory: A Reader,* ed. Mary Eagleton (Oxford: Basil Blackwell, 1986), pp. 213–16.

9. Loreto, in the Marche region of Italy, claims a cottage, presumably transported there by angels, in which the Virgin Mary was born.

10. Klaus Theweleit, *Männerphantasien II: Männerkörper—Zur Psychoanalyse des weissen Terrors* (Reinbeck by Hamburg: Rowohlt, 1980), p. 358. Although he refers to events during and after World War I, Theweleit suggests a distinction that Novalis makes explicit through the introduction of the crusaders—the distinction between a journey of formation (*Bildungsreise*) and unabashed raid (*Raubzug*). Heinrich's inital enthusiasm for the crusades corresponds to a sexual awakening (as indicated by his response to the sword he is given), and Novalis is generally sensitive to the libidinal structure of war-making. This is exemplified by the language used by Ginnistan to describe her sexual union with the child Eros: "Wie ein himmlischer Räuber schien er mich grausam vernichten und stolz über sein bebendes Opfer triumphiren zu wollen" (Like a heavenly marauder he seemed to want to cruelly annihilate me and to triumph proudly over his trembling victim, 305).

11. Ibid.

12. Letter to J. J. Eschenburg of 31 December 1777. *Lessings Leben und Werk in Daten und Bildern,* ed. Kurt Wölfel (Frankfurt: Insel, 1967), pp. 149–50.

13. Jill Ann Kowalik, "*Nathan der Weise* as Lessing's Work of Mourning," *Lessing Yearbook* 21 (1989): 1–17. See also Dennis F. Mahoney, " 'Stages of Enlightenment': Lessings's *Nathan der Weise* and Novalis's *Heinrich von Ofterdingen*," *Seminar* 23 (1987): 200–215.

14. Helmut J. Schneider, "Die Aufklärung, das Schenken und der Tausch: Bemerkungen zu einer Thematik in Lessings Dramen." Paper presented at the annual conference of the German Studies Association, St. Louis, October 1987. Schneider locates the question of natural parenthood within an economy of gift giving and identifies the "gift of life" via childbirth as an absolute debt that, from the standpoint of the Enlightenment, cannot be repaid, but only approximated through some ethical equivalent, in particular the saving of another's life. The Templar, by rescuing Nathan's adopted daughter from a burning house (and thereby preventing a repetition of the event that took the lives of Nathan's biological children), establishes himself as part of a "family" whose bond is ethical rather than biological, and the biological family that emerges with the discovery of a common parent is merely a simpler image of the Enlightenment family already in place.

15. John Ellis, *One Fairy Story Too Many* (Chicago: University of Chicago Press, 1983), p. 154.

16. Barbara A. Schapiro, *The Romantic Mother: Narcissistic Patterns in Romantic Poetry* (Baltimore: Johns Hopkins University Press, 1983), pp. 9–12.

17. Friedrich Kittler reads Klingsohr's *Märchen* (chap. 9 of *Ofterdingen*) as a matrilinear recoding of desire which begins with a prohibition of incest that issues from a mother and has rather the function of explicitizing the route of that desire than repressing it. Ginnistan, the enticing wet-nurse, vivifies a continuum between breast-feeding and lovemaking, and when she accompanies the child Eros on his journey, she assumes the form of his mother in order that he not succumb to her temptations. As a result of this metamorphosis, when Ginnistan and Eros consummate their passion (see above, note 10), any distinction between mother and lover is erased. Klingsohr's tale closes with the establishment of an ideal family where the mother is at its center—a mother-cult founded on the "myth of contiguity" between a mother and her children. Sophie, with whom the taboo against incest originated, compensates (in her role as universal mother) for the lack of milk that was the condition of incest. "Die Irrwege des Eros und die 'absolute Familie,' " in *Psychoanalytische und psychopathologische Literaturinterpretation*, ed. Bernd Urban and Winfried Kudszus (Darmstadt: Wissenschaftliche Buchgesellschaft, 1981), pp. 421–70.

18. Sigmund Freud, *Totem and Taboo*, trans. James Strachey (New York: Norton, 1950), p. 18.

19. Samuel Taylor Coleridge, *Poetical Works*, ed. E. H. Coleridge (London: Oxford University Press, 1967), Vol. 1, pp. 295–98.

20. Hartmut Böhme and Gernot Böhme, *Das Andere der Vernunft: Zur Entwicklung von Rationalitätsstrukturen am Beispiel Kants* (Frankfurt: Suhrkamp, 1985), pp. 435–37.

21. See above, note 14.

22. Gotthold Ephraim Lessing, *Werke*, ed. Herbert Göpfert (Munich: Hanser, 1970), Vol. 2, p. 278.

23. E. J. Hobsbawm, *The Age of Revolution: 1789–1848* (New York: New American Library, 1962), pp. 218ff.

24. Lawrence A. Rickels, *Aberrations of Mourning: Writing on German Crypts* (Detroit: Wayne State University Press, 1988), p. 36.

25. Lessing, *Werke*, Vol. 2, p. 208.

26. John Murray Cuddihy relates this experience to a number of theoretical moments in Freud's work—most important his reading of Sophocles' *Oedipus Rex*, the crucial scene of which now seems to be the encounter between Oedipus and Laius in which the former ignored the latter's command to make room for him (Laius) to pass. Freud wishes that his father had done to the anti-Semite what Oedipus did to Laius, namely strike him dead. Cuddihy argues that Freud could only avenge his father's humiliation in the sublimated form of theorizing, and this he did by unmasking the *goyim*, showing their highly civilized behavior as couched aggression. *The Ordeal of Civility: Freud, Marx, Lévi-Strauss and the Jewish Struggle with Modernity* (New York: Basic Books, 1974), pp. 48–57.

27. Carl E. Schorske, *Fin-de-Siècle Vienna: Politics and Culture* (New York: Knopf, 1980), pp. 191–92.

28. William J. McGrath, *Freud's Discovery of Psychoanalysis: The Politics of Hysteria* (Ithaca: Cornell University Press, 1986), p. 210.

29. Azade Seyhan, "Labours of Theory: The Quest of Representation in Early German Romanticism," *Seminar* 25 (1989): 194.

30. Paul Ricoeur, *Freud and Philosophy*, trans. Dennis Savage (New Haven: Yale University Press, 1970), p. 82.

31. Ibid., p. 106.

32. Ibid., p. 70.

33. Ibid., p. 96

34. Ibid., pp. 92–93.

35. Frank Kermode, *The Genesis of Secrecy: On the Interpretation of Narrative* (Cambridge: Harvard University Press, 1977), p. 2.

36. This phrase is commonly found at the beginning of German fairy tales, a variation of "Es war einmal" (Once upon a time). Brüder Grimm, *Ausgewählte Kinder-und Hausmärchen* (Stuttgart: Reclam, 1984), p. 5.

37. Tzvetan Todorov, *The Poetics of Prose*, trans. Richard Howard (Ithaca: Cornell University Press, 1977), pp. 218–33.

38. William Wordsworth, *Poems, in Two Volumes, and Other Poems (1800–1807)*, (Ithaca: Cornell University Press, 1983), p. 206.

39. See notes to the *Hamburger Ausgabe*, Vol. 1, p. 542.

40. Rainer Nägele, *Reading After Freud* (New York: Columbia University Press, 1987), pp. 4–5.

41. Novalis's fragment on the French Revolution is quoted and discussed in Chapter 1 of this study.

42. Georg Lukács, *Die Theorie des Romans* (Darmstadt: Sammlung Luchterhand, 1971), p. 21. On the same page, Lukács makes explicit reference to Novalis's fragment, cited earlier, describing philosophy as the "drive to be at home everywhere." See Michael T. Jones, "Twilight of the Gods: The Greeks in Schiller and Lukács," *The Germanic Review* 59 (1984): 50–51.

43. Arnold Ruge and Theodor Echtmeyer, "Der Protestantismus und die Romantik: Ein Manifest," *Hallische Jahrbücher für deutsche Wissenschaft und Kunst*, 1839 (267–69), 2136–52; partially reprinted in *Novalis: Beiträge zu Werk und Persönlichkeit Friedrich von Hardenbergs*, ed. Gerhard Schulz (Darmstadt: Wissenschaftliche Buchgesellschaft, 1970), pp. 1–19.

44. Herbert Marcuse, *Eros and Civilization: A Philosophical Inquiry into Freud* (Boston: Beacon Press, 1966), pp. 18–19.

45. Brooks, *Reading for the Plot*, p. 105.

46. Ibid., pp. 272ff.

47. Franco Moretti, *The Way of the World: The Bildungsroman in European Culture* (London: Verso, 1987), p. 70.

48. Catherine Belsey, "The Romantic Construction of the Unconscious," in *Literature, Politics & Theory*, ed. Francis Barker et al. (London: Methuen, 1986), p. 64.

49. See above, note 19.

## CHAPTER ONE

1. Freud defines "the uncanny" (*das Unheimliche*) as "that sort of frightful phenomenon that harks back to what is long familiar and intimate" (jene Art des Schreckhaften, welche auf das Altbekannte, Längstvertraute zurückgeht, *SA* IV:244).

2. Immanuel Kant, *Werke*, ed. Wilhelm Weischedel (Frankfurt: Suhrkamp, 1975), Vol. 9, p. 53. Cf. Christian Begemann, *Furcht und Angst im Prozess der Aufklärung* (Frankfurt: Athenäum, 1987), pp. 15ff.

3. Ricoeur, *Freud and Philosophy*, p. 160.

4. These remarks refer to a resistance to Freudian thought in general—a resistance not necessarily replicated in scholarship on Goethe's "Erlkönig." In fact, a number of studies exists in which the poem and sometimes Goethe himself are psychoanalyzed. Cf.

K. R. Eissler, *Goethe: A Psychoanalytic Study* (Detroit: Wayne State University Press, 1963), Vol. 2, pp. 780ff.; Raimar Stefan Zons, "Ein Familienzentrum: Goethes 'Erl-könig,' " in *Fugen: Deutsch-Französisches Jahrbuch für Text-Analytik*, ed. Manfred Frank et al. (Olten and Freiburg im Breisgau: Walter-Verlag, 1980), pp. 125–31. Richard Bertels-mann, "Goethe's 'Erlkönig'—psychoanalytisch," *Acta Germanica* 18 (1985): 65–97; Jean Bellemin-Noël, " 'Roi des Aulnes' ou Reine des Elfes,'' *Poétique* 18 (1987): 259–78. As diverse and insightful as these studies may be, they typically aim at an equivalency between elements in the poem and concepts in Freud's thought—for example, between the figure of the Erl-king and the "id" (Bertelsmann), the pre-oedipal father (Eissler) and the phallic mother (Bellemin-Noël). In this way they not only disimplicate psychoanalysis from the his-torical process, but they also ignore the discursive claims of a poem that is rather deliberate in locating itself within a debate on interpretation. More interesting are studies that, while they avail themselves of Freudian insight, destabilize psychoanalysis by linking it to the con-stituent flux and crisis of the text. For Richard Alewyn, "Erlkönig," along with the Gothic novel and eventually the horror film, marks an attempt to recapture the sensation of fear that the Enlightenment had rendered obsolete; Romanticism brings about the conversion of fear (*Angst*) into desire (*Lust*) because the Enlightenment had created the conditions under which fear returns as excitement, even arousal (*Reiz*). According to Alewyn, the convergence of *Angst* and *Reiz* embodies the figure of the Erl-king. "Die Lust an der Angst," in Alewyn's *Probleme und Gestalten: Essays* (Frankfurt: Insel, 1974), pp. 315–19. The broad implica-tions of Alewyn's analysis for Freudian theory become apparent in an essay by Odo Mar-quard that treats psychoanalysis as a continuation of a post-Enlightenment project, the aim of which was to establish the "safe presence of nature" (unriskante Präsenz der Natur). "Über einige Beziehungen zwischen Ästhetik und Therapeutik in der Philosophie des neun-zehnten Jahrhunderts," in *Literatur und Gesellschaft*, ed. H. J. Schrimpf (Bonn: Bouvier, 1963), pp. 22–55. Treating "Erlkönig" under the aspect of Freud's "Uncanny," Bernhard Sorg sees in Goethe's poem the emerging crisis of the lyrical subject, whose newfound in-tegrity is shaken and fractured by the recrudescence of unconscious, prerational, and phy-logenetic forces, the repression of which had been the condition of that integrity. *Das lyrische Ich: Untersuchungen zu deutschen Gedichten von Gryphius bis Benn* (Tübingen: Nie-meyer, 1984), pp. 72–77. Sorg's analysis is close to the general claims of Catherine Belsey, who asserts that Romanticism anticipated Freud's identification of the unconscious as the site of meaning and thus undermined the autonomy of the bourgeois subject (and concomi-tantly, the "Author"), which liberal humanism had instituted as "the origin and determinant of meaning and of history." The following remarks refer to an English gothic novel (M. G. Lewis's *The Monk*), but they are just as applicable to Goethe's poem: "it withholds from the reader the security of a single position from which the narrative as a whole is retrospectively intelligible. . . . The text is a product of two distinct discourses which are never reconciled." See "The Romantic Construction of the Unconscious," pp. 58, 66. One discussion of "Erlkönig" that might be brought into consonance with Belsey's thesis is by Sharon Larisch, who argues that Goethe's poem both represents a "literalization" of Plato's father-son met-aphor and "challenges not only Enlightenment rationality and the mature acceptance of nat-ural boundaries but the coherence of the dialogue form and dialogic investigation." See her "The Mixed Mode of Dialogue" (Ph.D. diss., University of Oregon, 1984), p. 136. The "not only" of Larisch's formulation perhaps detracts from the fact, underscored by Belsey, that the dialogic coherence which the Erl-king thwarts is indissociable from the rationality of the Enlightenment (to wit the importance of dialogue as a pedagogical tool in Les-sing's works).

5. This refers to the dream of the yellow-bearded uncle, discussed in the introduction to this study.

6. Bertelsmann, "Goethe's 'Erlköning,' " p. 67.

7. Peter Pütz, *Die deutsche Aufklärung* (Darmstadt: Wisenschaftliche Buchgesellschaft, 1987), p. 158–59.

8. Max Horkheimer and Theodor Adorno, *Dialektik der Aufklärung* (Frankfurt: Fischer, 1971), p. 17.

9. Begemann, *Furcht und Angst*, p. 4.

10. Böhme and Böhme, *Das Andere der Vernunft*, pp. 231ff.

11. Ibid., p. 247

12. Heinrich Adam Meissner, *Philosophisches Lexicon aus Christian Wolffs sämtlichen deutschen Schriften* (Düsseldorf: Stern Verlag Jannsen und Co., 1970; photo reprint of 1737 edition), p. 168.

13. See Wilhelm Grimm's 1818 preface to the *Kinder- und Hausmärchen*, in *Die deutsche Literatur in Texten und Zeugnissen: Sturm und Drang, Klassik, Romantik*, ed. Hans-Egon Hass (Munich: Beck, 1966), Vol. 1, p. 825.

14. Dietrich Fischer-Dieskau, *The Fischer-Dieskau Book of Lieder*, with English translations by George Bird and Richard Stokes (New York: Knopf, 1977), pp. 207–8.

15. Bellemin-Noël, " 'Roi des Aulnes,' " p. 263.

16. Bellemin-Noël, arguing that the Erl-king is a phallic mother who corresponds to the child's fear of castration, emphasizes the Erl-king's apparent preference for feminine activities, such as picking flowers at water's edge ("une occupacion de fillette"), hence his titular allusion to the "Elf-queen" (Reine des Elfes); see ibid., pp. 264–66.

17. Eissler, *Goethe*, p. 781.

18. Rupert Hirschenauer, "Erlkönig," *Wege zum Gedicht II: Interpretation von Balladen*, ed. R. H. and Albrecht Weber (Munich: Schnell und Steiner, 1963), pp. 166–67; Emil Staiger, *Goethe* (Zurich: Atlantis Verlag, 1952), Vol. 2, p. 345.

19. Böhme and Böhme, *Das Andere der Vernunft*, pp. 248–49.

20. Horkheimer and Adorno, *Dialektik der Aufklärung*, p. 18.

21. Friedrich Nietzsche, *Werke*, ed. Karl Schlechta (Frankfurt: Ullstein, 1969), Vol. 1, p. 57.

22. Freud, *Briefe an Wilhelm Fliess*, p. 285.

23. Ricoeur, *Freud and Philosophy*, p. 189. See also Freud's essay *Deckerinnerungen* (1899).

24. Freud, *Briefe an Wilhelm Fliess*, p. 293.

25. Marianne Krüll, *Freud and His Father* (New York: Norton, 1986), p. 43.

26. Freud, *Briefe an Wilhelm Fliess*, p. 213.

27. Marie Balmary, *Psychoanalyzing Psychoanalysis: Freud and the Hidden Fault of the Father*, trans. Ned Lukacher (Baltimore: Johns Hopkins University Press, 1982), p. 8.

28. Ibid., p. 18.

29. Ibid., p. 79.

30. Hirschenauer, "Erlkönig," p. 165.

31. Ned Lukacher, *Primal Scenes: Literature, Philosophy, Psychoanalysis* (Ithaca: Cornell University Press, 1986), pp. 19, 46.

32. William McGrath, *Freud's Discovery of Psychoanalysis: The Politics of Hysteria* (Ithaca: Cornell University Press, 1986), p. 197.

33. J. G. Fichte, *Gesamtausgabe*, ed. Reinhard Lauth and Hans Gliwitzky (Stuttgart/Bad Canstatt: Frohmann, 1977), I,1:170.

34. William J. Lillyman, *Reality's Dark Dream: The Narrative Fiction of Ludwig Tieck* (Berlin: de Gruyter, 1979), pp. 79–92; Heinz Hillmann, "Ludwig Tieck," in *Deutsche Dichter der Romantik*, ed. Benno von Wiese, 2d ed. (Berlin: Erich Schmidt, 1971), p. 123.

35. McGrath, *Freud's Discovery*, pp. 218 ff. Bellemin-Noël compares the Erl-king to King Henri IV, known for his preference for "effeminate" pastimes (p. 264), yet draws no political implications from the poem.

36. "Everything seems out of nature in this strange chaos of levity and ferocity." Edmund Burke, *Reflections on the French Revolution* (New York: Collier & Sons, 1909), p. 150.

37. Ronald Paulson, *Representations of Revolution (1789–1820)* (New Haven: Yale University Press, 1983) p. 9. See also Hermann Kurzke, *Romantik und Konservatismus: Das "politische" Werk Friedrich von Hardenbergs* (Munich: Fink, 1983), pp. 98ff.

38. Paulson, *Representations*, p. 9.

39. Ibid.

40. Dominick LaCapra, *Rethinking Intellectual History* (Ithaca: Cornell University Press, 1983), p. 96.

41. Normon O. Brown, *Love's Body* (New York: Vintage, 1966), p. 16.

42. René Girard, *Violence and the Sacred*, trans. Patrick Gregory (Baltimore: Johns Hopkins University Press, 1977), p. 209.

43. Lessing, *Werke*, Vol. 8, p. 508 (§ 85).

44. Ibid., p. 493 (§ 19).

45. Fichte, *Gesamtausgabe*, I,3:31.

46. Fichte, *Sämtliche Werke*, ed. Jost Perfahl (Munich: Winkler, 1972), Vol. V, p. 406.

47. Ibid., p. 261

48. Schorske, *Fin-de-Siècle Vienna*, pp. 133ff.

49. Gilles Deleuze and Felix Guattari, *Anti-Oedipus: Capitalism and Schizophrenia*, trans. Robert Hurley, Mark Seem and Helen R. Lane (Minneapolis: University of Minnesota Press, 1983), pp. 56ff.

50. Balmary, *Psychoanalyzing Psychoanalysis*, pp. 8–9.

51. Schapiro, *The Romantic Mother*.

52. Kittler, "Die Irrwege des Eros," pp. 427–28.

## CHAPTER TWO

1. Claus Träger, who regards Novalis as an outright reactionary, typifies the orthodox Marxist view of Romanticism, though even East German scholarship soon began to reappraise Romanticism by emphasizing its critical and emancipatory aspects. "Novalis und die ideologische Restauration," *Sinn und Form* 13 (1961): 618–60.

2. Hermann Kurzke, *Romantik und Konservatismus: Das "politische" Werk Friedrich von Hardenbergs* (Munich: Fink, 1983), pp. 67 ff. Despite his use of quotation marks, Kurzke, whose study is exhaustive, understands "politics" quite literally and examines Novalis's work against a vast and detailed background of German political thought. When he discusses Novalis's fragment comparing the French Revolution to "puberty" and the reac-

tion to "castration" (*Schriften* II:494), he does not activate the striking metaphor in his interpretation, but discusses only the political positions juxtaposed therein (pp. 98–119). In one of the truly superior studies on Novalis, Ulrich Stadler discusses the political writings in terms of their *micropolitics* (e.g., views on mechanization and money) and thus shares an analytical language with Franco Moretti, whose analysis of the *Bildungsroman* (below, note 4) explores the micropolitical implications of the symbol-allegory distinction. *"Die theuren Dinge": Studien zu Bunyan, Jung-Stilling und Novalis* (Bern: Francke, 1980), pp. 184–201. See also Wilfried Malsch, *"Europa": Poetische Rede des Novalis* (Stuttgart: Metzler, 1965); Klaus Peter, *Stadien der Aufklärung: Moral und Politik bei Lessing, Novalis und Friedrich Schlegel* (Wiesbaden: Athenaion, 1980); Gerhard Schulz, *Die deutsche Literatur zwischen Französischer Revolution und Restauration: Erster Teil, 1789–1806* (Munich: Beck, 1983), pp. 159–79.

3. Karl Marx, *Werke*, ed. Hans-Joachim Lieber and Peter Furth (Darmstadt: Wissenschaftliche Buchgesellschaft, 1975), Vol. 2, p. 824.

4. Franco Moretti, *The Way of the World: The* Bildungsroman *in European Culture* (London: Verso, 1987), p. 21.

5. In a passage from *Civilization and its Discontents* with important implications for the German Enlightenment's concept of *Glück*, Freud describes aim-inhibition as the prerequisite of happiness. *SA* IX:206–7.

6. Ulrich Stadler, "Novalis: *Heinrich von Ofterdingen*," in *Romane und Erzählungen der deutschen Romantik*, ed. Paul Michael Lützeler (Stuttgart: Reclam, 1981), p. 152.

7. Horkheimer and Adorno, *Dialektik der Aufklärung*, pp. 34–35.

8. Moretti, *Way of the World*, pp. 29–30.

9. Hartmut Böhme discusses alchemy and the body with specific reference to Novalis. *Natur und Subjekt* (Frankfurt: Suhrkamp, 1988), pp. 97–115. Also Tzvetan Todorov, *Theories of the Symbol*, trans. Catherine Porter (Ithaca: Cornell University Press, 1982), pp. 164ff.

10. "Optimum visibility" (*vollkommene Sehbarkeit*), which Goethe established as a criterion for the symbolic in art, is discussed in an important article by Neil Flax. "The Fiction Wars of Art," *Representations* 7 (1984): 10. Also Goethe, *HA* XII:142ff.

11. Moretti, *Way of the World*, p. 61.

12. In a unique and provocative study, Christoph Asendorf discusses *l'homme machine* and nineteenth-century technology in general against the backdrop of the works of E. T. A. Hoffmann and, to some extent, Novalis. *Batterien der Lebenskraft: Zur Geschichte der Dinge und ihrer Wahrnehmung im 19. Jahrhundert* (Giessen: Anabas, 1984), pp. 9ff.

13. Marx, *Werke*, Vol. 4, pp. 69ff.

14. Lessing, *Werke*, Vol. 2, pp. 274–75.

15. Ibid., p. 276.

16. Peter Pütz, *Die deutsche Aufklärung* (Darmstadt: Wissenschaftliche Buchgesellschaft, 1978), p. 10.

17. Susan Stewart, *On Longing: Narratives of the Miniature, the Gigantic, the Souvenir, the Collection* (Baltimore: Johns Hopkins University Press, 1989), p. 133.

18. Walter Benjamin, *Illuminationen* (Frankfurt: Suhrkamp, 1977), pp. 142, 178.

19. Stewart, *On Longing*, pp. 133–35.

20. Horkheimer and Adorno, *Dialektik der Aufklärung*, p. 21.

21. Erik Erikson, *Young Man Luther: A Study in Psychoanalysis and History* (New York: Norton, 1962), p. 58.

22. Ibid., pp. 59–60.

23. Ibid., p. 123.

24. Horkheimer and Adorno, *Dialektik der Aufklärung*, p. 8.

25. See Erikson, *Young Man Luther* for "The fact that he called defeat the devil only meant he was applying a diagnostic label that was handy" (p. 40).

26. Marx, *Werke*, Vol. 2, p. 816.

27. Ibid., p. 820.

28. Ibid., p. 821.

29. Herbert Marcuse, *Eros and Civilization*, pp. 18–19.

30. Ibid., pp. 16–17.

31. Marx, *Werke*, Vol. 4 p. 48.

32. Benjamin, *Illuminationen*, p. 176.

33. Geza von Molnár, "Another Glance at Novalis' 'Blue Flower'," *Euphorion* 67 (1973): 272–86.

34. Wilfried Barner, "Geheime Lenkung: Zur Turmgesellschaft in Goethes *Wilhelm Meister*," in *Goethe's Narrative Fiction*, ed. William J. Lillyman (Berlin: De Gruyter, 1983), pp. 85–109.

35. Ricoeur, *Freud and Philosophy*, p. 18.

36. Nietzsche, *Werke*, Vol. 1, p. 57.

37. Wendell Berry, *Standing By Words* (San Francisco: North Point Press, 1983), pp. 67–68.

38. Zons, "Ein Familienzentrum: Goethes 'Erlkönig'," p. 126; Avital Ronell, *Dictations: On Haunted Writing* (Bloomington: Indiana University Press, 1985), pp. 9–10.

39. Freud, *Briefe an Wilhelm Fliess*, p. 213.

40. Moretti, *Way of the World*, p. 64.

41. Marcuse, *Eros and Civilization*, pp. 173ff.

## CHAPTER THREE

1. Harold Bloom, *Poetry and Repression: Revisionism from Blake to Stevens* (New Haven: Yale University Press, 1976), p. 20; also *The Anxiety of Influence: A Theory of Poetry* (New York: Oxford University Press, 1973).

2. I deal with Freud's "Triebe und Triebschicksale" later in this chapter.

3. E. J. Hobsbawm, *The Age of Revolution*, pp. 218ff.

4. Kant, *Werke*, Vol. 9, p. 53.

5. J. G. Fichte, *Grundlage der gesamten Wissenschaftslehre* (Hamburg: Felix Meiner, 1956), p. 189. Cited by Harmut Böhme and Gernot Böhme, *Das Andere der Vernunft*, p. 129.

6. See Julia Kristeva, *Powers of Horror: An Essay on Abjection*, trans. Leon S. Roudiez (New York: Columbia University Press, 1982).

7. Böhme and Böhme, *Das Andere der Vernunft*, p. 129. Also Geza von Molnár, *Romantic Vision, Ethical Context: Novalis and Artistic Autonomy*. Minneapolis: University of Minnesota Press, 1987.

8. Barbara Schapiro, *The Romantic Mother*, p. xiii.

9. Böhme and Böhme, pp. 130–31.

10. Frank Lentricchia, *After the New Criticism* (Chicago: University of Chicago Press, 1980), pp. 321–25.

11. Peter Pütz, "Werthers Leiden an der Literatur," in *Goethe's Narrative Fiction,* ed. William J. Lillyman (Berlin: De Gruyter, 1985), pp. 55–68.

12. Thomas Weiskel, *The Romantic Sublime: Studies in the Structure and Psychology of Transcendence* (Baltimore: Johns Hopkins University Press, 1976), pp. 138–39.

13. See Jürgen Jacobs, *Wilhelm Meister und seine Brüder: Untersuchungen zum deutschen Bildungsroman* (Munich: Fink, 1972).

14. Marcuse, *Eros and Civilization,* pp. 169–71.

15. Herbert Anton, *Der Raub der Proserpina: Literarische Tradition eines erotischen Sinnbilds und mythischen Symbols* (Heidelberg: Carl Winter, 1967), pp. 91–95.

16. Heinz Kohut, *The Analysis of the Self* (New York: International Universities Press, 1971).

17. After Heinrich meets Mathilde, he wonders whether her face was not the one that appeared in the blue flower of his dream (*Schriften* I:277). In light of this query, and in light of the thesis that the blue flower is a metonym that links the mother to Heinrich's other erotic objects, it is interesting to note that in Ovid's *Metamorphoses* (Book III, verse 342), Narcissus' mother has a name that means "face of the blue flower" (Leiriope). See Victoria Hamilton, *Narcissus and Oedipus: The Children of Psychoanalysis* (London: Routledge, 1982), p. 111.

18. Elizabeth Stopp " 'Übergang vom Roman zur Mythologie': Formal Aspects of the Opening Chapter of Hardenberg's *Heinrich von Ofterdingen, Part II,*" *Deutsche Vierteljahresschrift* 48 (1974): 318–41.

19. Freud, "Triebe und Triebschicksale" (Instincts and their Vicissitudes, 1915).

20. Ricoeur, *Freud and Philosophy,* p. 125.

21. Kant, *Werke,* Vol. 3, p. 95. For a thorough discussion of the concept of "intellectual intuition," see John Neubauer, "Intellektuelle, intellektuale und ästhetische Anschauung: Zur Entstehung der romantischen Kunstauffassung," *Deutsche Vierteljahresschrift* 46 (1972): 294–319.

22. Kant, *Werke,* Vol. 3, pp. 95, 272.

23. Fichte, *Gesamtausgabe,* Part 1, Vol. 2, p. 261. See von Molnár, *Romantic Vision, Ethical Context,* p. 29; Hannelore Link, "Zur Fichte-Rezeption in der Frühromantik," in *Romantik in Deutschland,* ed. Richard Brinkmann (Stuttgart: Metzler, 1978), pp. 355–68.

24. Clemens Brentano, *Gesammelte Werke,* ed. Heinz Amelung and Karl Vietor (Frankfurt, 1923), Vol. 1, pp. 139–41.

25. Eckhard Heftrich, *Novalis: Vom Logos der Poesie* (Frankfurt: Klostermann, 1969), p. 87.

26. Ricouer, *Freud and Philosophy,* pp. 122–23.

27. Hugo Kuhn, "Poetische Synthese oder ein kritischer Versuch über romantische Philosophie und Poesie aus Novalis' Fragmenten," in *Novalis: Beiträge zu Werk und Persönlichkeit Friedrich von Hardenbergs,* ed. Gerhard Schulz, 2d ed. (Darmstadt: Wissenschaftliche Buchgesellschaft, 1986), p. 216.

28. Thomas De Quincey, *Collected Writings,* ed. David Masson (Edinburgh: Black, 1890), Vol. 3, p. 440.

29. J. G. Herder, *Sämtliche Werke,* ed. Berhard Suphan (Hildenscheim: Olms, 1967), Vol. 8, p. 19.

30. Ibid., pp. 52–53.

31. Ibid., p. 25.

32. Ibid., p. 9.

33. Gert Mattenklott, *Der übersinnliche Leib: Beiträge zur Metaphysik des Körpers* (Hamburg: Rowohlt, 1982), pp. 78–79.

34. Marquard, "Über einige Beziehungen zwischen Ästhetik und Therapeutik," p. 33.

35. Alewyn, "Die Lust an der Angst," pp. 315ff.

36. Horkheimer and Adorno, *Dialektik der Aufklärung*, p. 17.

37. Joseph von Eichendorff, *Werke*, ed. Joseph Perfahl (Munich: Winkler, 1970), p. 33.

38. Bloom, *Poetry and Repression*, p. 25.

39. Ibid., p. 3. The connection between influence and flood is made by Edward Said in a passage quoted by Bloom: "These threatening encroachments are described by Vico as the result of a divinely willed flood, which I take to be an image for the inner crisis of self-knowledge that each man must face at the very beginning of any conscious undertaking." Said, *Beginnings: Intention and Method* (Baltimore: Johns Hopkins University Press, 1975), p. 365. My own allusion is to Klaus Theweleit, *Männerphantasien I: Frauen, Fluten, Körper, Geschichte* (Reinbeck bei Hamburg: Rowohlt, 1986). See the introduction to this study, note 10.

40. August Langen, *Anschauungsformen in der deutschen Dichtung des 18. Jahrhunderts: Rahmenschau und Rationalismus* (Darmstadt: Wissenschaftliche Buchgesellschaft, 1965), pp. 5ff; Helmut J. Schneider, "Naturerfahrung und Idylle in der deutschen Aufklärung," in *Erforschung der deutschen Aufklärung*, ed. Peter Pütz (Königstein/Ts: Athenion, 1980), pp. 289–315.

41. Marcuse, *Eros and Civilization*, p. 182. In this same context, Marcuse quotes Novalis on the productive imagination, describing his as an important insight we have yet to digest (p. 160).

42. Ibid., p. 189–90.

43. Jean Baudrillard, *Selected Writings*, ed. Mark Poster (Stanford: Stanford University Press, 1988), p. 109–110.

44. Ibid., p. 105.

45. Stadler, *"Die theuren Dinge,"* pp. 130–49.

46. "Mutter, Heinrich kann die Stunde nicht verläugnen, durch die er in der Welt ist" (Mother, Heinrich cannot deny the hour thanks to which he is in the world), *Schriften* I:199.

47. Marcuse, *Eros and Civilization*, p. 194.

48. Linda Hutcheon, *Narcissistic Narrative: The Metafictional Paradox* (New York: Methuen, 1984), pp. xv–xvi.

## CHAPTER FOUR

1. Peter Gay, introduction to Edmund Engelmann, *Berggasse 19: Sigmund Freud's Home and Offices, Vienna, 1938* (New York: Basic Books, 1976).

2. Michel Foucault, *The Order of Things: An Archaeology of the Human Sciences* (New York: Vintage Books, 1973), p. xi.

3. Michel Foucault, "Language to Infinity," in his *Language, Counter-Memory, Practice*, ed. Donald Bouchard (Ithaca: Cornell University Press, 1977), pp. 53–67.

4. See Said, *Beginnings*, p. 302.

5. Foucault, *The Order of Things*, p. 297.

6. Jonathan Culler, *The Pursuit of Signs* (Ithaca: Cornell University Press, 1981), pp. 33–34.

7. Wilhelm von Humboldt, *Gesammelte Schriften*, ed. Berlin Academy of Sciences (Berlin: De Gruyter, 1968), Vol. 3, pp. 167–70.

8. Jacob Grimm, *Reden an der Akademie*, ed. Werner Neumann and Hartmut Schmidt (Berlin, GDR: Akademie-Verlag, 1984), p. 93.

9. See Helmut Jendreiek, *Hegel und Jacob Grimm* (Berlin: Erich Schmidt, 1975), p. 21.

10. That the vocabulary of archaeology continues to be informed by the metaphor of quest-romance is apparent in the title of Bruce Norman's recent popularization, *Footsteps: Nine Archaeological Journeys of Romance and Discovery* (Topsfield, Mass.: Salem House, 1987). See below, note 44.

11. Friedrich Hölderlin, *Sämtliche Werke und Briefe*, ed. Günter Mieth (Munich: Carl Hanser Verlag, 1978), Vol. 1, p. 272.

12. Freud, *Briefe an Wilhelm Fliess*, p. 430.

13. Ibid., p. 387.

14. Ibid., p. 320. See Steven Marcus, *Freud and the Culture of Psycho-Analysis* (New York: Norton, 1984), pp. 18–19.

15. Jacob Grimm, *Kleinere Schriften*, ed. Karl Müllenhoff (Berlin: Dümmler, 1864–71), Vol. 1, pp. 115–16.

16. Ulrich Wyss, *Die wilde Philologie: Jacob Grimm und der Historismus* (Munich: Fink, 1978), p. 51.

17. See the editorial note to Novalis's *Schriften*, I:183–84.

18. Friedrich Kittler, *Aufschreibesysteme 1800/1900* (Munich: Fink, 1985), pp. 11 ff. Neil M. Flax, "The Presence of the Sign in Goethe's *Faust*," *PMLA* 98 (1983): 183–203.

19. Foucault, "Language to Infinity."

20. Nietzsche, *Werke*, Vol. 1, p. 228.

21. In an unpublished manuscript (*Fables of the Subject*), Ashish Roy discusses the *Bildungsroman*, of which quest is a more ancient counterpart, as an allegory of what he calls the "normative economy of increase in narrative," a "hegemony of *recit*" that "demands that narrative kernels be developed through an increasingly meaningful series of events." As a modernist indictment of this structural movement, Roy offers the work of Kafka, which "contests the principle that the trials and tribulations of adventure be simply an agency of the quest, a carrier of preordained meaning." If the point is to situate a convention of credibility within a matrix of self-transcending detail, then the "scientific fables" of Grimm and Freud may be testimonies to the holding power of that convention.

22. Freud's paragraph on archaeology is analyzed at length by Mary Balmary, who hears in Freud's Latin phrase an echo of the curses of a biblical prophet: "Your schemes to overthrow mighty nations will bring dishonor to your house and put your own life in jeopardy. The very stones will cry out from the wall" (Habukkuk 2:9–11). *Psychoanalyzing Psychoanalysis*, pp. 95–98.

23. Benjamin, *Illuminationen*, pp. 395–96.

24. Raymond Schwab, *The Oriental Renaissance* (New York: Cornell University Press, 1984), p. 173. See also Hartmut Böhme, *Natur und Subjekt*.

25. See Jean Paul, *Vorschule der Ästhetik*, in *Werke*, ed. Norbert Miller (Munich: Hanser, 1973), Vol. 5, p. 33.

26. Jacques Derrida, "Freud and the Scene of Writing," in his *Writing and Difference*, trans. Alan Bass (Chicago: University of Chicago Press, 1978), p. 220.

27. Alexander Baumgarten, *Reflections on Poetry*, translated (from Latin) and introduced by Karl Aschenbrenner and William B. Holther (Berkeley: University of California Press, 1954), p. 39.

28. Peter Brooks, *Reading for the Plot,* pp. 60–61; Alice Kuzniar, *Delayed Endings: Nonclosure in Novalis and Hölderlin* (Athens: University of Georgia Press, 1987).

29. Brooks, *Reading for the Plot,* pp. 96ff.; Derrida, "Freud," p. 202.

30. Friedrich Kluge, *Etymologisches Wörterbuch der deutschen Sprache* (Berlin: De Gruyter, 1960), p. 189.

31. Ricoeur, *Freud and Philosophy,* p. 123.

32. Stadler, *"Die theuren Dinge,"* p. 207.

33. Ibid., pp. 130ff., esp. 134.

34. Ricoeur, p. 18. *Freud and Philosophy,* In a similar vein, Hans-Georg Gadamer asserts that the locus of hermeneutic understanding lies "between strangeness and familiarity" (zwischen Fremdheit und Vertrautheit). *Wahrheit und Methode,* 5th ed. (Tübingen: J. C. B. Mohr, 1986), p. 300.

35. Heinrich Schliemann, *Ilios: The City and Country of the Trojans* (New York: Benjamin Blom, 1881; reprint, 1968), p. 3. Schliemann has, like Freud, fallen prey to the accusation of having written "scientific fairy-tales" where scholars invoke historicist premises to indict the veracty of his accounts. William M. Calder III, who impugns Schliemann with considerable vituperation, not only points to individual inaccuracies in the latter's writings, but he also points to the literary strategy with which particular misrepresentations are incorporated into narrative: "The entry remains a masterpiece of its genre, the narration of outrageous untruth within the setting of accurate details. We have the precision of train times, traveling companions, hotels, oysters." "A New Picture of Heinrich Schliemann," in *Myth, Scandal, and History: The Heinrich Schliemann Controversy,* ed. William M. Calder III and David A. Traill (Detroit: Wayne State University Press, 1986), p. 24. See note 21 above.

36. In a passage that invokes the imagery of Romanticism, Walter Benjamin describes the aura as a "distance" ("Ferne") inscribed in the object, however close it may be; to bring something closer, which is the effect of technical reproducibility, is to destroy its aura. *Iluminationen,* p. 142.

37. Freud, *Gesammelte Werke,* ed. Anna Freud with Marie Bonaparte (London: Imago Publishing Co., 1940–52), Vol. 2, p. 537. (*Deckerinnerungen* is not contained in the *Studienausgabe*).

38. Foucault, *The Order of Things,* p. 298.

39. Marx, *Werke,* Vol. 4, p. 50.

40. Schiller, *Sämtliche Werke,* Vol. 4, p. 744.

41. Ibid., p. 747.

42. Regarding the impossibility of translation that the Romantics asserted, Kittler (*Aufschreibesysteme*) discusses meaning in terms of general equivalency, which came to be of crucial importance to Marx (pp. 76ff.).

43. Stadler, *"Die theuren Dinge,"* p. 11.

44. A postscript to this chapter is furnished by the French anthropologist Claude Lévi-Strauss in his autobiography, *Tristes Tropiques,* trans. John and Doreen Weightman (New York: Atheneum, 1984). Lévi-Strauss implicates his own discipline in a nostalgia for romance when he states: "I wished I had lived in the days of *real* joureys" (p. 43); "Journeys, those magic caskets full of dreamlike promises . . . " (p. 37). He recalls a boyhood fascination for geology much like that of the old miner in *Ofterdingen,* and he describes it as "a quest . . . which I took upon as the very image of knowledge" (p. 56). Indeed, he uses the geologist's excavations as a metaphor for both Marxism and psychoanalysis (p. 57).

## CHAPTER FIVE

1. Seymour Chatman, *Story and Discourse: Narrative and Structure in Fiction and Film* (Ithaca: Cornell University Press, 1978), pp. 41–42.

2. Frank Kermode, "The Secrets of Narrative Sequence," in *On Narrative*, ed. W. J. T. Mitchell (Chicago: University of Chicago Press, 1980), pp. 82–83.

3. Todorov, *The Poetics of Prose*, pp. 45ff.

4. Arthur Conan Doyle, *The Sherlock Holmes Mysteries* (New York: New American Library, 1988), pp. 112–15.

5. Walter Benjamin, *Das Passagenwerk*, ed. Rolf Tiedemann (Frankfurt: Suhrkamp, 1983), p. 274.

6. Ibid., p. 272.

7. Ibid., p. 279.

8. Franco Moretti, *Signs Taken for Wonders: Essays in the Sociology of Literary Forms*, trans. Susan Fischer, David Forgacs, and David Miller (London: Verso, 1988), p. 137.

9. See Claude Lévi-Strauss, *The Savage Mind* (Chicago: University of Chicago Press, 1966), p. 11.

10. Among other things, Natalie learns that Mignon, for whom Wilhelm was both father-figure and object of desire, was witness to an erotic encounter between him and Philine (*HA* VII:523–24)—a scene similar to the *Urszene* deduced by Freud in his case-study of the "Wolfman," who as a small child observed his parents engaged in intercourse. Such "primal scenes" fall under the category of fabula not only because of their sequential propriety but also because they are "products of construction" (Ergebnisse der Konstruktion, *SA* VIII:168), that is, not accessible to memory.

11. Nägele, *Reading after Freud*, p. 14.

12. Jochen Hörisch, *Gott, Geld and Glück: Zur Logik der Liebe in den Bildungsromanen Goethes, Kellers und Thomas Manns* (Frankfurt: Suhrkamp, 1983), 17–19, 51–52.

13. Nägele, *Reading after Freud*, p. 10.

14. John H. Smith, "Cultivating Gender: Sexual Difference, *Bildung*, and the *Bildungsroman*," *Michigan Germanic Studies* 13 (1987):218.

15. The letter in which Lessing anticipates the loss of his wife in the wake of the death of his son concludes with a wrenching economy: "Ich wollte es auch einmal so gut haben, wie andere Menschen. Aber es ist mir schlecht bekommen" (For once I wanted to be happy like everyone else. But I fared badly). Wölfel, ed., *Lessings Leben in Daten und Bildern*, p. 150. The emblematic importance of this episode for the Enlightenment's notion of autonomy is discussed in the introduction to this study.

16. Both Moretti (*The Way of World*, pp. 69–70) and Brooks (*Reading for the Plot*, pp. 110–11) discuss Lukács in this context.

17. Kuzniar, *Delayed Endings*, p. 102.

18. Moretti, *The Way of the World*, p. 70.

19. Franz Kafka, *Tagebücher 1910–1923*, ed. Max Brod (Frankfurt: Fischer, 1986), pp. 327–38 (entry of 19 December 1914).

20. Franz Kafka, *Diaries II: 1914–23*, ed. Max Brod, trans. Martin Greenberg and Hannah-Arendt (New York: Schocken, 1976), p. 104.

21. The idea that the castle of Kafka's novel may refer to Lothario's castle is an insight I owe, along with much else, to Ashish Roy, and looking back on his manuscript now,

I realize that his words contain the seeds of an argument I thought was my own: "That everywhere in his work Kafka should make free with the conflation of animal and human, particularly powerfully in the investigative pieces like 'The Burrow' and 'Investigations of a Dog', that too remains embedded in this matrix [of the exaggerated exhortation issued to the bodily members, the bodily 'answer' expected in response to a 'psychic' command]. Such a jackdaw-like 'freedom' not only points an accusing finger at the kind of mythic tendency inherent to Enlightenment that Horkeimer and Adorno have expounded. It critically reinscribes the attempt, and the failure, of the *Bildungsroman* to free Enlightenment of its mythicizing determinants. It should not be hard, therefore, to understand how Kafka's 'organological concern' with narrative as it 'bears its completed organization within itself even before it has been fully formed' takes hold of the concept of *Bildung,* and how that concern determines Kafka's position in a historically emerging German modernism." *Fables of the Subject,* unpublished. See also Chapter Four of this study, note 21.

22. Brooks, *Reading for the Plot,* p. 12.

23. G. W. F. Hegel, *Vorlesungen über die Ästhetik* (Frankfurt: Suhrkamp, 1970), Vol. 2, p. 220.

24. Franz Kafka, *Erzählungen,* ed. Max Brod (Frankfurt: Fischer, 1986), p. 107.

25. See Ralph Freedman, *The Lyrical Novel* (Princeton: Princeton University Press, 1963), pp. 27ff.; Oskar Walzel, "Die Formkunst von Friedrich von Hardenbergs *Heinrich von Ofterdingen,*" in *Novalis,* ed. Gerhard Schulz (Darmstadt: Wissenschaftliche Buchgesellschaft, 1970), p. 53.

26. "Di Schreibart des Romans muss kein *Continuum*—es muss ein in jeden Perioden gegliederter Bau seyn. Jedes kleine Stück muss etwas abgeschnittenes—begränztes—ein eignes Ganze seyn" (The composition of the novel should not be a continuum—its structure must be articulated at each stage. Every small part has to be severed—limited—its own whole" (*Schriften* III:562).

27. See Ernst Behler, "Der Roman der Frühromantik," in *Handbuch des deutschen Romans,* ed. Helmut Koopman (Düsseldorf: Bagel, 1983), pp. 273–301.

28. Walter Benjamin, *Ursprung des deutschen Trauerspiels* (Frankfurt: Suhrkamp, 1972), pp. 197–98. With reference to the premature deaths of Franz Schubert, John Keats, and Novalis, Thomas McFarland writes: "Early death is not merely early demise—it is a diasparaction that emphasizes the sense of incompleteness and fragmentation. Diasparaction that incorporated the sense of ruin was also pervasive, whether the ruin was conceived as work uncompleted or as edifice decayed. . . . Novalis, his own life soon to be shattered by consumption, hails in his early 'Ans Kloster in Ruinen' a ruined medieval monastery: 'Da liegst du nun und bist gefallen,/Zerstöret von der mächtigern Zeit'—there liest thou now and art fallen, shattered by the mightier Time.' " *Romanticism and the Forms of Ruin: Wordsworth, Coleridge, and Modalities of Fragmentation* (Princeton: Princeton University Press, 1981), pp. 13–14.

29. Freud, *Bruchstück einer Hysterie-Analyse* (Fragment of an Analysis of a Case of Hysteria), 1905.

30. Kuzniar makes disparate references to the *Nebeneinander/Nacheinander* distinction (109) and to Lessing's *Laokoon* (192).

31. David E. Wellbery, *Lessing's Laocoön: Semiotics and Aesthetics in the Age of Reason* (Cambridge: Cambridge University Press, 1984), pp. 35 ff.

32. Toril Moi, "Representation of Patriarchy: Sexuality and Epistemology in Freud's Dora," in *In Dora's Case,* ed. Charles Bernheimer and Claire Kahane (New York: Columbia University Press, 1985), p. 186.

33. Ibid., pp. 196–97.

34. This is Moretti's contention in *The Way of the World*, p. 71.

35. This according to the account of Sulpiz Boisserée, to whom Goethe showed Runge's *Vier Jahreszeiten* (fig. B), which Goethe owned and had displayed in his music room. *Traum und Wahrheit: Deutsche Romantik aus Museen der Deutschen Demokratischen Republik*, ed. Jürgen Glaesmer (Teufen, Switerland: Arthur Niggle, 1985), p. 142.

36. Paulson, *Representations of Revolution*, p. 8.

37. Vitruvius, *De Architectura*, quoted in Paulson, p. 170.

38. Friedrich II, "De la littérature allemande" (1780), in *Sturm und Drang, Klassik, Romantik*, ed. Hans-Egon Hass (Munich: Beck, 1966), Vol. 1, p. 216. On the specific "unethical" and "unnatural" connotations of *bizarrerie* in relation to the French Revolution, see Jan Starobinski, *1789: Emblems of Reason*, trans. Barbara Bray (Charlottesville: University Press of Virginia, 1982), p. 74.

39. Girard, *Violence and the Sacred*, pp. 74–75.

40. See Thomas P. Saine, "Über Wilhelm Meisters 'Bildung,' " in *Lebendige Form: Interpretationen der deutschen Literatur*, ed. J. L. Sammons and E. I. Schürer (Munich: 1970), p. 71.

41. See Kittler, "Die Irrwege des Eros."

42. Thus when Heinrich first kisses Mathilde, whom he later recognizes as the face that appeared in the blue flower of his dream, his mother becomes the receptacle of his new-found passion: "Heinrich stand, wie im Himmel. Seine Mutter kam auf ihn zu. Er liess seine ganze Zärtlichkeit an ihr aus" (Heinrich stood as if in heavan. His mother came over to him. He showered his full affection on her, 276; *PH* 104).

43. Paulson, *Representations of Revolution*, p. 173.

44. For example: "Er pflückt die blaue Blume—und wird ein Stein. Die Morgenländerlinn opfert sich an seinem Steine, er wird ein klingender Baum. Das Hirtenmädchen haut den Baum um und verbrennt sich mit ihm. Er wird ein goldner Widder. Mathilde muss ihn opfern. Er wird ein Mensch. Während dieser Verwandlungen hört er allerley wunderliche Gespräche" (He plucks the blue flower—and turns into stone. The Oriental woman sacrifices herself on his stone, and it becomes a singing tree. The shepherd girl cuts down the tree and burns herself with it. It becomes a golden ram. Mathilde has to sacrifice it. It becomes a man. During these transformations he hears all kinds of wonderful conversations, *Schriften* I:348).

45. McFarland, *Romanticism and the Forms of Ruin*, pp. 41–42.

46. Kuzniar's analysis in *Delayed Endings* (pp. 105–7) of the blue flower of *Ofterdingen* as derivative—that is, as a false origin—is crucial.

47. Paulson, *Representations of Revolution*, pp. 174–75.

48. Flax, "The Fiction Wars of Art," p. 10.

49. John Keats, *The Poems of John Keats*, ed. Jack Stillinger (Cambridge: Harvard University Press, 1978), pp. 372–73.

50. Jens Christian Jensen, *Philipp Otto Runge: Leben und Werk* (Cologne: DuMont, 1978), p. 180.

51. Ibid., p. 182.

52. Ibid.

53. Freud, *Briefe an Wilhelm Fliess*, p. 213; Sigmund Freud, *The Origins of Psychoanalysis: Letters of Wilhelm Fliess, Drafts and Notes, 1887–1902*, ed. Marie Bonaparte et al., trans. Eric Moosbacher and James Strachey (New York: Basic Books, 1954), p. 170.

## CHAPTER SIX

1. Jakob Böhme, *Sämmtliche Werke,* ed. K. Schiebler (Leipzig: Barth, 1846), Vol. 1, p. 247. See Carl Paschek, "Novalis and Böhme," *Jahrbuch des freien deutschen Hochstifts* 1976, pp. 138–67; Warren Stevenson, *Divine Analogy: A Study of the Creation Motif in Blake and Coleridge* (Salzburg: University of Salzburg, 1972), pp. 42ff.

2. In *Ofterdingen,* Klingsohr tells Heinrich: "Im Kriege . . . regt sich das Urgewässer" (In war . . . the primordial waters are stirred, 285).

3. Samuel Taylor Colerige, *Poetical Works,* ed. E. H. Coleridge (London: Oxford University Press, 1967), Vol. 1, pp. 295–98.

4. James Joyce, *A Portrait of the Artist as a Young Man* (New York: Penguin, 1979), p. 217.

5. Ibid., p. 223. These lines bear comparison to the following passage from Klingsohr's tale in *Ofterdingen:* "Die Frau . . . tauchte den Finger in die Schaale, und sprützte einige Tropfen auf sie hin, die, sobald sie die Amme, das Kind, oder die Wiege berührten, in einen blauen Dunst zerrannen, der tausend seltsame Bilder zeigte" (The woman . . . dipped her finger into the bowl and sprayed a few drops at them, which, as soon as they touched the wet-nurse, the child or the cradle, ran together into a blue mist, which displayed a thousand strange images, 294).

6. Ibid., p. 218.

7. Irving Wohlfarth, "The Politics of Prose and the Art of Awakening: Walter Benjamin's Version of a German Romantic Motif," *Glyph* 7 (1980): 131–48.

8. Emphasis added.

9. Elinor Shaffer, *"Kubla Khan"* and The Fall of Jerusalem: *The Mythological School of Biblical Criticism and Secular Literature 1770–1880* (Cambridge: Cambridge University Press, 1975), p. 95; also McFarland, *Romanticism and the Forms of Ruin,* pp. 237–38.

10. Joyce, *A Portrait of an Artist,* p. 215. The same analogy is found in Lessing's *Hamburgische Dramaturgie:* "Aus diesen wenigen Gliedern sollte er [der Dichter] ein Ganzes machen, das völlig sich rundet, wo eines aus dem andern sich völlig erkläret, wo keine Schwierigkeit aufstöss, derentwegen wir die Befriedigung nicht in seinem Plane finden, sondern sie auss ihm, in dem allgemeinen Plane der Dinge suchen müssen; das Ganze dieses sterblichen Schöpfers sollte ein Schattenriss von dem Ganzen des ewigen Schöpfers sein" (From these few parts the poet ought to make a whole, which rounds itself off completely, where one thing explains itself completely out of the next, where no difficulty appears because of which we do not find gratification in his plan, but rather have to seek it beyond, in the universal plan of things; the whole of this mortal creator should be a shadow drawing of the whole of the eternal Creator). *Werke* IV, 598.

11. Manfred Frank, " 'Intellektuale Anschauung': Drei Stellungnahmen zu einem Deutungsversuch vom Selbstbewusstsein," in *Die Aktualität der Frühromantik,* ed. Ernst Behler and Jochen Hörisch (Paderborn: Schöningh, 1987), pp. 107–8.

12. Coleridge's definition of the "Subject" as a "realizing intuition," as a "subject which becomes a subject by the act of constructing itself objectively to itself," is virtually identical to Schelling's. *Biographia Literaria,* ed. J. Shawcross (Oxford: Oxford University Press, 1907), Vol. 1, p. 183.

13. While the poem was written in 1798, the preface was likely added just before the poem's publication in 1816.

14. Joyce, *A Portrait of the Artist,* p. 218.

15. Marilyn Butler argues for an apolitical reading of Coleridge's poem, charging him with "rewriting a narrative previously in the public sphere so that it becomes a private fable, political no longer." "Plotting the Revolution: The Political Narratives of Romantic Poetry and Criticism," in *Romantic Revolutions*, ed. Kenneth R. Johnston et al. (Bloomington: Indiana University Press, 1990), p. 152.

16. Horkheimer and Adorno, *Dialektik der Aufklärung*, p. 18.

17. Hans Peter Duerr, *Traumzeit: Über die Grenze zwischen Wildnis und Zivilisation* (Frankfurt: Suhrkamp, 1985), p. 26.

18. Ibid., p. 46.

19. Ibid.

20. Duerr, *Traumzeit*, pp. 39 ff.

21. Moi, "Representation of Patriarchy," pp. 189–90; Luce Irigaray, *The Sex That Is Not One*, trans. Catherine Porter (Ithaca: Cornell University Press, 1985), pp. 60–61.

22. Freud, *Briefe an Wilhelm Fliess*, p. 213.

23. Duerr, *Traumzeit*, p. 92.

24. Ibid., p. 79.

25. Ibid., p. 85.

26. Coleridge's "A savage place! as holy and enchanted" is echoed in Joyce's novel when a wooded sacristy, symbolic of Stephen Dedalus's unshakeable Catholic upbringing, is described as "A strange and holy place" (p. 41). John Smith, *Imagery and the Mind of Stephen Dedalus* (Lewisburg: Bucknell University Press, 1980), p. 183.

27. Heinrich von Kleist, *Sämtliche Werke und Briefe* (Munich: Hanser, 1961), p. 151.

28. Ibid., p. 156.

29. Ibid.

30. Ibid.

31. Foucault, *The History of Sexuality*, p. 65.

32. Edward Said, *Orientalism* (New York: Vintage, 1979), p. 19.

33. As exhibited by the romanticism of Jakob Grimm, discussed in some detail in Chapter 4 of this study.

34. Stadler, *"Die theuren Dinge,"* pp. 221–22.

35. Benjamin, *Illuminationen*, p. 142.

36. Zulima speculates as to the deeper motivation that impels the crusaders eastward: "und vielleicht ist es dieser dunkle Zug, der die Menschen aus neuen Gegenden, sobald eine gewisse Zeit ihres Erwachens kömmt, mit so zerstörender Ungeduld nach der alten Heymath ihres Geschlechts treibt" (and it is perhaps this dark impulse which, with the coming of an age of awakening, drives men with destructive impatience from new regions back to the homeland of their ancestors, 237).

37. Kittler, "Die Irrwege des Eros," p. 433.

38. Theweleit, *Männerphantasien*, Vol. 1, p. 224.

39. Ibid., pp. 113–14.

40. Gayatri Spivak, "Sex and History in *The Prelude*," in Gayatri Chakravorty Spivak, *In Other Worlds: Essays in Cultural Politics* (New York: Routledge, 1988), p. 57.


## EPILOGUE

1. Claude Lévi-Strauss, *The Savage Mind* (Chicago: University of Chicago Press, 1966), p. 264.

2. Ibid., pp. 16–21.

3. Erikson, *Young Man Luther*, p. 40.

4. See Schorske, *Fin-de-siècle Vienna*, and McGrath, *Freud's Discovery of Psychoanalysis*.

5. Freud, *Briefe an Wilhelm Fliess*, p. 345.

6. Alexander Mitscherlich, *Society Without the Father: A Contribution to Social Psychology*, trans. Eric Mosbacher (New York: Harcourt, Brace & World, 1969), pp. 150–51. Also Max Horkheimer, *Studien über Autorität und Familie* (Paris: Felix Alcan, 1936).

7. Kleist, *Werke*, vol. 1, p. 197.

8. Theweleit, *Männerphantasien*, Vol. 2, p. 252.

9. Ibid., p. 238.

10. Mitscherlich, *Society Without the Father*, p. 268.

11. Ibid., p. 269.

12. Compare Kittler, "Die Irrwege des Eros," pp. 437–42.

13. The nostalgia behind the theories of Horkheimer and Mitscherlich is the focus of Jessica Benjamin's essay that is brilliant in both its clarity and compression. "Authority and the Family Revisited: or, A World without Fathers?" *New German Critique* 5 (1978): 35–57.

# Index

Alewyn, Richard, 169–70 n.4
*Alte und der junge König, Der,* 163
Anti-Semitism, 5, 13–19, 25, 46, 96, 162
*Arabian Nights, The,* 110
Archaeology, 7, 22, 97–100, 102, 104–7,
    114–15, 129–30
Asendorf, Christoph, 173 n.12

Balmary, Marie, 35–36, 177 n.22
Baudrillard, Jean, 95
Belsey, Catherine, 23, 169–170 n.4
Bellemin-Noël, Jean, 169–70 n.4, 171 n.16
Benjamin, Jessica, 184 n.13
Benjamin, Walter, 54, 63, 106, 118, 136,
    178 n.36
Berry, Wendell, 67–69
Bertelsmann, Richard, 169–70 n.4
*Bildung,* 22, 111, 119, 121, 122, 124, 126–
    27, 131–33
*Bildungsroman,* 22, 50, 70, 111, 118–19,
    124, 127, 131–32, 177 n.21, 179–80 n.21
Bloom, Harold, 71–73, 92, 176 n.39
Blumenbach, Johann, 111
Böhme, Hartmut, 173 n.9
Böhme, Jakob, 142–43, 160
Brentano, Clemens, 85
Brooks, Peter, 21
Brown, Norman O., 42–43
Burke, Edmund, 40

Coleridge, Samuel Taylor, 87, 142; *The Fall
    of Jerusalem,* 145; "Kubla Khan," 12–
    13, 23, 141, 142–47, 150–52, 155,
    159–60
Critical Theory. *See* Frankfurt School
Cuddihy, John Murray, 168 n.26

Death instinct, 110–16
De Quincey, Thomas, 87–88
Detective story, 117–20
Diderot, Denis, 136
Dream-interpretation, 7–8, 11, 14–16, 18,
    22, 26, 69, 77–79, 88–90, 103–4, 117,
    127–29
Drive, 111–14
Duerr, Hans Peter, 23, 147–50
*Düringsche Chronik,* 102

Echo, 82
Echtermeyer, Theodor, 20
Eichendorff, Joseph von, 91–92
*Einbildungskraft,* 142
Eissler, K. R., 169–70 n.4
Engels, Friedrich, 60
Enlightenment, 6, 10–11, 13–16, 17, 19–20,
    25–26, 28, 32–33, 36, 43–44, 49, 52–
    55, 59, 61, 66, 67, 71, 90–91, 98, 105,
    131, 132, 142, 147
Erikson, Erik, 56, 161

Family romance, 5, 6, 70, 71, 93, 96, 142, 147, 152
Fascism, 158–59, 163–64. See also *Freikorps;* National Socialism
Fetishism, 21, 50, 52, 54, 63, 64–65, 115, 156
Fichte, Johann Gottlieb, 21, 39, 44, 46, 72–73, 84–85, 88, 92, 143, 145
Flax, Neil, 173 n.10
Fliess, Wilhelm, 34, 35, 149
Fontane, Theodor, 120
Foucault, Michel, 8, 97–98, 103, 153
Frankfurt School, 54–55, 61, 67, 161–62
*Freikorps,* 158, 161
French Revolution, 5, 20, 22–23, 25, 28, 38–44, 49, 55, 72, 131–33, 160
Freud, Jakob, 5, 15–17, 35
Freud, Sigmund, 5, 12, 18–19, 22, 35–38, 42, 88, 97–99, 104, 149–50, 161–62, 164; *Aus der Geschichte einer infantilen Neurose* [*"Der Wolfsmann"*] (From the History of an Infantile Neurosis ["The Wolfman"]), 33, 37–38, 42, 118; *Bruchstück einer Hysterie-Analyse "Dora"* (Fragment of an Analysis of Hysteria "Dora") 129, 131, 149; "Der Familienroman der Neurotiker" (Family Romance for Neurotics), 6–7, 11, 13–14, 49, 93, 152; "Deckerinnerungen" (Screen-Memories), 114; *Das Ich und das Es* (The Ego and the Id), 83–84, 86; *Der Mann Moses und die monotheistische Religion* (The Man Moses and Monotheism), 116; *Eine Teufelsneurose im siebzehnten Jahrhundert* (A Demonic Neurosis in the Seventeenth Century), 149; *Totem und Tabu,* 42–43; "Trauer und Melancholie" (Mourning and Melancholia), 166 n.1; *Die Traumdeutung* (The Interpretation of Dreams), 14–16, 18, 26, 27, 35, 46–47, 97, 106, 118, 127; *Triebe und Triebschicksale,* (Instincts and Their Vicissitudes), 71, 82–83; *Das Unbehagen in der Kultur* (Civilization and Its Discontents), 61, 129–30, 172–73 n.5; "Das Unheimliche" (The Uncanny), 169 n.1; *Zur Ätiologie der Hysterie* (On the Aetiology of Hysteria), 104–6. *See also:* anti-Semitism; archaeology; death instinct; dream-interpretation; drive; family romance; fetishism; Fliess, Wilhelm; mourning; mourning labor; narcissism; oedipal theory; Oedipus complex; pre-consciousness; primal scene; repetition-compulsion; screen-memories; seduction theory; sublimation; superego
Friedrich II (Frederick the Great), 133, 163
Friedrich Wilhelm I, 50, 163
Friedrich Wilhelm III, 64

Geology, 87, 107
Girard, René, 43
Goebbels, Joseph, 163
Goethe, Johann Wolfgang von, 65, 69, 132, 136; "Auf dem See," 73–74, 76; "Erlkönig," 9, 19–20, 21, 25–32, 36, 38, 39–40, 55–56, 58, 64, 69, 156, 162; *Faust,* 47, 51, 64, 102–3, 124, 143, 164; *Die Leiden des jungen Werther* (The Sorrows of Young Werther), 73–75; *Römische Elegien* (Roman Elegies), 106; *Von deutscher Baukunst* (On German Architecture), 137–38; *West-östlicher Divan,* 153; *Wilhelm Meisters Lehrjahre* (William Meister's Apprenticeship), 22, 51–53, 119–21, 124, 126–27, 131–32, 133–34
Gothic, the, 133, 137–38
Gottfried von Strassburg, 94
Goya, Franciso, 33
Grimm, Jacob and Wilhelm (Grimm Brothers), 11, 25, 98–102, 104–5, 141
Grotesque, the, 121, 133–36, 138

Hamlet. See Shakespeare
Hannibal, 16–17
"Hänsel und Gretel," 9, 11–12, 26. *See also* Grimm, Jacob and Wilhelm
Hardenberg, Friedrich von (Novalis): *Die Christenheit oder Europa* (Christianity or Europe), 122; *Glauben und Liebe* (Love and Faith), 20, 63–67; *Heinrich von Ofterdingen,* 6–13, 45, 58, 65, 66, 70–82, 84–86, 88–89, 92–96, 101–4, 107, 119, 121–22, 127–29, 134–36, 144, 147, 153–158, 162, 164–165; *Die Lehrlinge zu Sais* (The Novices at Sais), 106–7
Hegel, Georg Wilhelm Friedrich, 124–25, 145
Herder, Johann Gottfried, 88–89
Hermeneutics, 15, 18–19, 21, 42, 90
Hieroglyphics, 106–8, 115–16, 130
Historicism, 55, 103–4
Hobbes, Thomas, 45
Hölderlin, Friedrich, 98
Holmes, Sherlock, 117–18

## Index

Horkheimer, Max and Theodor Adorno, *Dialektik der Aufklärung* (Dialectic of Enlightenment), 14, 25, 28, 33, 38, 41, 49, 54, 57, 91, 147, 162, 179–80 n.21. *See also* Frankfurt School
Humboldt, Wilhelm von, 98

Idealism, philosophy of, 8, 21, 48, 71–73, 82–90, 145
*Iliad*, 114
Intellectual intuition, 83–87, 159, 182 nn. 11,12

Jannings, Emil, 163
Joyce, James, *A Portrait of the Aritst as a Young Man*, 142–44

Kafka, Franz, 121, 123–26, 132–33, 179–80 n.21
Kant, Immanuel, 13, 21, 26, 70, 71–72, 83, 95, 145
Keats, John, 138
Kittler, Friedrich, 168 n.17, 178 n.42
Kleist, Heinrich von, *Das Erdbeben in Chili* (The Earthquake in Chile), 152–53, 160; *Der zerbrochene Krug* (The Broken Jug), 163
Krafft-Ebing, Richard von, 45
Kristeva, Julia, 166 n.8
Krüll, Marianne, 35
Kurzke, Hermann, 172 n.2
Kuzniar, Alice, 181 n.46

Lacan, Jacques, 21, 98
Landscape, 8, 9, 13, 23, 76–77, 100, 148, 155–56, 165
Larisch, Sharon, 169–70 n.4
Lenau, Nikolaus, 46–47
Lessing, Gotthold Ephraim, 10–11, 68–69, 92, 120, 123, 179 n.15, 182 n.10; *Die Erziehung des Menschengeschlechts* (The Education of the Human Race), 43–44, 46, 67; *Laokoon*, 130; *Nathan der Weise* (Nathan the Wise), 11, 14, 16, 49, 52–54, 162–63; *Wie die Alten den Tod gebildet* (How the Ancients Portrayed Death), 139
Lévi-Strauss, Claude, 161, 178 n.44
*Locus amoenus*, 94
Louis XVI, 42, 44. *See also* French Revolution
Lukács, Georg, 20, 59, 120, 169 n.42
Luther, Martin, 41, 54–57, 62, 161
Lyrical novel, 144

McFarland, Thomas, 136, 180 n.28
Marcuse, Herbert, *Eros and Civilization*, 20–21, 50, 61–62, 66, 70, 75, 95–96
Marquard, Odo, 90, 169–70 n.4
Marx, Karl, 50, 53, 60, 63, 95; *Das Kapital*, 115
Marxism, 20–21, 50, 52, 54, 61, 120, 147
Mitscherlich, Alexander, 162–64
Moi, Toril, 131
Moretti, Franco, 50–52, 172–73 n.2
Mourning, 5, 10–11, 80–81, 135
Mourning labor, 5, 144

Nägele, Rainer, 120
Narcissism, 7, 12, 17–18, 21, 26, 28, 47–48, 58, 62, 72–96, 110–11, 135, 143, 145–47, 157, 161
Narcissus, 12, 70, 74, 82–83, 87
Narratology, 117, 131,136
National Socialism, 161. *See also* Theweleit, Klaus
Nietzsche, Friedrich, 33, 68, 103
Novalis. *See* Hardenberg, Friedrich von

*Odyssey*, 66
Oedipal theory, 9, 26, 28, 31, 33–43, 56, 119–20, 133, 139, 158, 163
Oedipus, 28, 33–38, 40, 46–47, 68, 149–50
Oedipus complex, 43, 78, 98, 134, 158
Orientalism, 8, 23, 98, 104, 112–13, 145–46, 153–55
Orpheus, 45, 70
Ovid, 135

Paulson, Ronald, 41–42, 133
*Pharmakos*, 150
Philology, 7, 98–110
Picasso, Pablo, 130
Preconsciousness, 27–28, 130
Primal plant (*Urpflanze*), 136
Primal scene (*Urszene*), 19, 34, 36–38, 41, 56, 101, 136
Protestantism, 41, 55–59, 62. *See also* Luther, Martin
Provençal, 101, 102, 108, 121, 127
Psychoanalysis, 5, 7, 14, 18–19, 21–23, 26–27, 42, 54, 60, 72, 82–83, 86, 147, 161, 164

Rank, Otto, 7
Ranke, Leopold von, 104
Reformation, 41, 49, 54–63
Repetition-compulsion (*Wiederholungszwang*), 33

187

Ricoeur, Paul, 18–19, 66, 83
Riefenstahl, Leni: *Der Triumph des Willens* (The Triumph of the Will), 163
Romanticism, 5, 6, 10, 11, 13–15, 17, 19, 32, 37, 39, 47, 50, 67, 72–73, 82–83, 85, 88, 98, 103, 130, 133, 142, 147, 161, 164
Rosetta stone, 115
Rothe, Johannes, 101
Roy, Ashish, 177 n.21, 179–80 n.21
Ruge, Arnold, 20
Runge, Phillip Otto, 22, 121, 133, 138–41
Russian formalism, 117, 130

Said, Edward, 153, 176 n.39
Savigny, Friedrich Carl von, 99
Schapiro, Barbara, 72
*Schauderromantik,* 91
Schelling, Friedrich, 21, 73, 83–84, 86–91, 95, 145, 159
Schiller, Friedrich, 45–46; *Anmut und Würde* (Grace and Dignity), 45; "Die Götter Griechenlands" (The Gods of Greece), 139; *Die Räuber* (The Robbers), 16; *Die Sendung Moses* (The Divine Legation of Moses), 115–16; *Über die ästhetische Erziehung des Menschen* (On the Aesthetic Education of Man), 44–45
Schlegel, Friedrich, 17
Schleiermacher, Friedrich, 62

Schliemann, Heinrich, 98–99, 114, 178 n.35
Screen-memories (*Deckerinnerungen*), 34
Seduction theory, 20, 34–38
Seyhan, Azade, 168 n.29
Shakespeare, William, 131, 133, 149
Sorg, Bernhard, 169–70 n.4
Spivak, Gayatri, 160
Stadler, Ulrich, 172–73 n.2
Steinbach, Erwin von, 137
Strachey, James, 12
Sublimation, 45, 93
Sublime, the, 25, 73, 90–92, 94, 147
Superego, 5, 17, 27, 42–43, 120
Supernaturalism, 26–27, 32–33, 36–37, 40, 45, 55–56, 59, 124, 148

Theweleit, Klaus, 158–59, 161, 163, 167 n.10, 176 n.39
Tieck, Ludwig, 39
Todorov, Tzvetan, 117
Träger, Claus, 172 n.1

Unconscious, 23, 27, 37, 39, 78, 83, 90–91, 95, 97, 98, 121, 129–30, 145

Virgil, *Aeneid,* 35–36, 46, 153

Wartburg, 102
Werner, Abraham Gottlob, 107
Winckelmann, Johann, 17
Witchcraft, 11–12, 148–51
Wordsworth, William, 19, 160